Y0-BRM-463

STEP ON A CRACK

(You Break Your Father's Back)

The True Story of Vanessa Morelli Ferris
written by Pamela Camille

Freedom Lights Press, Chimney Rock, Colorado

STEP ON A CRACK
(You Break Your Father's Back)

by Pamela Camille

Cover design by Michael Hughes
Cover artwork by Michael Hughes

Published by   Freedom Lights Press
P.O. Box 87
Chimney Rock, CO 81127

Copyright © 1987 and 1988 by Pamela Camille
Library of Congress Catalog Card No. 88-080654
ISBN 0-945985-00-2

I dedicate this book to Bonnie, who taught me the meaning of loving; to my husband, who taught me commitment; to my children, who give us hope for the future; also, to my beautiful friends who are a constant source of strength and wisdom, and who have helped make my dreams come true.
vmf

For my little brother, Michael Casey, who had he lived, would have reminded everyone that the first book I ever wrote was all about him; and for my husband, Michael, who has so completely and lovingly supported me—in this and through all the dark days.
pc

Special thanks to: Ida Bucher, who gave support and direction from the start; Marlene Nanus, Director of the St John's child Study Center; Barbara Droher, Sexual Abuse Coordinator for Alameda County, who spent forevers on the phone with me, pointing me toward the best resources; and everyone at the National Center for the Prevention and Treatment of Child Abuse and Neglect, in Denver, Colorado—especially the film loan department. Thanks also to the Institute for the Community as Extended Family, in San Jose, CA, for their reams and reams of resource materials.

AUTHOR'S PREFACE

The first few times I read the statistics on the sexual abuse of children, I was certain that the numbers were a typo. It couldn't be true that one in every four women is sexually abused by the time she reaches eighteen, and more often by her own father than by anyone else. Could it? It could not possibly be that common, I told myself. But the numbers kept reappearing: one in four, one in four. (I sometimes found "one in three", but one in four was the figure I read most often. One in four is the American Humane Society's most recent statistic.)

I live in a somewhat rural area, with houses separated from each other by empty acres and hills. In short, there aren't that many neighbors. Yet, once the word was out that I was writing a book about child sexual abuse, four different neighbors came to me with their own stories of sexual abuse within their families: two father-daughter incest stories, one older brother-younger sister story, and one stepfather-daughter story. The crimes were committed in four vastly different areas of the United States. I could ignore the statistics no longer. When I went to the book store to buy more books on the sexual abuse of children, the woman at the cash register told me, with tears in her eyes, that she, too, is a survivor of sexual abuse. For me, the numbers now have faces.

In 1987, in one of the wealthiest sections of San Francisco, parents' worst nightmares have been realized. Thirty-seven children staying at the Presidio's Army Day Care Center complained of sexual abuse. When they were examined, two of the children tested positive for the AIDS virus. Many of the others tested positive for Clamydia--another sexually transmitted disease that can cause sterility and blindness. For all of the public's awareness of the problem, then, sexual abuse of children has not ended.

The abusers have threatened and sweet-talked their victims into silence: silence that gives the abuser power. The abuser can then go about his business as a (most often) well respected member of society, and (most often) as a well respected member of the Church. It has always been the victim who bears the shame—in silence. May it end NOW, forever. We must all do what we can to shatter the fake silence and the torture of children. The price—pain—is high, but the eventual reward is freedom.

pc

* * *

Dear little sisters and brothers,

I never planned to tell any one in my new life about all the bad days. I wanted to erase as completely as possible my father's gross abuse of me, until my neighbor's daughter tried to poison herself to death. She was a beautiful sixteen year old girl who'd put up with her stepfather raping her repeatedly for two years, The night she almost died, she and her mother came to my house from the hospital. Kathy, the girl's mother, was in absolute shock. She blamed herself.

They stayed at my house until they could find a new place to live, and a new life without the jerk stepfather. (He vanished—skipped bail and poofo-split forever.) It really hit me that no matter how far I've come from my rotten past—I live in the hills above Los Angeles in a quiet, beautiful area—it's still right next door. I realize now that I have to help girls, boys, young women and men get out of that ugliness.

So this book is for you, the victims. It is not for your parents, your church, your library, or your school. It is not for critics. I won't ever take out the words that Church people might think are "not nice" for young girls and boys to read. If you've lived through anything like this, you've lived through uglier stuff than any words could ever be. I hope this book helps you take charge of your life, make

ii

choices, and mostly, to get OUT. There really are better times ahead. I wish I could hug each one of you. I'm older than you are, with small daughters of my own. When I was going through all of this, nobody talked about sexual abuse of kids, and there was NO PLACE to go. It's much better for you now, but if I could make it through the RIDICULOUS shit the "authorities" put me through, you'll get through it, too. It's been hard, going over the past again. Especially the first part, and, of course, the last part nearly killed me. But I reported the abuse in 1959, and I want all of you to see how much better it is to report in the 1980's. I want you to know everything, so you don't suffer so much as I did.

There are MANY places to go, now, and I'll try to take you through every step. It's a long, terrible road you're on, and only people who've really been on it know how bad it is. Unfortunately, it's also a very crowded road. You have lots of company; one out of every FOUR girls is molested by the time she is eighteen. One out of SEVEN boys is sexually abused by the time he is eighteen. Think about that, the next time you're in a movie theatre with, say, two hundred people. There is a good chance that FIFTY of those people were or are being sexually abused. Can you tell which fifty? Probably not. All of you need each other, to stop this hideous abuse forever. We need to work together, and take some power for ourselves. It's a hard road, but when you get off it for good, you can love yourself a lot because you survived it. I want to help you get there.

Vanessa is not my real name, but I always liked that name, so that's why I chose it. I'm hiding behind it, because I don't want my daughters to know how much cruelty their mom had to put up with. They love me a lot. One time my older daughter noticed the scar above my eye, and she asked me about it. She has a big heart, and I hated to tell her that my daddy did that to me with a knife. I lied a little, and told her my daddy hit me there. She cried and cried. So that's why; it's not that I'm ashamed. Well, it IS a little embarrassing, but NOT because there's anything wrong with ME. It is a horrible shame that there are so many SICKOS out there, but I'm going to try to help you beat them. You deserve a happy life, so go for it!

(Every other name in this book is fake, also. I don't want to get sued or anything.) So.
With all my heart,
(But not the best grammar in the world)
Vanessa Morelli Ferris

How This Book Came To Be Written By Me:
(A note from the Author)

When I was ten, Vanessa Morelli came to live at my house with my little brother, my older brother and me. I had no idea at the time why she wasn't living with her own parents. Vanessa was fifteen, and she slept in my room with me, in the other twin bed. I loved having a big sister, especially one who was so kind to me. (My real life older brothers and sisters were not very kind.) She often referred to my parents as her "foster parents", which I didn't completely understand. As they were both extremely busy, important figures in the business community, my parents didn't have time to say much of anything. Vanessa was simply there, without any explanation at all. My parents were Vanessa's interim foster parents for a short time only, as my father was ill.

Over the years, I would see Vanessa here and there. Recently one summer, she and I lived in the same big city, and one day she drove up in a big limousine offering to give me a free tour. We shared some great memories, and Vanessa was proud, the way a REAL big sister would be proud, of my achievements as a writer. But that day I also learned that the reason Vanessa was taken from her parents, and had come to live with my family years ago, was that her mother beat her and her father had forced sex on her for years. I was horrified; this was the first time the ugly reality of child abuse had ever come close to me. And fifteen year old Vanessa, who had gone out of her way to give so much to me, the gangly-insecure ten-year-old, had borne all of this silently. She who'd seemed so wise, serene and kind, had kept all these nightmares inside. My love for her blossomed big and rich.

Vanessa is not only a survivor; she is a lover of life. With humor, courage, and hard work, she has become a happy-ending woman. She wanted to tell her story because she knew she could help other women and children who are going through the same thing, or who have gone through the same thing. Basically, she wants to help others say, "yes, this terrible thing has happened, but now let's get on with life—to the good times we deserve." She has offered her short cuts toward healing. I felt deeply moved and honored when she asked me to write her story.

Hopefully, our joint efforts will give some children, young men and women, and grown women and men courage, strength, and hope. And phone numbers, of real places to go that are staffed with kind, believing people to help them. That is our goal.

Sincerely,
Pamela Camille

STEP ON A CRACK
(YOU BREAK YOUR FATHER'S BACK)

When I was three, before the dirty stuff started, we lived in Seattle. My mother was a real clean freak; she had this thing about white. I remember one time she dressed me in a white party dress to take me to the beach, and she laid out a beautiful white bedspread on the sand. Then she told me, "you get one speck of sand on ANYTHING and you'll be in for a big spanking." I stood there, trying to identify a "speck of sand" so I would know what that bad thing was, but all I could see was a whole beach full of black mud. It was all stuck together in wet globs—the kind of mud you really love when you're a kid.

Okay, I thought, sand castles are out. I'll try the water. (I wanted to be good. I wanted them to like me—especially her, because I thought she was perfect.) No way. Fifty degrees, at the most. I'm pretty sure my toes turned blue. For awhile, I happily busied myself with the sky, making beautiful horses from the clouds over my head. I found a dancing unicorn with flowers tumbling from her horn, but then the wind blew the clouds and unicorn away. There was nothing else to do except roll in the mud until lunchtime. (I forgot.)

He saw me first. My father. I don't like to call him that, or even to think about him. He scared me. My mother was ignoring him, I think, because he was drunk. He stomped over to me, and lifted me by one arm. He carried me to my mother as if I were a stinking piece of dead fish that had washed up on the shore. They took turns hitting me, all over. I had screwed up again.

Even then, I was clever enough to know that it was insane to beat a child for getting sand on a white dress at the beach. But it didn't matter—not too much—because right in the middle of this nutsy beating, I started flying, up and away. I mean, I was IN the sky, and my dress was clean again. It was beautiful, and my best friend, Rama,

1

was beside me. Rama was the baby deer who came with her mother to our front yard outside Seattle. Rama's mother loved her; they were always together, kissing, sort of, with their noses. And Rama was lucky; she didn't have a father—at least he was never around to bother her. Anyway, Rama flew with me in the sky, and told me we were going to a new kingdom called Moravia. Rama had the longest black eyelashes in the world, and the kindest eyes.

The queen of Moravia was pure class. She didn't even have to tell me her name, because in my head I instantly knew: Queen Shalimar. She was wearing a glittering coat made of pink and silver clouds. It was Saks Fifth Avenue expensive, and she wore diamond rings about the size of tennis balls. She was perfectly skinny—not at all fat like me—and she had a perfect suntan. She had thick black hair, like me, only she was movie star gorgeous. Beside her sat two leopards, one spotted and one black. They growled and purred at the same time; they loved their queen, I could tell. They would do anything for her. My eyes got huge; I couldn't say anything, I was so amazed. Queen Shalimar scratched the black leopard's chin and smiled.

"Would you like to have a leopard of your own, Vanessa?" She knew my name automatically. She waved her hand, and the tennis-ball-diamond lit up the sky. Poof! A pink limousine appeared. Inside the limo, a beautiful black leopard smiled at me. His name was Krayta. I smiled back, then remembered my manners.

"Thank you!" I said.

"Fuckin' smart ass! I'll give you something to smile about!" My father whacked me again. Suddenly, I was back at Black Mud Beach again. But I knew, I just knew inside, that the beautiful queen would let me come back to Moravia any time I wanted. That was my comfort, and that is how I survived the early years. I flew off to Moravia whenever I could. It was a kingdom made of satin and rubies. I could play with the crystal there whenever I wanted, because it never broke. It was always summer weather in Moravia, (a pretty normal thing for a kid in the rainy old

Northwest to dream), and you could paint with the colored prisms that jumped out from the crystals. Krayta was my Royal Bodyguard; he could rip any one apart with his claws if I asked him to, but with me, he was gentle. It was Krayta who taught me how to purr. Thirty years later, I can still purr better than any human I know. Moravia became my real home, my paradise, where every one loved me.

My father started the dirty stuff when I was five. It seems as if I've talked to a hundred shrinks about it, down through the years, but still, every time it comes up, I want to puke. I have to tell it, though! I have to tell everything, so that other girls and boys who it's happening to will know: I really know how terrible your days and nights are. Because no one else in the world, I mean NO ONE, knows, except for other people it's happened to. Maybe he did it to me a little differently than other creep-guys do it to other young girls and boys, but it's really all the same ugly nightmare thing going on. And if it's happening to you, only you know HOW weird and HOW gross it is.

So anyway, I was five, and I was helping my mother do the dishes. I was drying them, trying to be perfect and dry every drop so she wouldn't yell. My father was lying on the couch in the living room. He was in a weird-happy mood. Looking back as an adult, I realize he was drunk. Then, I only knew that he scared me. He called my name.

"Vanessa! Come here right now!"

I looked up at my mother like, "please, tell him I'm busy," but she looked mean at me and said, "go in and see what your father wants."

He was lying there on the couch. His pants were unzipped, and this big tall thing, like a fat giant slug, had grown up out of his pants. (There are an awful lot of slugs in Seattle—huge ones.) Startled, I couldn't figure out why my father was letting this slug crawl on him—and he liked it, even. I was horrified. Well, I'd never seen a penis before, which is what the "slug" really was. But then, that night, all I knew was that it was a poisonous slug that had maybe bewitched my father and now wanted to get me. I hesitated, holding my breath. Maybe my father had forgotten, maybe he didn't know I was there. Maybe he'd forget that he had called me. I made my whole body silent—made everything stop shaking, hoping he'd fall asleep, but he knew.

"Want an ice cream cone?" he asked me.

"No, thank you, Sir." (I had to always call him "Sir".) I sort of jumped when I heard him talk, because I wanted to run away. The slug was watching me.

"Come here and lick this ice cream cone, or I'll beat the shit out of you."

"Yes, Sir." I had to. God, how could he call a poisonous slug an ice cream cone? His mind was poisoned, I guessed. I walked in slow frozen motion, afraid of him, afraid in a strange way about what he wanted me to do. I knew that it was no ice cream cone; it didn't look like one when I stared at it. It was a poisonous slug, and I knew that licking it would make me go insane. He shoved me onto it. I took one lick, and it sure as hell didn't taste like any ice cream cone! Disgustorama—I could feel vommit coming up in my throat, so I swallowed hard. I tried to get away, but he yanked my hair and kept me there.

"Keep it up. You're doin' great," he said. He smiled, but he acted mean, like he was about to hit me. My body was trapped there, doing that strange ugly thing to my father's poisonous slug.

But my head floated up, fast. By now I could beam up to Moravia without even flying if I had to get there in a hurry. Queen Shalimar was so incredibly beautiful, dressed in a silver satin kimono. I'm sure she never had a weight problem; her body was perfect, naturally. She smiled at me—a movie star's smile like when they're in love. Krayta nuzzled me when he saw me, and put his heavy black paws around me. He always knew the best ways to comfort me.

"Vanessa," the Queen said, "all of Moravia wishes you to be the Royal Artist. From now on, you shall be called Lady Vanessa, and your gowns will all come from Saks Fifth Avenue."

But my mother was screaming, and I had to beam back

fast. My mother screamed and pulled me off my father's slug. My whole body jolted, but I didn't even care that I wet my pants. I was only glad to get away from him, until she yelled at me. "Go to your room! You're disgusting!" As if she was mad at me.

I remembered to say, "yes, Ma'am," but then I started to cry. "He told me to do it!" I yelled at her—maybe the only time I ever did. She wacked me on the head hard, and really sent me flying.

"I said, get the hell to your room!" And she punched me. Now, my mother is a hard, tiny person, but whenever she punched me, she punched like an angry King Kong.

I felt powerless, and much too blecky-depressed to beam up to Moravia. I wanted to die—I hoped the poison worked fast. Nothing cheered me, even though I could see out the window that both our yard and the forest beyond it were bright and frosty in full moonlight. Silver shadows danced on everything. On a better night, I would have made beautiful dreams, or painted with the prism-colors Queen Shalimar had given me. Rama and her mother were nibbling at frosty grass in the yard outside my window. They waited for me to come feed them. Rama could take me to the kingdom, I knew she could, but I just felt lost. The slug had poisoned me; it had poisoned my life. I would die, but I was too sad and tired to care. I spoke to Rama, trying to explain through my mind—that's how Rama and I always communicated. Certain "looks" meant certain things. She tried to cheer me up by calling me my new Royal name.

"Lady Vanessa! Queen Shalimar is lonely without you. You must come! "

God, I thought, even Queens get lonely. So I beamed up to Moravia—I'd do anything to help the beautiful queen. She was wearing a brown satin dress, and she pointed her perfectly painted, long fingernails at me.

Lady Vanessa," she said softly, "I know everything, and you must remember that you are the Royal Artist. You must write a letter to the President, and change things forever. I love you, Vanessa. From now on, you are my daughter." That was the best news of all: the Queen was my real mother, and she loved me.

*   *   *

The thing is, telling all this about my parents, no one could imagine them as normal, charming people—which, if you saw them on a good day, they are. They don't look the least bit evil; they look normal. They do the laundry, and stand in grocery store lines. They love pasta. They aren't all bad, because no one is. I tried to totally hate them, but it didn't work. They're my parents; I came from them, and that'll never change. So every now and then, I have to say something good about them, because it's the truth. In the most monstrous person in the world, there is some good.

So one of the good things about my parents is that they taught me to read and write by the time I was four. Not using the nicest methods, maybe, but fear was a powerful motivating force with me. I knew that they knew I was smart, because my parents never talked to me like I was a "cutsie wootsie itsy bitsy Vannikins." Never; they always talked to me as if I were an intelligent adult. So I knew exactly what Queen Shalimar was talking about when she told me to write to the President. I swore to her that if my father ever waved his poisonous slug at me again, I'd write to the President of the United States.

Meanwhile, the nightmares started, the hot-then-freezing, sweaty nights when I dreamed I was a midget in a giant, ugly-dead garden. It was the same, every night: I was running, terrified, and sweating all over. Trying to get away, but every leaf was the size of a house. I was puny, and I knew that the hideous poisoned slug would get me. I screamed and screamed for Krayta, but no sound came out, no matter how hard I strained to make a scream. In the ugly-dead garden, there was no scream—I couldn't make it come out, but my mother would shake me hard.

"GodDAMMIT, Vanessa, you're screaming again! Look

at you, you've wet your bed. Take a shower, and wash these sheets and clothes immediately."

So I learned to sleep with a pair of socks stuffed in my mouth, so that when the ugly garden's silent scream came, it was also silent here, in my terrible bed.

* * *

In our family, it was my mother who worked a real job, as an accountant to Chevron Oil Company. She got up every morning and wore tailored business suits, almost like men's suits. She looked very tidy and fashionable in them. She was slim and never had to diet, unlike me. Even at five, I was plump. My mother never forgave me for that, and she always rubbed it into my face that my little brother—oh, I forgot to mention my little brother, Johnny, three years younger than I—was slender. And coordinated. Yes, even at two; it was often pointed out to me that I'd been a klutz since day one, UNLIKE my brother.

My father, meanwhile, stayed home and slept late in the mornings. About noon, he went to bars and talked to people until they gave him money. At least, that's the way it seemed to me then. He took my brother and me once; it was awful, because I had to carry his crimes. (My father never did, and my brother never understood, because he was too young. So I suffered the guilt that was rightfully my father's.)

He took us into a dark, dark bar with dumb red lamps that hardly made any light. We sat with him at the bar, and a bartender with a round, happy face gave us a soda while my father laughed and joked with him. Everyone seemed to like him; I always noticed that with wonder when we went anywhere. I kept very, very still when my father went to Pay for all the drinks and said, "God DAMMIT! Somebody stole my wallet!" I just had a feeling I should keep silent, though I knew he'd put his wallet in the glove compartment just before we left the car and entered the bar.

Then my father and some other men looked all around the bar stools for my father's wallet. I started to speak up and say, "hey, Sir, don't you remember leaving it in the glove compartment," but before I'd opened my mouth, my father gave me a cruel "shut your mouth" look. If any of those men had seen that look, they would have put him in jail right then. I was terrified he would kill me, later, for even thinking of speaking.

After looking awhile, my father said, in a very sad voice—as if he were going to cry, "God, it was all I had to feed the children with." He cried a little, but I wasn't fooled. "Could I get anyone here to . . ." and his voice choked a little, "buy my father's watch? It's the only valuable thing I have, but it's worth at least a thousand."

My heart was slamming against my chest so hard, I thought it would plop right out and mess all over the bar. My father had a huge bag of watches exactly like the one he was wearing—in his room, on the dresser. I knew they only cost five dollars each, because he and my mother talked about them, "the Hong Kong specials". No one ever saw my tears when the happy-faced bartender pulled out two one hundred dollar bills to give my father, because I was looking down at my soda glass. I was so ashamed, and angry, and certain we would all go to jail. There was a name for this, my father's only "job": zagering. When people asked me what my father did, I told them "I don't know", and my face would blush red, because it was a lie. He was a zagerer. Here was yet another reason to avoid children my own age.

Summers were hell for me, with the days even worse than the nightmares, because there was nowhere for me to run after my mother went to work. I would hang onto her leg and cry, "please don't go," and "please take me with you," but that behavior disgusted her. She kicked me away, and went to work hating me. When she was gone, I would hide under the bed, or anywhere. When my father woke, he'd call me into his room. I sat stone hard, in hiding, until he finally got Johnny to "go get your sister, Johnny." Johnny thought it was a game, and he'd toddle over to me under the bed or wherever I hid. I held my finger up to my mouth like "SSHH!" And he'd giggle.

"Daddy! Here!"

So I'd walk in hating Johnny's guts, and there was my father, in bed with his poisoned slug sticking straight up under the covers. Johnny always cried when my father said, "close the door, Johnny, and leave us alone. I need to talk to your sister alone." Usually, what he wanted from me was the ice-cream cone thing. But sometimes, he would drag me into bed beneath him, and he would climb on top of me. I was positive I would suffocate to death. I couldn't breathe. It was dark, and hairy, and he smothered me. He rubbed the poisoned slug on me, "down there", until it felt red and sore. I could cry, though, into the hard darkness of his chest. He didn't know, or he didn't care.

"Um, please, Sir, I don't feel well," I would try sometimes, or sometimes I would look at him sad and say, "do I have to?". One time I said, "but Mommy doesn't want me to," but all these ever got me was a smash in the face. Especially mentioning my mother. He always reminded me that "if you ever tell your mother about this, I'll kill you." I believed him—he would kill me; he had knives, and he shoved them in my face sometimes.

I finally did tell my mother once, and it was a disaster. It was a summer day, which meant I had to "do it" to him. I don't know, my mother seemed nice to me when she got home, and she and I were alone—my father was out at a bar, and my brother was asleep or something—so I told her. My father came home soon after I told her, and through my closed door, I could hear them yelling wildly at each other.

"You are disgusting!" My mother yelled at him. Then she smashed up something against the wall.

My father told my mother quietly, "she's a fuckin' liar!" I knew he meant me. But then he said, "well, you won't do it!" Then everything got quiet and strange. I guess they made up, because when they came out, they turned all their hate onto me.

My mother hated to cook, so my father made spaghetti

sauce that night to make everything up to her. (I must not have been very special, huh, if a little spaghetti sauce could make it all right with her.) I crouched in a corner like he told me to do. Every time he passed me on his way to the refrigerator, he smacked me good and hard. He smelled like garlicky whiskey, and he kept saying, "I told you I'd kill you if you told her, and I will." By the time his spaghetti was ready, my mouth was too swollen to eat. My mother smiled and said "a diet-night would be good" for me. I sat in my bedroom while they ate, hugging a pillow and pretending it was Krayta. I could feel him purring on my neck trying to comfort me, but my tears squeezed out hard, like crystal turds at my eyes, and they would not stop. I wanted Krayta to rip out their throats, and I wanted to live anywhere but on this bitterly unfair planet.

So after that I learned to just do it to my father and get it over with. Every summer night I went to bed hoping I'd never wake up, and every summer morning, I'd wake up crying because I was awake. I'd cry and shake and feel nauseous while I made breakfast for Johnny, and dread my father's sicko call. After he was done, . . . I can't stand this part, it's really hard and horrible to remember, but I have to remember I'm writing all this for my little sisters and brothers who maybe are going through it right now. Or maybe it happened to them and they feel all alone. SO I HAVE TO SAY IT ALL. I HAVE TO TELL THE WHOLE TRUTH so they won't feel so alone like I did. Anyway, after my jaws hurt from doing it so long, and tears were all over my face which I kept down so he wouldn't see them, all this yucky hot junk shot up from the slug. Hot poison. It was really scary the first time it happened, because I thought he had peed on my face, but after a few times I realized that when the poison shot up in the air, it always meant "the end" — I didn't have to do anything else after that. He would go to sleep right afterwards. I would beam right to Moravia after I washed my mouth out with Extra Strength Listerine, and the truth is, I enjoyed some beautiful summer afternoons while my father snored.

Summers in Moravia, on the other hand, were excellant. All the fruit trees were packed full of Hostess Twinkies and Ho-Hos, and you could eat all you wanted and never get any fatter. No one called you "Fatty" there, either, because in Moravia, the more twinkies you ate, the thinner you got! Sometimes, Queen Shalimar would vacation on her royal yacht with the whole kingdom. This always seemed to be when my father went on "business trips" – zagering in out-of-town bars – and my Mother was working. Rama and I would hang out in the forest just beyond our property, waiting for the Queen's Royal Yacht to come sailing down the creek. It was paradise for me then, maybe the only happy days of my childhood. My little brother and I would just lounge around on the grass, and Rama would come and eat apples from our hands. Johnny was cool enough to take care of himself – I only got beat for forgetting about him once, and that was only because I was in Moravia. We both knew my parents liked him better – it was pretty obvious – but Johnny was only snotty about it sometimes. Hardly ever. Even as a tiny kid, I think he felt sorry for me. He really didn't bother me much. He liked my stories about the kingdom of Moravia; he always begged me to let him come. The Queen, however, considered him inferior, and never invited him. I told Johnny that if he always remembered to call me Lady Vanessa, perhaps when he was older, he would be allowed. So he did.

I spent a lot of time writing letters; I wrote six letters to the White House one summer. I remember them very well, especially the last one.

> "Dear Mr. President:
> I would like to know if children have any rights. I mean, is it right for a father to make his daughter lick his you-know-what? My mother would beat me if she knew I was still doing it, but my father says he would kill me if I tried to tell her again like I did one time, so what is the right thing? I would like very much to live in another house, with other par-

ents. I am the Royal Artist for the kingdom of
Moravia, but my parents don't let me live there all
the time. I want to, very much. Please help me. I will
only tell you my real name if you promise to protect
me with the FBI so my parents don't kill me.

Thank you. Love, Lady Vanessa of Moravia."

I mailed it to the White House, but maybe I forgot the
return address. I waited for months for the FBI to show up
and save me from my father (who was never out of town for
more than two weeks at a time in summer—he missed his
free lunch from my mother), but it never happened. Looking back, it makes sense that no one came—especially if
they had no return address. Even if they did have a return
address, this was in 1958, and NO ONE, in those days,
believed that such things as sexual abuse happened. No one
wanted to admit that incest-rape among the middle class
was possible, that it happened, not out in backwater
marshes to poor, ignorant people, but also on the outskirts
of a metropolitan city. No one wanted to open that crate of
uglies. It amazes me, looking back, how mature I was at
seven, which was when I wrote that particular letter. I'd
been "doing it" to my dad for two years, off and on during
the summers except when he was gone. It was just sort of a
rotten thing about summers.

School months were better, that way. I wasn't the smartest kid, and I got in a lot of trouble for doodling and daydreaming, but I could tiptoe out of the house every morning long before my father woke up. I was FREE, almost the
whole school year, from doing that strange thing that I
knew other kids didn't have to do. I had absolutely no
social life with kids my age, probably mostly because I
avoided all of them. I felt too polluted; I felt that what I did
showed, and made me different—ugly and gross. I liked the
teachers at school, though, and I worked hard to please
them. I hated coming home; I dreaded him being there
alone, drunk, and wanting you-know-what. It happened
sometimes, but not too often, because I dawdled too much,

walking home. He was usually either passed out or at the bars by the time I got home.

I did everything I could to kill him secretly, especially on the walks home. You see, in Seattle, the sidewalks are practically all lines and cracks, so it's easy to secretly weaken and kill people. You just have to step on every single line and crack. It made my walk home take forever—part of my plan, of course!—But the beating I got was worth it. For a long time, I actually believed my father would drop dead someday because of me. I hoped it, with all my heart. Every day, walking home, I stepped on every single line and crack, solemnly reciting, "step on a line, you break your father's spine. Step on a crack, you break your father's back." Other children ran home in the freezing rain, and they called me a Weirdo-with-cooties as they raced passed me. I *was* a weirdo, stomping hard on every single line and crack, and doing my ritual chant. Even in the most pouring rain, I never speeded up the procedure; I never missed a crack. His death was my most fervent prayer, and to do it right, you had to firmly plant your entire foot on the crack or line, and recite the words with your voice fat with hate, and your teeth clenched: "step on a line, you break your father's spine, step on a crack, you break your father's back." Unfortunately, it never worked. He was always there to knock me around at night. ("If you'd walk home faster, you might not be such a BUTTERBALL!") I started to realize that evil people NEVER die when you need them to.

* * *

Dear Little Sisters,

There is something you must do. You must help your little sisters fight child abuse. If you have a little sister, no matter how young she is, there is a 53% chance that she is also being abused. If she's not being abused now, she will be.

Maybe you have a friend who is always sad and silent, the way I was. She has no friends, and she doesn't seem to want any friends. Maybe you have another friend, and her little sister is being abused. Maybe you know a boy who plays with himself a lot, or tries to hump like a dog on other kids. Instead of just calling these kids weird, you should try to find out why they are so sad. You must be gentle when you talk to her or him. If she or he is being abused in her home, you must help her tell. Or, you can tell your teacher.

Here are the things to look for in small children:

If they know too much about sex, that is a real sign. Young kids don't don't usually know about sexy things, so if they seem not only to talk a lot about sex, but really understand the whole sexual process, that is a red-alert sign.

If they do strange, sexy things to their friends at school and to their dolls, that is another red-alert sign. When I worked with small children at a day care center, there was one four year old boy who always "humped" on his friends, the way dogs do with their penises and legs. We contacted the authorities, who discovered that, yes, his older brother was abusing him.

If they are ALWAYS, ALWAYS masturbating, or playing with themselves "down there", that is a sign.

If they are always trying to touch their teachers in the genital area, ("down there"), that is a sign. One three year old girl would touch any man she saw, there, in his genitals. That was what her father had told her to do with him. She thought it was the only way she would get affection and love. The court decided to put her in a foster home because her parents were bad for her, but the father in the first foster home couldn't handle it. The little girl kept touching him there, even in front of the neighbors when he was watering his flowers. She would touch little boys there, too. It was embarrassing! She was sent to another foster home, this time with a very kind minister and his wife. They slowly showed her that she didn't have to touch him there to get affection.

If you know a little kid who has trouble going to the bathroom, or eats weird, or has too many nightmares, or wets her bed a lot, or sucks her thumb constantly, these can all be signs. If they are afraid to go to sleep, or they can't concentrate, and they stop caring about school, these can all be signs. Help these kids if you can.

If the kids are older, even teenagers, they might totally withdraw, or be really depressed. They might talk about suicide. They might not ever wash themselves, or they might take three showers a day. (They might be the way I was, always stinking of Listerine.) If they are weirdos, and can't make friends, you might try to slowly make friends with them. They don't want to be weird, but their home life might be terrible. If they run away, or take drugs, or drink, these can all be red-alert signs. If they refuse to dress for P.E., or hate their bodies, that's a sign. If they arrive at school early and leave late, maybe there's something they don't want to go home to. If they cry for no reason, or are afraid of everything, that's a sign. If they are fearful of rest rooms or showers, or if they set fires, these are signs. If they are terrified of all men, that could be a sign. If they suddenly have a lot of money, new clothes, or presents with no reason for it—it's not their birthday, and they won't tell you why they have them—this can be a sign. If your girlfriend tells you it really hurts her to go to the bathroom, or she seems to have a hard time walking or sitting because it hurts so much, down there, be kind to her. Ask her about it, and help her get to the school nurse. If she always has a headache or stomach ache, ask about it. Help her get to the school nurse.

You can save lives by opening your eyes and helping them get help.

* * *

Queen Shalimar and I stayed tight, during those rough times; she helped keep me sane, especially when this asshole hunter shot Rama, right near our property.

It was during one of those perfect weeks in summer, when my father was out of town. Rama and I were on a secret mission, wading through a giant alligator swamp getting magic blossoms from the creek near our house. We were sacrificing ourselves this way because we needed to find the most beautiful flowers in the world for Queen Shalimar's birthday.

When the shot came, it was instant. Rama was down. The bullet had come within a few inches of me, so my ear was still "thud-ringing". Mushy fear-apples exploded in my head, so I couldn't move, but the Queen screamed at me mentally to run to Rama and help her. I ran out into the clearing screaming at the hunter.

"AAAAH! AAAHI AAAAH!" Then I collapsed onto Rama and covered her with my body; I laid down in Rama's blood. I couldn't believe it: she was still moving. She was alive. I told the Queen in my head all about how Rama and I had been searching for swamp blossoms for her birthday, and she comforted me, telling me everything would be OK. She said that Rama would not die, but then this ugly man with a big gun walked up to us. I was still lying on top of Rama. I was dead silent—because I'm better than any one at crying without making a sound. The hunter was terrified—he thought I was dead and he wanted to run. I could feel it; his fear smelled really bad, so I knew I had some power over him.

"Kill me, too, Mister! Please, kill me, too!" I screamed up at him, crying.

The man got nicer; he was surely glad I wasn't dead. "Honey, I'm so sorry. Did I shoot your friend? Sh, sh, there, there, honey, it'll be O.K. Let me look at you, see if you're hurt. I feel so damned bad about this. C'mon, let's make it better." He tried to touch me, to see if I was shot anywhere, but I hit his hand away. I'd never ever do that to an adult, normally, but I felt so strong this one time with the power that I knew I had over him. I had all the power of rage: rage at everyone, for everything ugly in this world. This rage was always inside me, but that day I had none of the fear that usually ate up all my rage.

He checked Rama out. She was terrified of him; her eyes were crazy with fear, but I wouldn't let her go. She weighed a hundred pounds more than I did, at least, but all my love and hate and fury held onto her so she wouldn't leave me. The man held her, too. He was a big guy.

"It's only a leg wound, hon. I tell you," he was trying so hard to talk while Rama was squirming, screaming like crazy. "Promise not to tell any one," (my body got all tense the second he said that) "bout me shootin' out here, and I'll get her leg all fixed up. Let's get her over to my house." He yelled loudly. "Hey, Bobby! Hank! Tom! Ginny! C'mon over here, right NOW!"

And these three big guys came running up to poor Rama and me. Also, a pretty housewife-type lady also ran up to us. She looked at me all scared, at all the blood all over me, like she thought I was shot. She looked at me as if she loved little girls. I loved her hair; she had tons of it, and it was this incredible shade of reddish-brown, all braided and piled up like a queen's. I felt happy all of a sudden. Queen Shalimar was right; everything was going to be fine.

It sounds unbelievable, but every one managed to hold onto Rama and get her into the barn. The housewife-lady called the vet, who came right over. Rama was screaming like anything, even though I kept petting her and saying, "they're going to SAVE you, Rama—you'll be perfect again.". He sedated her and then pulled the bullet out. They told me this after they bandaged her up; I had to be carried away when I saw the vet pull out the big hairy needle to sedate her. I started screaming, so the lady with all the beautiful hair took me away.

"Sh, sh, honey, your little pet's gonna' be fine, you'll see! C'mon, let's go in the house, and get you all cleaned up. I've just finished a fresh peach pie. Does that sound good?"

Boy, she was nice. And beautiful. Her name was Ginny Barnes. I couldn't get over her amazing hairdo. You see, my mom got her hair cut at a Barber shop. It was just like a man's: super short and straight, and sort of gray-colored. On her, though, it looked pretty. But as much as I hated it, she made me cut my hair like that so "it wouldn't be any trouble to take care of." She always said, "if you had to mess with longer hair, you'd thank me for having the sense to keep it short," but I never did. Short hair on my slender, pretty mother looked good, but short hair made me look like a fat round boy, and EVERYONE at school told me so.

Ginny Barnes' house was the most magnificent house I'd ever seen. They were rich, I decided; they had all these antique vases on top of antique furniture. The house was huge, with a big balcony, and fancy stairs. Everything smelled good.

"This house is so beee-yoooo-tiful!" I exclaimed.

The lady laughed. "Just like you'll be, little muffin, once I get you all cleaned up!"

In my whole life, no one had ever talked so nice to me except Queen Shalimar. When I called her Mrs. Barnes too many times, she said I could just call her Ginny. I couldn't believe it. I fell instantly and madly in love with her. It was the turning point of my life, maybe: when a real person I didn't make up treated me nice.

I was embarrassed when she took off all my clothes, though. After all the stuff going on with my father, I felt that my body was filthy – that you could read it, and know everything. Especially "down there". My father rubbed his slug on me there, and so I knew I was poisoned, there. I know that a lot of girls who this sex abuse stuff happens to have it ten times worse, because they get touched harder, even fucked there. But even though he never did fuck me there, my "hole" and all around it felt ugly. So I really hated it when Ginny was staring at me there.

"Vanessa, you have a bad rash here, honey. Does your mama know about this?"

I started crying. "No, Ma'am. I mean, pul-lease don't tell her. Please, OK Just please?" I was hysterical.

Ginny looked at me, gently worried. She hugged me. "Poor baby. You're gonna' be fine, you'll see. Sh, sh, it's all right. You go ahead and cry all you want."

I was sobbing, shaking and sobbing, and I couldn't stop. It was the only time in my life another human being had treated me as if they didn't hate me – as if I hadn't done something wrong. (True, there were times my father liked what I was doing to him – a lot – but I hated doing it, and I hated the way his voice got all weird like shaky satin saying "good, that's so good". I knew it was a terrible thing, so his niceness then didn't count at all.) But I was also terrified, because just as my good times in Moravia always ended, this beautiful time would end, and my parents would kill me. I would be cut up with a knife, I imagined – my father had this huge knife collection. I would be fed to the alligators in the swampy creek. OK, so there are no alligators in Seattle, Washington, but it surely looked like a place alligators would love to hide and eat up little girls. When I wasn't having nightmares about my father, I was wide awake at night, listening for alligators who might come in my room and eat me. I always tried to keep a can of my mother's hair spray next to my bed to spray in the alligator's eye.

Ginny gave me a bath, making me laugh with soap bubble games. She washed my face slowly, as if I were a beautiful jewel. Her eyes were a little happy, but also a little sad. I could tell right then that she wished I were her daughter, and with all my heart, I wanted to be. Then she told me all about her life.

"Robert—that's my husband—he and I always wanted a little girl, but . . . well, we had one, Jennifer, but she died just an hour after she was born."

So that was it. I looked up at her, old and serious, I bet, for a 7 1/2 year old. "I'll be your daughter, Ma'am, I mean Ginny, if you like. I'd love that more than anything."

Ginny laughed and hugged me, even with the soap bubbles all over me. She didn'tcare. "Course I'd love it, honey, but what about your mama? She'd be lost without you."

When my clothes were all clean and dry, I went to the barn to see Rama. She really would be fine; I couldn't believe it. Mr. Barnes was there, petting her with me.

"Looks like I just nicked her. Good thing I'm a lousy shot, isn't it, Vanessa?" He joked. He was nice, after all, but I'd never love him the way I loved Ginny after he'd shot my best friend. They sent me home with some peach pie "for my parents", which I gobbled up on the short walk home through the forest so I wouldn't get in trouble. I asked if I could come back tomorrow, "to check on Rama." I danced and floated all the way home after they said yes.

I went to the Barnes' house every day for the rest of summer. It was all I lived for. Sometimes I'd remember Queen Shalimar and feel guilty for never visiting her, but I must admit I didn't think too much about her. Some one as gorgeous and wonderful as her didn't need me all that much, I reasoned, but Ginny Barnes did need me, and boy, I needed her.

Rama forgave me a little for becoming friends with the Barnes family. She was soon perfect again, and we were all really excited when we set her free. Mr. Barnes made a solemn oath NEVER AGAIN to hunt so close to our houses, and Rama even let him pet her. Then she bounded away, graceful and perfect as ever, and I didn't see her too much after that, because she was soon busy getting married and having children. Her babies looked exactly the way she had looked when she was a kid. She came to our yard every now and then to show them off. Rama's little ones liked our apples, also.

* * *

The FBI never came to rescue me, and I lost a lot of faith in "the system" as a result. All of a sudden, my father was back, and that meant more of the horrible ice cream cone scenes every morning, but it didn't matter so much, now. All that mattered was that Ginny never found out, because I figured she would be grossed out and never want to see me again if she knew. I just guzzled gobs of Extra Strength Listerine, which my mother never noticed because she, being the clean freak, guzzled it after every meal anyway. The nightmares continued, worse than ever. The giant, ugly-dead garden, and me running, sweating. I tried to hold my eyes open when I went to bed, so that I wouldn't go to sleep and fall into the garden. I always did; it got so that even the most splendid sunsets made me sick to my stomach—they always meant that bedtime-then-morning would happen again.

Ginny and I did everything together the last few weeks of summer. Ginny loved to grow millions of flowers and make bouquets, and I loved helping her. (I always had to scrub like crazy to get the black dirt out from under my fingernails before my mother came home, but it was worth it. Ginny said I was "very artistic" at arranging flowers.) When I wasn't with her, I was working on a big prism-painting I was making for her. It was a painting of Rama and me and Queen Shalimar in the kingdom of Moravia. I wanted her to know about all of it. When I gave it to her, she cried.

"Your kingdom is so beautiful, 'Nessie." (She called me 'Nessie—no one else had ever called me a nickname. I loved it.) "You are a real artist, that's the God's truth of it." Wow, the "God's truth" sounded so important, I couldn't believe

it. She gave me a big hug, and asked me if I wanted some
chocolate cake. I mean, she never hassled me about my
fatness, which my mother did constantly. Ginny thought I
was a "cute little muffin", and let me eat any fattening
thing I wanted.

Having a real person love me made all the difference; it
meant that my parents' home became more and more
unbearable in comparison. I probably never would have
committed my "criminal act" if it hadn't been for the Barnes
family making me feel as if I was lovable. As if I deserved
better.

It was one of the worst kinds of summer days: I'd been
awake all night with my mouth stuffed with socks, screaming and screaming in the ugly garden nightmare. I'd wet
my bed, and jumped up to bathe before my mother discovered it. Morning came, and, I'll be honest: I was cranky.
"Ornery", my parents called it. My father wanted you-
know-what after my mother left, but I felt sick after no
sleep. The poisonous slug in the ugly dead garden had been
chasing me all night, and I just couldn't face my father's
slug.

"Come here," my father demanded. I stood where I was,
at the entrance to his room. I did nothing; I went blank, all
over.

"What are you, retarded? I said COME HERE."

But there was nothing on my face, and nothing in my
body could move. My father always grew angry very
quickly, and I remember he seemed just a little bit uneasy
with my strange behavior. I'd never done anything like this
before: a total blackout. He reached to his bedside table and
pulled out his shiniest Indian knife—the big one. I didn't
move.

He smiled, and came toward me. "This'll put the fire back
in you."

And I shot from the house. Instantly. Faster than I'd
ever moved. I ran to the forest, where I knew my father
would never find me. I knew the forest too well, and the
forest knew me. All the secret paths that Rama had shown

me—they covered me, and swallowed me up. I hid beneath
The Giant Fern by the creek, and held my knuckles in
between my teeth so they'd stop clattering. If he found me,
I was dead. He was screaming my name in a wild way that
I'd never quite heard before. I might have smiled if I
weren't so terrified, because he was way off my track, on
the other side of the creek. I'd lost him, now, and I'd never
go back. Never.

* * *

I waited for my father to go back to the house for what
seemed like hours. Hours of his swearing and threatening
that almost made me quit. I didn't, though. I shook, and
tried to keep from peeing into the damp forest mulch
beneath me. (He might hear the tinkle. I couldn't.) I waited
for him to slam the back door, then, with tears racing down
my face. I had to pee so bad, but I waited until I was
positive it was safe. I listened, tortured, while he yelled at
Johnny. He must've hit Johnny, because Johnny started
crying. I wanted to run up and sock my father for hitting
Johnny, but Johnny could take it. Through my tears, I
silently laughed when Johnny yelled, "why don't you just
go get a cocktail, you senile old man?" God, where did he
get his courage? I could hear Johnny run, laughing, even.
My father gave up. Finally, the car started, and he drove
away. I was free, and I raced, dragging my haggard old
heart to Ginny's. If she didn't take me, I would live in the
forest, but I would be free until I died of the cold.

When I got to her house, I was still shaky all over, and
grimy from tears, sweat, and the mud beneath the Giant
Fern. I took many deep breaths before I went in the Secret
Entrance, an old pantry that led to the kitchen that Ginny
said I could use ANY time. I wanted to pretend as if nothing unusual had happened. I would tell her later that I was
never going home.

She was cutting some cake for herself, because she liked

cake, too. See, she had big boobs and was a tiny bit plump, so my mother would probably say she was "a fat pig", but really she wasn't. She was very attractive. Anyway, Ginny asked me if I'd like a piece. She didn't seem to notice that I was still shaking, but she must have known something, because she asked me about "down there". My "vagina," she called it. She LOOKED "down there" at my shorts when she said it—"vagina"—so I knew what she meant. I nearly choked. I thought she knew what I'd done with my father, maybe, or maybe she knew that I'd run away that very morning. I knew it was all connected—the stuff my father did with me and the rash "down there", on my vagina. I figured God made the rash, to let me know how gross I was. At any rate, I got really scared when Ginny mentioned it.

"Nessie, honey, remember that rash, you know, that you had on your vagina? Is it still there?"

I started to cry. "Please, Ginny, please can we not talk about it?"

"We have to, honey. You've been real different the last couple weeks, and I'm worried about you. That's because I love you. Now if you're not healthy, we're gonna have to get a doctor. Remember how the doctor fixed Rama?"

GOD, she was talking about a DOCTOR looking at me THERE. Shit, I almost ran out of the house! I jumped up and screamed and yelled, "no! no! no!" All the fear from the forest returned, and I shook and shook while I cried.

Ginny grabbed me and held me hard, and just kept saying, "I care about you, Nessie. I'm your friend, and I'm not gonna let anything bad happen to you, I swear it. Now there's something going on that's not right with you, and I'm gonna fix it. Do you hear? You and me are gonna make it better, but first I gotta know what it is."

All I could do was scream and cry. "No, no, no! Please, no!" But she got a little mad and shook me.

"Now you listen to me! You're a tough little girl, and you think I don't notice things, but honey, I'm your next door neighbor, and the last two weeks since your daddy came back, you've been creepin' in here like some kind of criminal, smellin' to high heaven like some awful horse liniment. What the hell is goin' on? I give you presents to take to your folks, and you either eat 'em up fast or hide 'em in the bushes. I mention your father and you jump. Now what is it, child?" She knew everything, it seemed – all my tricks I'd done to lie about everything, but she didn't care. She still loved me.

"I, I, I've run away!" I cried and shook. "If he finds me, he'll KILL me, Ginny – he told me he'd KILL me, and he would! He has these gigantic knives he puts in front of my eyeballs, and he says he'll slice up my eyes. Even the FBI can't save me from him, like I asked them to. What could YOU do?"

"I swear, if he's hurting you, I'll kill him! Now, come on! We've got to change whatever horrible thing's goint on. You won't have to go back. Now do like I tell you, and tell your friend Ginny what he's done to you, to make you run away."

So I told her. Everything. She went to the kitchen sink and started to puke, I thought. I thought she'd hate me when she turned around, and I sort of wanted to run away so I wouldn't have to look at her hating me. But I waited to see, just in case, and when she turned around, it wasn't there. No hate at all. She loved me more, it seemed, more than ever. She held me and cried, really hard. She used language I never in my life would imagine her saying – she called my father "that fucking son of a bitch. I'll get my gun right now, and KILL him. I swear it."

"No! He'd kill you! Ginny, don't do anything, please!"

Ginny looked worried and angry at the same time, but not angry with me. She told me she had a friend who was a Judge, and I was pretty impressed, but all I wanted to do was just be Ginny's real daughter. She said she'd adopt me "in a minute, after we put that evil man in jail."

We both agreed that if I could stay away from my father just three more days until school started, I'd be safe. I'd stay with the Barnes family. Mr. Barnes arranged it with

my mother. Boy, was I happy about that! I thought my
mother might kill me if I'd gone to ask her, but I knew she'd
be charming and wonderful to Mr. Barnes. (But not to Mrs.
Barnes.) They would make it all right, Ginny said; I felt so
good thinking I'd never have to do that awful thing with
my father again. I was absolutely in heaven, because even
though all these terrible things had happened to me, I was
still young and naive enough to believe in happy endings
coming quick, like in the movies. In that way, I was really a
dumb kid. Because real life ain't the movies, and when
things get bad, the truth is, sometimes bad things get
worse.

But for the moment, not imagining any of this, I must
say, I was really, really happy, sitting around the dinner
table that night with the Barnes family. Ginny and
Robert's three teenage sons were incredibly nice to me:
they pretended I was their cute little sister. I have to admit
I had terrible crushes on all of them, and blushed like crazy
when they teased me. I'd never known a house could be so
happy like this, with every one laughing at the table.
(Johnny and I were not allowed to speak at the dinner
table, let alone laugh!) No one even cared if people talked
with their mouths full, or spilled food all over the table
cloth. My mother would have said they were all slobs, but I
thought they were the handsomest richest happiest people
I'd ever known. This was better than the kingdom of Moravia had ever been—not so glamorous, but warmer. But just
like the kingdom, it would end too soon.

* * *

School started, and even though I had to leave the
Barnes' house, I had hope. I carried Ginny Barnes around
in my heart all day at school, so it never felt lonely there. I
loved being away from my father at school. I got straight
A's the first semester, in every single class. I did it for
Ginny. Miss Benko was my teacher, and her eyes sparkled

sometimes when she talked to me. I think that was because she could see how much I needed her to be pleased with me. I liked it on rainy days when the lights in the classroom seemed orangey-yellow. Everything smelled warm, and we all huddled around the teacher with our reading books. I imagined that Ginny made herself miniature so she could sit on my shoulder while I read to her. The classroom was a safe, cozy place, and I was in the medium-smart reading section: not so smart that every one hated me, but not so dumb that kids laughed when I stumbled over words. I also knew enough about cruelty that I never let myself laugh at the dumb readers in the class, even when they made the most hilarious mistakes. I mean, even the teachers laughed at some of the mistakes, but I never, never did.

Then everything changed, horribly. It was a cold, sunny-windy day, and we were all playing in the playground. A police car zipped into the school driveway with the red lights flashing. Wow! Were we kids excited, but unfortunately, I was the one they were after. They called me into the principal's office, and this big greasy cop treated me as if I were a criminal. I couldn't believe it: I was eight years old, hadn't done one single thing wrong except been born. Every kid in the school watched while I got in the police car with a red face, and we drove away. This was the beginning of a strange three years. I can't say too much good about my "institutional years", but I'll try to pick out only the most interesting things, because if there's anything worse than bleak, it's boring.

* * *

I was driven to a weird, prison-like place. It isn't really a prison, but it has bars on all the windows, inside and out. There are bars around each tiny cell, so if you get up from your little bed too quickly, you bump into bars. Everyone in charge there walks around on edge, as if they have to be prepared at all times for some kind of prison riot. Like the

Little Munchkin Revolt, you know? Little eight year old girls wacking off heads with their crayons. Right! No, I don't care WHAT they called it. "Such-and-such Child Center", to be precise – I don't want to get sued or anything for telling the truth about how bad it was. They've ignored all the requests for access to my files I've made as an adult, so maybe they're afraid of something. It was a prison. When I got there, this really bad-ass, hairy woman, with a gross black moustache and beard, gripped me by the arm. She looked at me mean while I took off all my clothes and showered. I was a sensitive child, so my memories of this big, hairy lady glaring at me while I washed with this horrible-smelling soap are awfully bad.

The medical exam and interrogation that followed are among the hardest memories of my life to recall, hard because they are so ugly and brutal. Lying on a metal table, I, the eight-year-old child, can see the stark white lamp. The large cop who'd pulled me out of school is looking down at me as if I am a prostitute he has busted. He is smoking a cigarette.

"Tell the truth," he says, "because we'll find out anyway in a minute. DID YOUR FATHER ENTER YOU?"

I am crying, because there is a hot white burning lamp "down there", on me. On my rash, like a spotlight. They have spread my legs, it hurts, and everyone – FIVE MEN AND A NURSE – are looking into me. I have no idea what they are talking about. "Enter". What do they mean, "enter"?

"Answer the question!" Someone shouts at me from beneath a sheet that is covering my legs. I feel something – God, no! Something shoving into the OTHER hole – where I go "number two". "Relax! You've got to RELAX!" The man – a doctor – is disgusted. He throws down a metal tool that clangs on the ground. I jump and cry. "Tsk! She's not cooperating."

Pity I hadn't yet developed my sense of humor. I might have said, "hey, fella, I'd like to see YOU relax while five people watch ME stick something up YOUR ass!"

I cried and cried and cried. I felt degraded, ugly, and criminal, but I couldn't understand, really, WHAT it was that I'd done, or what I could've done differently. Something, clearly, because I was definitely on trial. I think I passed out, because I remember they were nicer to me when I woke up.

After I'd been told to dress, a cold, scholarly man questioned me. He did not believe me; he asked me assinine questions such as, "have you never, never stolen candy from a grocery store?" Now, of course, I understand perfectly: he was judging MY MORAL FIBER. People, if I had a lovely life at home, why would I tell a lie that would get me thrown onto a table with cold metal things prodding me?

There was one fairly cool lady there who seemed to believe me. She was kind to me. She gave me a paint set, and I jumped on it like a starving person. I painted Moravia, and Queen Shalimar dancing in the sky. I still remember it; the Queen was wearing her favorite silver cloud jumper. Shalimar's black hair was done up just the way Ginny Barnes wore her hair, but it made me cry to think that Ginny Barnes had caused all this. She said she loved me, so I didn't understand why she didn't just kidnap me and take me to some wonderful universe. I tried to shrug off my sadness, though, saying, "oh, well, nothing so far is fair, or makes any sense, anyway."

I painted feverishly in this cell for what must have been hours. Then the fairly cool lady came and led me by the hand into a cold, clammy room. It was a bleak, stale-smelling room, with one long table. I was on trial, I could instantly see that. There were three lawyer-shrink looking types with remarkably clean fingernails all sitting around the table. They pretended to be nice, but they hated me; they were trying to trick me. Really dumb. I mean, I had never in my life heard words like "penis" or "oral copulation" or "intercourse". Never. I had no idea what these words meant, but these tricky men were saying those words over and

over. They acted as if I was a liar. It was the loneliest day of
my life; it went something like this.

"Now, Vanessa, I want you to tell us if you recall your
father ever coercing you into oral copulation," one of the
men said.

In my heart, where I hid tons of dirty swear words
against every one, I wanted to unlock the words, and say,
"Does any one here speak a goddamned word of English?"
Jesus! I can't think of too many eight year old girls who
know what "coerce" or "oral copulation" means. I now have
a daughter about that age, and I've never heard her refer to
either one. But, as a terrified little eight year old girl, all I
could say was, "um, excuse me, Sir, but I don't know." Like,
what the FUCK are you talking about?

He got tense, and cleared his throat. He was annoyed.
"Do you understand what those words mean?" "Like, every
kid knows automatically, right? So you must be a dumb
shit," is what he MEANT, but didn't say. I remained my
frightened, silent self. My heart and mind were raging
against these people, screaming, "HOW DARE YOU
TREAT ME THIS WAY? I HAVE DONE NOTHING
WRONG." But if I didn't say "Sir" and keep silent, "seen
and not heard," I figured they would beat me, torture me, or
put me in jail without my dreams, forever. Therefore, I
refused to let them see my hating-thoughts.

"No, sir."

So they tried a bunch of other grown-up words I'd never
heard before. I was feeling smaller and lonelier. I felt that I
would soon become microscopic and slip out of the chair.
Finally, the woman-shrink in the crowd had a brainstorm.

"Vanessa, can you tell us in your own words what you
remember your father doing?"

By that point, I was a sweaty mess, on the verge of tears.
But also a little survivor. I can look back so easily and
become that plump, nervous little girl again, and cheer for
the way she stood up to those people in that room. I told
them everything—the whole ice cream cone scenario, using
MY words, and the words my father used.

"HOW MANY TIMES?" They immediately badgered. Suddenly, rage made my voice grown-up ugly. We were getting down to the matter at hand. "Every single day in summer for the last three years, except when he was gone or I slept over at the Barnes' house," I said. I looked them straight in the eye and told them. Everything. As if it was partly THEIR FAULT—that's what my eyes and my voice said, and they got it, because a couple of them squirmed in their seats. Maybe their fannies were sweating and sticking to the plastic seats, just like mine. I hope so. And it WAS partly their fault, because they were stupid adults who were treating the wrong person like a criminal. They were part of the grown-up world who said to kids, "Obey, obey!" And that's all I'd done: I'd obeyed my father, who had big knives.

Then they tried to make me a liar. This killed me. Like an eight year old kid is really going to make up something like that, just so she can be wheeled away in a police car in front of the whole school, and then get locked up in prison. Grow up, people! This was no balloon party for me.

But they did all these tricks—especially the shrinks. (I didn't know THEN that they were shrinks, but looking back, I am certain of it.) One guy said, "We understand you draw WITCHES!" Emphasis on the word "witches" was his emphasis. He held up my drawing of Queen Shalimar for everyone at the table to see. What a dumbshit he was—like that painting really proved something, right?

I was mad at him for calling Queen Shalimar a witch. Knowing how terrified I was, I am SO proud of the little girl Vanessa standing up to all of them. "Sir, that is NOT a witch. She is a queen, a very good queen." The other people at the table looked at him like he was a Jerk. So for a few moments, I had power that I could feel. Ginny and Queen Shalimar were strong in my heart, so when I talked, they helped the power come into my mouth. I lectured everyone at the table, like a wise little teacher: "Do you know of the Good Witch of the North, in the Wizard of Oz? Well, Queen

Shalimar is like that, only she rules ALL of Moravia." So
THERE, you creep. That shut him up.

My first courtroom trial came soon after that. Why was
there a trial? Because my mother and father "contested" my
"allegations". They said I'd made the whole thing up, so it
was my word against theirs.

The same fairly cool lady took me by the hand. I let her
be nice to me, but I'd already decided that I would hide my
paintings from her, under my little mattress. She led me to
the courtroom. It was hideous. I had to SAY it–what my
father did to me–in a courtroom, while my father himself
sat there glaring at me. My whole body shook, and my
fanny got so sweaty, I thought I'd peed in the chair. He was
going to kill me, I knew it. But I couldn't lie, at that point. I
was as good as dead, but by then, I didn't care. It was true,
and I had to say it. He stared at me, with more cruelty than
on any television or movie screen, beccause it was cruelty
that was real. For a second, I gave it back: all the ugliness
and cruelty. I put it into MY stare, at him.

"He told me to lick the ice cream cone. He MADE me lick
it."

What saved me was Ginny Barnes. She sat in the courtroom loving me with her eyes the whole time. I took some
power for myself when I stopped looking at HIM and
focused my whole heart and eyes on Ginny. I told the stinking lawyers and shrinks everything, over and over. Tears
streamed down my face, and my voice wobbled, but I kept
talking, even when one lawyer yelled at me.

"Vanessa, I want you to tell the truth. Didn't you WANT
to sexually arouse your father? Wasn't it always your
desire that your daddy love YOU and not your mother?
Wouldn't you do ANYHTING to make him love you?" This
is what they did–and still do–in court; they try to make
people believe that the child is a little sexpot coming onto
her daddy, uncle, whoever. All I can say is, children can be
stronger than all these assholes put together, if they need
to, and I needed to.

"NO!" I screamed back at him. "I HAVE NEVER

LOVED MY FATHER! I WISH HE WERE DEAD! I'VE STEPPED ON EVERY CRACK, TRYING TO BREAK HIS BACK!" When I was finished, my knees were shaking so badly that the fairly cool lady had to carry me back to my chair.

Then I sat while my mother told the court that I had always been a liar. She said I made up stories about queens and kingdoms, and deer that had mental telepathy. When the lawyer asked her "then you never walked in while your daughter was performing fellatio with your husband?" She said no.

I started screaming. It all just hurt too much, so I cried and cried. Some one finally carried me away, so I didn't hear anymore of that trial. I sat in my cell praying to God to please please kill me. I told Him I'd do ANYTHING for Him, wash the dishes or anything if He'd just let me die,

After awhile, my mother's clomp-clompey high heels were coming down the floor to my cell. She came in after the hairy lady guard unlocked my cell. (I called the guard "Brutus" in my mind, after the hairy man in the Popeye cartoons who always beat up poor old Popeye.) My mother sat on my bed next to me. I moved away from her.

"Vanessa," she said after Brutus left, "I want you to know that the reason I lied today was because if I told the truth, they would put your father in jail." And I looked up from her about six inches past my bed, to the ugly black bars all around me, and I understood everything. That it was better for her to put me in jail than to put her drunk-ass, child molesting leech of a husband in jail. I never said a word to her; I just understood. The world opened up its ugliest, blackest heart to me, that day, but you know something? I also decided that day to survive whatever stuff they dumped on me. Someday, I would be strong and happy, and live in a beautiful place. "Forget it, God," I told Him. "I don't want to die, after all. Damn You, I'm going to be happy someday. I've seen happiness, and You do everything You can to keep me from having it, but I WILL take it. I WILL have it. Someday." That was my choice, my decision; I deserved a happy ending, and I was going to goddamned stick around until I got it.

* * *

Dear Little Sisters and Brothers,

All this sounds pretty bad, right? And now you're thinking, "Oh, my God! Forget this! I'm not telling ANYBODY!"

Yeah, it was awful after I told, but it was still ten times better than doing that strange thing with my dad. And guess what? It doesn't have to be ANYTHING like what I went through, with the cops and mean, yucky doctor and cruel shrinks, anymore! When I was little, shrinks were trained that little girls only IMAGINED sex abuse—it didn't really happen, they said to each other. But now, the cat's Out of the bag, folks, and policemen, lawyers, psychiatrists, and all the social workers are trained to FACE FACTS. They've started to get their acts together—and what a difference! Mothers, and feminists, and volunteers—both men and women—who were once abused just like you, have all worked their tails off to make it better for you, today. It's still not perfect, of course. If it were perfect, there'd be no abuse. But they have done great things. I told you all the stuff I went through, not to scare you, but to say," "hey, if I could survive that old time torture treatment, you can definitely survive the modern day routine, which is a piece of cake in comparison."

So here is the plan: first, you TELL. I know. It's hard. But you must, to save yourself, and to save your dad, stepdad, brother, uncle, or whoever. Tell your best friend, NOW. If you have a fairly cool teacher at school, tell her or him. A woman teacher might be more sympathetic, but tell whichever teacher is the coolest—TELL YOUR TEACHER. Just TELL! Silence is bad for everyone. There is a law, called a mandatory reporting law, that says a teacher MUST report every case of suspected child abuse. If it turns out not to be true, no one can sue this teacher, because she or he acted on good faith.

If you don't have a best friend, or a teacher you like, that's OK. I understand about feeling weird around people your own age. You feel dirty, and so you just haven't made any close friends. You can still get out.

If you live in a medium or big town, you have many options. First, check the very first page of your telephone book. Under "Emergency Calls", or "Crisis Intervention Agencies", you'll see either a CHILD ABUSE HOTLINE, or EMERGENCY SHELTER PROGRAM FOR WOMEN AND CHILDREN. If you call either of those numbers, you will find people who have sexual abuse crisis training. Many of these people know exactly what you are going through, because when they were younger, it happened to them, too. Also, check the yellow pages— that's right: let your fingers do the walking. Look under "Crisis Intervention Services", or "Child Abuse", or "Human Services". You will find a 24-hour hotline number, or maybe you'll see a "Women Against Rape" agency number. Women Against Rape can help you find just the right people: people who will believe you and be nice to you. People who will tell you, "it's not your fault. You are not a bad person."

Another place to call or go, especially in a larger town, is the County Hospital. Most county hospitals now have a Family Crisis Center. And, just as teachers HAVE to report suspected child abuse, doctors are also required, under the same law, to report.

If you have run away, or if you know someone who has run away because their dad (or stepdad, grandfather, uncle, brother) was sexually abusing her, YOU ARE NOT A CRIMINAL. SHE IS NOT A CRIMINAL. YOU ARE NOT A BAD PERSON. On the very first page of any phone book, again, under "Crisis Intervention Agencies" or under "Emergency Numbers", you will find a RUNAWAY HOTLINE number, or a number for an EMERGENCY SHELTER PROGRAM FOR WOMEN AND CHIL-

DREN. Call, then go there, to the emergency shelter. They will help you, for free, to put your life back together. They won't hassle you. They are trained in how to get it all rolling for you. If they can't do the perfect thing for your particular case, they will help you find the people who can. If you or your friend have run away, and you run into one of those phone booths where the phone book's been ripped off, try to remember: 1–800–4-A-CHILD. Twenty four hours a day, seven days a week, you can call. They will tell you how to find help in your area. AND, you'll get your dimes back. (Unless, of course, it's one of those really great days, and the phone booth eats all your dimes. Never run away without LOTS of dimes.)

DON'T sleep on the street; there are some REALLY bad people out there on the street.

If your town is too tiny to have a phone book, you can call this same number, 1–800–4-A-CHILD, any time of day or night, whether you live in Tennessee, Montana or New Jersey. If your town doesn't have a phone, get a really nice person to let you use their telephone. Tell them, "it's a toll-free number, so it won't cost you anything." You will be calling the National Center for Child Abuse Studies in Denver, Colorado. They will help you get the BEST POSSIBLE help. They know all the best sex abuse/ child abuse programs in your county. Also, check the back of this book, to see if there are any sexual abuse treatment programs in your area. They are all over the country.

If you live on an Army, Air Force, or Navy base, there is probably a Child Advocacy Program, or maybe it's called a Family Advocacy Program. Check it out. They are there for YOU, and they are trained in Child Abuse/ Sexual Abuse. Tell the nicest person there what's going on, no matter who it is that's abusing you. They will immediately see that you are SAFE, and they will do everything they can to help your family deal with all the problems.

OK, so now, somehow, you've told someone. At first, you will feel relief, that this hard, heavy secret is finally off your little shoulders. If the person you are telling is an idiot, and doesn't make you feel better, or doesn't comfort you, tell them to shove it. Tell someone else. Because the most important words that you can hear are: IT IS NOT YOUR FAULT. YOU DID NOTHING WRONG. If the person you tell does not say those words, then tell someone else. And keep chanting the words to yourself, like a little Buddhist monk: "IT WAS NOT MY FAULT. I DID NOTHING WRONG. HE WAS OLDER/ HE WAS AN ADULT. HE TOOK ADVANTAGE OF ME."

If the person you tell does not believe you, don't work at trying to convince her or him. Tell someone else. One case study comes to mind, of a girl who told her Bishop at Church that her father was raping her. The Bishop told her she was imagining it; her father was a very nice man, very active in the Church. The girl believed the Bishop; she wanted to believe, because her dad WAS a nice man, and she loved him. But then her younger sister finally told her that "Daddy" was doing it to her, too! Young people's imaginations DON'T work that way. Sure, you might have sex fantasies about your favorite hunk movie star, but that's REALLY different. That's natural, and doesn't make you shrivel up and hate yourself.

* * *

THE PROBLEMS

Every one of you is different. Your families are different, and your neighborhoods are different. Child abuse happens in rich families, middle class families, and in poor families. Black, white, red, brown, yellow families. And each case of sexual abuse is different.

For most of you – 56% – it is your natural father who is sexually abusing you. 99% of sexual abusers are men, so I will say "man", but some of you were abused by women. For 60% of you, the man who abused you did NOT use force. He didn't HAVE to, because he was your dad. You were taught to obey. If you were very young, you saw nothing wrong with it, because Daddy could never do wrong. For many of you, then, your father /stepfather/ brother/ was gentle. For many of you, your father/abuser started when you were a very young girl, or boy – doing little things, like sitting you on his lap, and moving funny, beneath you. You liked that! Anyone would. That's OK. He hugged you and loved you, and told you that you were "Daddy's girl", or "that's my boy"; he made you feel special. You were his favorite, and the honest truth is, you LOVED being his favorite!

This happens a lot. The typical age sexual abuse begins is five to eight years old. The average age of all sexual abuse is 9.3 years, which maybe surprises you. Our society may have helped put an idea in your head that maybe the usual age for this sort of thing is, say, fifteen or sixteen, because young women that age are just so sexy, AND MAYBE THEY ASKED FOR IT, right? Here's the thing: *NOBODY* ASKS FOR IT, BECAUSE NOBODY WANTS TO BE SEXUALLY ABUSED! And if you were five or if you were fifteen, and if you think it's your fault that this man did this, THINK AGAIN! Maybe he started by rubbing you, and that felt good. It felt like Daddy (or Grandpa, Uncle, whoever) loved you. DO NOT BE ASHAMED. IT IS STILL NOT YOUR FAULT. He is the adult. It was HIS responsibility NOT to do that. He should have given you affection without using you for sex. He corrupted your relationship with him by taking advantage of his power over you. He took advantage of your need for love. What HE did was WRONG, WRONG, WRONG. YOU, on the other hand, did NOTHING wrong.

So then the problem, if your story is like this, is that you love your abuser. Well, you loved him more when he wasn't doing this strange thing to you. You're confused, because of your mother, and you feel used. You HATE the secrecy and shame of what he is doing, but he's told you that IF YOU TELL ANYONE, DADDY WILL GO TO JAIL, AND THE FAMILY WILL BE SPLIT UP. Wow! What a heavy guilt trip that is! Maybe you're the oldest daughter in the family (very common), and maybe you feel like you have to keep doing this with your dad—YOU FEEL SORRY FOR HIM, AND HE NEEDS YOU. I know of one case history with an older daughter where she bargained with her father: I'll do this if you swear you'll never do this to my little sister. When he broke his promise, she told. She had felt it was all up to HER to keep the family together.

When I say "fathers", that includes stepfathers. It's the same thing. If your mother is living with a boyfriend who is abusing you, you might stand a better chance. It might be easier for you to tell, and your mother might totally take your side and help you through it. But then again, she might not. Whatever happens, TELL, stick to the truth, and be strong.

If your abuser is your brother, don't let him bully or frighten you. Tell your teacher and tell your parents. Don't stop telling until your brother gets professional help. He needs that help, for his sake, and for his someday-children's sake. The odds are that if he doesn't get therapy now, he will grow up to abuse his own children. His abuse of you was an act of hostility, not an act of sex. He is PISSED, at you and at your mother. You must help him, by telling. It won't be any easier for you than for girls telling on their fathers, or on strangers. Your brother will maybe lie, and say it was your fault, so be strong. It was NOT your fault. Stick to the truth, and be strong. It's hell, I guarantee it, but you'll make it.

You might be afraid that if you stop giving in and letting them abuse you, it will destroy the family. So you will be the martyr and let your own life be ruined. But, hey! Honest! You are NOT helping your father/brother like himself better, and you are NOT helping your mother and father face THEIR problems with each other.

Maybe your father has warned that if you tell, he will go to jail, you'll all be starving and on the street, and Mom will hate you. WRONG. That doesn't have to be the case. Your dad (or stepfather or uncle, brother, grandfather) is sick. He doesn't feel good about himself, doing this with you—no matter WHAT he SAYS. HE NEEDS PROFESSIONAL HELP. In fact, YOUR WHOLE FAMILY NEEDS HELP. The problems are too much for you alone to deal with, and the good news is that there are people out there who can help your family become like a regular-normal family again. Honest, a normal dad can hug his child without sex, and a normal, grown man has sex with a grown woman, preferably his wife.

I know. You've already guessed it: it AIN'T normal, what's going on. It AIN'T healthy, not for you, him, Mom, or your brothers and sisters. It is, unfortunately, an illness that spreads, like cancer. He can move on to your little sister or brother, and—worse--the odds are terrible that, unless all of you are helped, one of YOUR kids will be sexually abused. More about that, later. The point is, there are a million reasons why you MUST tell. Sexual abusers NEVER stop on their own. YOU must make it stop, or it won't.

The properly trained professionals can help your dad/ stepfather stop doing this thing. They can help your parents TALK together about THEIR problems with each other, they need that! And Professionals and they can help YOU feel happy and good about yourself again. YOU DESERVE THAT!

All this good stuff starts happening when you get in touch with two treatment center groups, DAUGHTERS AND SONS UNITED and PARENTS UNITED. When you call any of the above numbers, the people you talk to will see that you get in touch with the treatment center groups closest to your area. HONEST, if your situation is anything like this one, with the non-violent dad/ stepdad/ brother, your family CAN grow normal together again. These groups have succeeded with something like 95% of the families they've worked with. The Courts like these treatment center groups, and some of dads/stepdads often get to keep their jobs while they're working out their problems. The first goal of the treatment center group is to get dads to ACCEPT RESPONSIBILITY, to tell their wives and daughters, "It was MY FAULT. My daughter was NOT to blame." Dads learn to stop abusing their daughters or sons, and to treat them normally again. Mothers and daughters work to develop a strong relationship, and Mom and Dad talk about what went wrong between THEM. They all start to work things out. Sound too good to be true? It is true. Sometimes. Happy ending city. In one teenager's case, her dad came to her and thanked her many times for turning him in. I saw it in a documentary film about Child Sexual Abuse, THE UNTOLD SECRET. These are her direct quotes from the film:

> "He said I saved his life when I told, because he stopped drinking and everything. He said he was proud of me for telling."

(She was real lucky. Don't hold your breath waiting for that scene, but if a sexual abuser learns to like himself, he WILL be a nicer, happier man.) OK, so that's the good news. The bad news is that all the happy ending stuff comes later. Sometimes it takes a full two years' worth of treatment before everything is wonderful. And I can tell you that when you tell, basically, the shit is going to hit the fan. I guarantee that your dad/stepdad/brother will choke on his Wheaties, and your mother will be WRECKED by the news. This is called a MAJOR CRISIS. It will STINK. You have to get through it, though, and you will need PROFESSIONAL HELP. If your dad's a reasonable kind of person, the police will talk HIM, not YOU, into leaving the house immediately. They even have temporary emergency shelter for abusers in many places. Sometimes, other men who used to be abusers will help your abuser get through his crisis while you and your mom are going through major crises at home. If there's nothing like this in your town, if he can afford it, he can go to a hotel. Otherwise, he can go to an emergency shelter.

If both your parents are too intense about everything for you to feel safe—like, if your dad AND mom are denying everything, and are REALLY PISSED AT YOU—I'm sorry to say it, but you'll be the one packing your bags. Too many mothers get scared, and turn on their kids. Only they WON'T lock you up like a lunatic criminal, the way they did me, thank God! You'll go to an Emergency Shelter for one or two days, where everyone will be really kind and gentle to you. They'll listen to you, and work to find the best place for you to stay until it's safe for you to return home. IF IT IS SAFE. These Sex Abuse Treatment Centers have a GREAT track record for getting victims back in their own homes, fast. There are lots of these Treatment Centers with the humanistic approach; they are in every state. If you don't see an address near you, call/ask around; they're starting new centers every day, ALL over.

What if you were abused by a neighbor, or by a total stranger? Or your brother? What if your stepdad did it, and he's a super-violent guy? These sex abuse treatment centers will help you—to get over it, and to get on with life. Start NOW, to get it in gear.

What about THE MONEY? Like, how much does all this therapy cost? You pay whatever you can afford. Counties provide some funds, and there are some kind, rich people out there who were abused and who contribute. (So, hey! When you're over all this, and you're rich and happy and successful, remember to pitch in, OK? Send money--they need it!)

So. There will be Tough Times. Really Bad. Each county is different, so I can't promise what your exact experience will be. I can only promise that it will be better for you than it was for me. Still, you will probably have to tell at least one total stranger exactly what happened in your abuse case, with all the hairy, gross details. One question they'll pester you with is "how many times did he abuse you?" Be ready for that one. (If you're like me, you WEREN'T counting!) It's a big deal to the professionals, so have your answer ready, and stick to that number. I didn't have a calculator handy, so I just said, "every day in summer for three years." They have calculators; they can figure it out.

The important thing is to BE STRONG with your answers. TRY not to wimp out.

Some counties will videotape your report, so that you won't have to repeat your ugly tale over and over. Or, more amazing, the different agencies will BELIEVE each other, so you'll only have to tell the story once. They're working on that one; everyone knows it's crazy to make a kid tell their teacher everything, then the policeman, then the child welfare worker, then the lawyer, then the court, then the therapist. God bless videotapes!

You will definitely have to have a medical exam. They need evidence, and there are now some very fancy machines that don't hurt but do get evidence. Young girls' bodies are not ready for sex, and sex can rip their insides. Sometimes, these rips are microscopic, but that is evidence. The medical exam is NOT fun. However, the medical profession is now TRAINED to be gentle with child abuse victims. They will make it as painless as they possibly can. In the best places, a kind, trained woman or nurse will hold your hand through the whole thing.

Some counties will assign you a "child advocate" who will sort of hold your hand and interpret all the Legalese gobble-talk for you. The basic thing to remember is, you are NOT a criminal. Don't let the authorities give you any shit. You have the right to be treated with respect. If the people you tell don't believe you, or hassle you, tell them to shove it. Go somewhere else until you are treated with respect. There are good shrinks and bad, nice cops and mean cops, sensitive social workers and nasty social workers. Demand respect, because you deserve it. If the shrink or social worker they assign to you makes you feel worse, tell them, "you are making me feel worse. You are hurting me. I want someone else." And don't stop until they GET you someone else, or until that person lightens up on you and is kind to you.

Again, I can't promise, but for most of you, you won't even have to go to trial. Ther's a new law that says, wherever possible, kids should not have to watch their parents fight in court. So, basically, your dad's lawyer will meet with the Judge and your dad, and your dad will promise to go to a Treatment Center and get well. If he's lucky, he'll go to jail-with "work furlough". This means he will go to work every day, just like normal. And, he'll go to the Treatment Center. He'll sleep in jail, maybe, until he's well. Maybe you don't want him to sleep there, but it's important for you AND your dad/stepdad to know that society says that it's WRONG to do that to a child. If the abuser is your brother, and he's a kid, he'll go to a treatment center, alone and with the whole family. If he was really violent, that's different.

If your dad is really violent — as mine certainly was — it won't be so happy. He will simply go to jail. My father never did, because my mother swore up and down to high heaven that I made the whole thing up. She was his protector, and I had no witness who SAW him get sexy with me. They need proof, medical or otherwise. What the court DID figure out, though, is that they were NOT good parents for me. Witnesses testified that he was violent with me. So the court "terminated their rights as parents", just so that I could go to a nicer home. A foster home. IT SAVED MY LIFE!

The main thing to remember is that the law considers "the welfare of the child", *you*, the most important thing of all. THEY CARE ABOUT YOU, BECAUSE YOU MATTER. You deserve better, so fight for it and GET better.

Your parents' house might be the worst place on earth for you to be, and the courts will do their damndest to find a foster home that will be good for you. This is what they did for me, and you can read about it in the chapters to come. If you're happy in the first foster home, great. If you're not happy, they'll find a better foster home for you. I had some strange times in foster homes, but I also had some great times! It was a hundred times better learning the rules in strangers' homes than living in terror at my natural parents' home. It was hard, but it was better.

So. I've thrown a huge load of info at you packed in a tiny nutshell. I'll go into it more later. For now, kick back and read about the time I spent in a nuthouse. And be glad that you won't EVER have to experience anything quite like it!

* * *

I spent the next three years locked up in the Child Center with a hundred other girls who'd been abused, neglected, or were just plain crazy. At night, a hundred girls screamed in their nightmares. Looking back, I rage at the way they treated us, forbidding us to TALK with each other about our lives before the Child Center—about what terrible thing had really happened to us. We were only allowed to tell our psychiatrists our real reasons for screaming in the night. There we were, injured little people only allowed to fake it; we were admonished, in every silent way possible, to act as if it was the most normal thing in the world to be living in an institution, without a home, family, or love. There were a million other rules, too—and you really couldn't break any of these rules, because you were ALWAYS watched. Through secret one-way windows in the walls, and glass windows in the ceiling. Because little girls are such a high security risk, right? I mean, what were we going to DO—divulge national secrets or something? It would have saved all of us so much lonely suffering if we'd known that OTHER little girls had similar hideous things happen to them, and felt exactly as rotten. If all my little sister-victims get nothing else from this, my story, I hope you realize this: that there are THOUSANDS of little girls, boys, and young women and men just like you, and if you can TALK to them about it, you will HEAL yourselves and each other. In numbers, you will have comfort, and you will have POWER. FIND THOSE FRIENDS!

I was institutionalized in 1959, which was almost thirty years ago. So much has happened since then! Back then, no one wanted to believe that such a thing as sexual assaults on children really happened. When Freud, the father of modern psychiatry, treated depressed women a hundred

years ago, and patient after patient described sexual
assaults on them as children, he got tense. The numbers of
fathers abusing their daughters made him think that he
would upset the status quo too much if he told the truth.
As in, IT WOULD HURT ALL THESE NICE MIDDLE
CLASS MEN AND THEIR STATIONS IN LIFE. So
instead, he sacrificed all those women: he told them and the
world that they imagined the abuse, BECAUSE IT WAS
REALLY THEIR SECRET DESIRE TO SLEEP WITH
THEIR FATHERS! (What a guy!) Later, in some of his
letters published after his death, the world discovered his
big coverup. Unfortunately, the damage had been done.
Shrinks were still into Freud when I needed comfort, and
shrinks were TAUGHT TO IGNORE incest and sex abuse
confessions from their patients.

First of all, do you believe that anyone could be so STU-
PID? Secondly, this very fellow Freud is the Father of
Modern Psychiatry. Revered! His ideas were IT—many
shrinks used his ideas as THE BIBLE all through the fifties and into the sixties. OK? So women and women-
children didn't stand a chance, back then. The men in
charge still couldn't face the fact that American men who
saluted the flag and ate apple pie could go home and rape
their children. And I think they would've liked keeping the
whole ugly mess under the covers; the problem was, it grew
too big to ignore.

The thing is, there are good shrinks and there are bad
shrinks. I never knew that at the time, because basically,
the shrinks at the Child Center were all insensitive mon-
sters who did NOT know or care what it felt like to be
treated like a criminal and locked up because my father
made me lick his penis. The shrinks got really uncomfortable when I talked about it—not that I was real comfy talking about it, either!—but it really bothered them, because
they couldn't quite plug their tidy little Freud theories into
it. Hell, what good could Freud do *me*? He had his own
incestuous desires, so his theories were not terribly sympathetic or useful to me. "No," I had to say, over and over, "I

never tried to seduce ANYONE. I was NOT jealous of my mother, and I did NOT desire my father." Everything I've learned about Freud and Jung has convinced me that they were women-haters parading as healers. Women today have a lot of work to do, undoing all the harm to women and their self esteem done by those two men. I'm glad they're dead, and not the big shots they once were, but I wish they hadn't fucked up my life indirectly right then. It didn't exactly need the help.

None of the girls in the Child Center were juvenile delinquents; we were all considered "Emotionally Disturbed". That's what they called it then; now they call it Emotionally Handicapped, which sounds much better. "Emotionally Wrecked because you got raped or beaten by your parents" is what it really meant. Or wacko. There were some definitely other-world types in there. For the first few weeks, I had hope that Ginny Barnes would adopt me, but I was told that my mother would not allow it. Nor would my mother allow me to be placed in a foster home of any kind. It was the Institution for me; thanks, Mom! She was never a great mother, but I'll tell you, I longed for her ferociously. I painted beautiful pictures in Crafts Class of the most grandiose version of my parents' little brown home. I just wanted to go home—AFTER they put my father in jail, of course. They never did, because my mother wouldn't let them. It was not to be.

I figured out that the Child Center was for wacko-heads when they put Elizabeth Forsey in with me. I mean, I don't want to sound like I didn't feel sorry for her—I really did—but a huge red light flashed in front of my head when she walked in all curled in a ball, cawing like a crow. "They think I'm that crazy, too," my mind said while I watched Elizabeth. She jumped on her skinny crow-feet, screeching, "Caw . . . Caw . . . Caw!" It was a scary-lonely feeling, watching her, and even though I swore I'd be tough and not let any one see me cry, the hot silent tears came and I couldn't stop them for anything.

But crying was the best thing I could have done. Elizabeth, it turned out, was wonderful; if she was a little nuts, I wanted to be nuts, too, because she was genius-nuts. The second she noticed I was crying, she stopped the hopping bird act and came over and hugged me softly. (My very first hug since Ginny Barnes. It felt like a skeleton-hug, but it was heavenly, anyway.) She whispered—sort of a horror-movie scary whisper—right in my ear so my stomach caught on fire.

"Never let them know . . . ANYTHING . . . I will never hurt you and we can be Secret Friends forever."

Elizabeth was eleven, which at the time, seemed old and wise. She taught me that nothing in the world is so bad, you can't laugh at it. She was the first girlfriend I ever had that was my own age; I mean, she didn't even care that I was chubby and had boobs, sort of. (I think some girls at school were jealous of them, because the boys ALL noticed them, and teased me, which I must admit I enjoyed. Why did I enjoy the teasing? Because I got to tease back, HARD; once they started, it was fair to tease back: their braces, cowlicks, buck teeth—NOTHING was sacred. Funny how young all that stuff starts—we were only eight.)

Elizabeth was pretty, in a skinny, pale way. She had pale hair, pale skin, and pale eyes like a Malamut dog's, all on this tall body you could almost see through, she was so skinny.

When I knew I could trust her—after about two hours—I told her everything about Moravia. Elizabeth made the institution grand; we were political prisoners, she said, because we were both from Other Kingdoms. She perfectly understood, because her REAL home was Heronta, a land of birds. She could become any bird in the world, anytime she wanted. I was amazed at how perfectly she could imitate a meadow lark.

"Ah, but don't you see?" She said, mysteriously. Tears streamed down her face. Elizabeth had no problem with weeping; there was something magical, and crazy-strong about her. "My wicked enemies have stolen every single feather off my wings."

"That's so GROSS!" I said, letting tears, for once, come freely to MY eyes.

"But they will all grow back. I have been told this by Raininda, the Queen Eagle. She says that when this happens, I will become a giant condor, and you can climb on my back, and we will fly fast and far away from this ridiculous place."

All these things we whispered to each other under the covers on cold nights. God bless Elizabeth – she was an insomniac, just like me! (Many victims of child abuse have trouble sleeping.) When I couldn't sleep, I would whisper "Elizabeth", and she would silently and solemnly pull up her bedcovers. I would climb onto her cot in super slow motion so it didn't creak. Sometimes it DID creak, and it seemed like a loud explosion in the sleeping dark, and we would giggle silently so hard we thought for sure we'd pee all over the bed. But we never ever talked about, you know, the real reasons we were there. I no longer wanted to, at that point; talking to the professionals had given me no comfort. I guess it was the same with Elizabeth, because she never ever mentioned her home before the Child Center. I think we just wanted to be children, at that point, with children's dreams and giggles.

Elizabeth loved me for naming the nastiest guard "Brutus". Everyone hated her. Even now, when I as an adult can understand and forgive a lot of people and what they did, I cannot understand Brutus. She seemed to just HATE little girl victims. Like Claire, the ten year old girl who lived in the room next to ours. Claire was undersized and autistic: basically off in her own sad world. She never said a word. She clung to a stuffed ostrich, "Ozzie", at all times; that toy was everything to her. There was absolutely no reason in the world to take Ozzie away from Claire. He never made messes or bothered any one. But Brutus became obsessed with Ozzie one day in the cafeteria when all of us were eating lunch. She badgered Claire to give Ozzie to her.

"It's time you grew up and joined the rest of us!" Brutus
said to Claire. "Now give me the damned bird."

Claire sucked her thumb harder when people tried to talk
to her. And she tightened her clutch on Ozzie. Brutus was a
round, tough woman, but Claire's tiny body held the power
of both fury and madness. It was obvious that something
terrible would happen if Brutus didn't leave Claire alone.
Elizabeth was the only brave one in the room.

"Please Bru—er, Mrs. Mitchell, Claire can't LIVE without Ozzie. PLEASE just let her keep him."

"Whoa, shit!" I thought, when I saw Brutus whirl around
and look at Elizabeth. "Elizabeth is DEAD, now!" That
woman was evil, and the evil look Brutus spit from her eyes
froze Elizabeth solid, almost like that woman in the movie
THE TEN COMMANDMENTS that turned into one big
salt statue.

Meanwhile, Claire and Ozzie were intensely communicat-
ing, much the way Rama and I had once communicated:
mind-to-mind. Brutus sprang on them, and ripped off
Ozzie's head. A few girls screamed. Stuffing flew, or maybe
it stuck in the air in that bloodied, awful moment; twenty
five years later, I still cry thinking of Claire's ruined face
while she stared at Ozzie's decapitated body. She wet the
floor, and her whole body shook; another nurse came and
shot her up with tranquilizers, then carried her away. Ozzie
was thrown in the trash with all the uneaten corned beef
hash.

Elizabeth was wild that night; if I hadn't stopped her, she
would've killed Brutus. "The scummy bitch-witch MUST be
eliminated! I will take a knife and string up her guts all
over these bars, and we can watch MAGGOT wormies eat
them!" Elizabeth always talked melodrama, but never so
violent as that. It terrified me. She paced back and forth,
planning different ways to kill Brutus. But I was practical
in my thinking: I would lose Elizabeth if she did anything
too radical.

"Elizabeth, please can't we just get Ozzie out of the trash
so Claire doesn't completely go Croako?"

Elizabeth lit up like a Mundo-Mama woman. (Elizabeth and I had invented a colony of madwomen-of-the-jungle in South America, the Mundo-Mamas, who were inching their way to Seattle to free us.) "BRILLIANT ONE! We shall. We shall."

We waited until the deepest blackness of night. Even though my knees banged against each other I was so terrified, I followed Elizabeth into the cafeteria dumpster. SO gross, with all the smelly rotting food—but Elizabeth was so determined, I didn't say a word. We were risking "Isolation City", but we fished out poor Ozzie's head and body anyway.

Claire was still doped up, and she started making painful whimper noises when we tried to wake her, so we waited till morning. You had to use sign language with Claire, but she understood that we'd get some glue or thread or string or something from Crafts Class to put Ozzie together again, IF she'd keep Ozzie out of sight. She could at least sleep with him, now. I can't say Claire jumped up and down or anything like that; she just looked slightly less ruined when she saw Ozzie again. I could even say she smiled a bit, and I wouldn't be lying.

"Brutus must be PUNISHED," became Elizabeth's new anthem. Actually, I agreed, but in the Child Center, no one was big on giving us power. All we could do was little stuff, like make up songs under the covers at night.

"Broootus, Brooootus/ I stab you in the face/ and pull all your skin off/ and it is an improvement/ Doo Lang, doo lang, doo lang!" Pretty brutal stuff, but it comforted us somewhat.

There was one excellant day, though, when Elizabeth yanked a huge tomato skin out of her zucchini-tomato goulash at lunch and heaved it, RIGHT at the section of the floor where Brutus always marched back and forth, glaring at us. NO ONE ELSE ever walked there, because of all the Brutus-cooties emanating from the area, so all of us just ate quietly and waited for something great to happen.

We were not disappointed. Old Brutus marched in, right

to her area with full gusto. Whoooo-hooo, she slipped and slid and fell right on her big, hard ass. THUD! The whole cafeteria broke out into a riot of pent-up hate- laughter being liberated. Even Claire gleamed with joy. It was a small revenge, but it was the best ecstasy I ever knew at the Child Center. God, I loved Elizabeth that week! We all did. Needless to say, we would starve for a WEEK before we would answer "who did this?" So after two days' worth of starvation, they let us eat again. Small price to pay for such sweet justice.

* * *

Elizabeth was the one who taught me I could sing. Not so great as her, because her bird and human songs were so beautiful that everything else in the world stopped dead when Elizabeth sang. She first had to help me with Math, my worst subject, so I could get all A's and B's at the Child Center school. This was a big deal, because you could only take "EXTRACURRICULAR" (meaning "fun") classes like painting and Glee Club if you didn't have any C's. Terribly cruel, if you think about it: we'd been through so much in our tiny lives, where did they get off expecting our grades to be perfect? We were Children, for Christ's sake, and FUN and PLAY should not have had to be something we EARNED with good grades. We'd already more than earned it with our suffering and anguish.

But anyway, I would never have joined the Glee Club if Elizabeth hadn't talked me into it. She made me feel so great, she said incredible things like, "my GOD, Vanessa, not only are you a gifted artist, but you have a MAGNIFI-CENT voice!" She was always hyper-dramatic, and she knew the biggest words of anyone in the whole Child Center. My voice was nothing like hers; I mean, she sang "Somewhere, Over The Rainbow" so much better than Judy Garland, it was a miracle. I stared at her body sometimes while she sang, wondering WHERE all that wind was coming from. Me, on the other hand, I should have been able to belt it out hard, like Aretha Franklin or something, but no way: I sang like a squeaky fish—you know, the way whales and dolphins squeak to each other underwater? But then it started coming—more sound, more wind, with practice. It all whooshed up inside of me, and I never wanted to shut up. Ever. The music set me free and let me fly.

You see, in our household, we had had to keep QUIET. Both of my parents would always say this really DUMB thing: "Children should be seen and not heard." Of course, in my case, they made it very clear that it gave them no great pleasure to LOOK at me, either. My little brother and I would sit at the dinner table in terror of my father, who was always in a terrible mood—especially when he was sober. If we cleared our throats, he'd look up at us like an angry bull. I always expected smoke to come out of his nostrils, I swear, he looked so much like an angry bull. He was huge like one, too. So Johnny and I ate silently, and when I started to choke on my food, I would choke silently, with hot tears pouring out of my eyes when I choked.

What I'm saying is that mine was not a home where you went around singing your heart out. So I never knew how until Elizabeth loved me enough to let me sing. And then I never stopped. We sang and sang and sang; I could feel some real power coming into my voice. It was turning into a pretty good voice, and we sang all these songs in Glee Club that had three part harmony. There was this one song, "Michael Rode the Boat Ashore" that made me feel holy inside when I sang it, because there was this magical place you rowed to in the song that had "milk and honey on the other side" of the river. I put that place into my dreams, with myself being rowed in this exotic barge, and coming upon a land of milk and honey.

Unfortunately, the music cost me Elizabeth. She was the Glee Club soloist for our big Talent Show one year. We put on these shows at the Child Center every year, to show off for prospective parents who might want to adopt a screwed-up little girl if they knew she could sing or paint well. Ginny Barnes had come to visit me at the first one of these. I'd painted her house with myself radiantly happy, sitting inside it. But that was when Ginny told me that my mother would probably never allow me to be adopted, or to get into a foster home.

So, anyway, Elizabeth and I practiced really hard, me because singing made me feel fantastic, and Elizabeth because – she told me this under the covers, one night – she wanted to get adopted more than anything in the world.

"I want," she whispered, "just for a little while, before I grow boobs and get married, to know what it's like to hear someone call me 'honey', and kiss the top of my head because they're so tall and nice." She said it so sadly, I really wanted it for her, too, but I cried anyway.

"But I'll miss you too much," I reminded her.

Elizabeth smiled. "But Lady Vanessa, of course you will come, too."

So when the big day came, I used my colored markers mixed with spit to make Elizabeth's cheeks look a little pinker. "They don't want to spend all this money on a kid who looks like she's going to DIE on them," Elizabeth explained. I also gave her the red tie out of my pajama bottoms – no big sacrifice, as my tummy'd gotten big enough to hold them up without the tie. I did my best with her hair, which was horribly skimpy and straight-limp, so she ended up looking a LOT cuter. I made two braids and wound them around on top, then made a big bow in the back. After that, I was busy doing EVERYONE'S hair for the Glee Club recital, so Elizabeth must've looked pretty good.

"Remember to look and act YOUNG," I said, in a brave, self-sacrificing tone. That is tremendously important if you want to get into a foster home, and especially if you want to get adopted – the youngest kids always go first. I said this as if I wanted her to get adopted, which I guess for HER I did. In my most secret heart, though, I dreaded her ever leaving me.

Elizabeth stepped out in front of the Glee Club onstage,

and sang "Summertime" in the spotlight like you've never heard it sung. Tears ran down my face, she sang so beautifully. I also knew I would lose her; they'd be fighting to adopt a kid who could sing like that. Weird shivering spasms cut across my body, because I loved her so much. I was proud of her with my whole heart, but how much I loved Elizabeth was being tested to the limit.

Three days later, Elizabeth was bouncing all over our room, talking about her new foster parents. I pretended to be happy for her. She'd tried to talk the family into adopting me, too, but I knew they couldn't because of my mother, even if they'd wanted to. I gave her the self sacrificing act. All of us were good at that.

"Just shut Up about that, Elizabeth! You'll screw it up if you try to make them take me. You just go. I'm really happy for you." I probably didn't sound too happy; I turned away so I could cry in peace.

Elizabeth visited me once, a couple months after she'd gone. It was my tenth birthday, and I was wishing I had some kind of quick painless cancer so I could die. It was great of Elizabeth to remember my birthday. I swear, she was like a different person! Her rosy, plumped-up body said "happy happy happy." I loved her enough to honestly be happy for her, then, instead of just feeling sorry for myself. She made me laugh, rambling on and on about her foster family.

"And they've got this goofy little dog, Boo Boo, that was like their only child before me, so little Boo Boo eats right along with us at the dinner table, with a baby bib tucked into his collar. Boo Boo, though, has serious sibling rivalry problems with me. It's a real pain. Right after dinner, he runs upstairs and barfs all over my bed." Elizabeth laughed. Tears bubbled in my eyes when I laughed, and she came over and hugged me.

"I miss you a lot, Lady Vanessa," she said, gently messing up my hair. We both hated it when she left—too much to go through with it another time. I knew I'd never see her again, but it helped a little, knowing that she still loved

me—that she always would. She sent me a few letters. The
last one was postmarked "Van Nuys, California". Elizabeth's family had moved there. She liked California, she
said, and I dreamed about her, a bird with all her feathers
back on, flying and singing in a sunny place.

Fanny was the girl who moved in after Elizabeth left. She
was really a sweet girl, only eight years old, so I sort of
took care of her. They brought her to the Child Center after
she tried to drink a whole quart of Liquid Plumber. She
cried a lot about everything, so it kept me busy trying to
comfort her and cheer her up. Someone had really done a
number on her, she was a super sad kid. She was definitely
NOT as much fun as Elizabeth, but at least I felt needed. I
learned to be a much nicer person, taking care of Fanny all
the time. Like the rest of us, she didn't talk about the bad
times she'd left at home, but with Fanny you could easily
figure things out. If I picked up a brush to brush my now
rather long and beautiful hair, Fanny would scrunch up in a
ball, as if I was going to beat her. Things like that: she
always went around like a dog with her tail between her
legs, afraid everyone would beat her.

There was one teacher at school who was also a shrink—
Miss Grant. She helped me a lot, more than any grown-up
had so far. She actually said "I believe you," the first time I
told her about my father, mother, and all the sex abuse.
That meant everything to me, and she even went on, saying
things like, "it wasn't your fault." She had a kind, pretty
face, with freckles and a perky nose. Her hair was always
bouncy and clean. She liked me a lot, and she always did
little things to let me know she cared. Once, I couldn't
believe it—she smuggled in Grumbacker paints for me.
Those are the most expensive paints, and she sure wasn't
rich, so I knew she probably cared more than shrinks are
supposed to. I will always love her for that. She was definitely a Great Shrink. She tried to help me love myself
more, and make me realize that she thought I was lovable,
even if my mother and father didn't. "That's THEIR problem," she'd sigh, "they threw away a treasure—YOU!—and

I almost feel sorry for them." Boy, she made me feel special. She made me tell her every single time I had the nightmare.

"God, Miss Grant, I HATE telling you that," I'd say. She always started each session with, "so, Vanessa, anymore Ugly Dead Garden nightmares?"

It was easy for her to tell by looking at me, she said, because my eyes looked red and frightened after a Dead Ugly Garden Night. She'd make me tell the whole hideous thing—live through it, start to finish.

She'd interrupt me, RIGHT when the huge hideous slug was about to crunch me in its green slime teeth. I was hysterical, sweating and crazy. Sometimes, I even wet myself, but either she never noticed, or she never cared. She acted like it never happened.

"Vanessa, PUNCH HIM!" She screamed at me. "Go back to sleep, FIND THE HIDEOUS SLUG BEFORE HE FINDS YOU, AND KILL HIM! KILL HIM, DAMMIT! He's hurt you long enough—now you hurt HIM right back!"

Sometimes, it worked. Miss Grant helped me start sleeping better. If I woke up in the garden at night, I WOULD go back to sleep—yes, terrified, but I'd start looking for the Giant Poisonous Slug, anyway. Sometimes, I took a knife with me, and in the garden once, I found HIM sleeping, and snuck up on him, and sliced him into slushy bits, and fed him to the garden's garbage disposal.

"Well, you look positively triumphant, today, Vanessa. What happened? I love seeing you like this."

"I KILLED him, Miss Grant! I killed the slug!"

I swear to God, her face was five-years-old-happy. She jumped up from her chair, yelled "YAY!" just like a little girl, and took my two hands. We started jumping up and down, and dancing in a circle together, singing, "the slug is dead! The slug is dead! Hoooo-ray, Vanessa!" God, she was cool!

* * *

One time, Fanny tried to swallow all this toilet paper. She almost choked to death, and it was GROSS when I found Fanny in the bathroom. Her face was bluish green. God, I didn't know anything about saving choking people. I pounded her on the back, and jumped around screaming and crying. Miss Grant came running, and Fanny was rushed to the Emergency Hospital. While she was in the hospital, Brutus yelled at Fanny because she'd "disobeyed the rules of this institution". As if she were a hip James Dean rebel or something!

Miss Grant and I stood outside Fanny's room at the hospital—Miss Grant had gotten me in after Fanny kept screaming, "Vanessa! I'm so afraid!" Both of us were really depressed.

"Vanessa, what are we going to do to make Fanny feel loved?" Miss Grant asked me, as if I were an intelligent adult. Her voice sounded lost and sad. I wanted more than anything to have an answer for this kind, pretty lady with the freckle-stars all over her face.

"Hey, Miss Grant, I know!" I said. I was filled up with happy air inside, I felt so alive and smart. "Her birthday is only three days away. Why don't we give her a huge surprise party? I mean, Brutus would kill me if it were MY idea, but she would let YOU give a party!"

Miss Grant jumped up and down like a happy little kid. That's what I liked best about her. She never acted old. "YES! That's IT! Vanessa, that's GREAT, we'll DO it!" She squeezed my hand, wanting to do more. She and I would have skipped down the hospital corridor arm in arm singing "put another candle on the birthday cake, the birthday cake, . . ." or something equally joyous, but at that precise, go-crazy instant, Brutus looked at us like we were sucking on porno magazines. (She was suspicious of every smile.) It was, after all, AGAINST THE RULES to be "loud"—read "happy". I would not really be free to release the rejoicing, skipping child inside me until many years later. Oh, well. Miss Grant and I got away with a hand squeeze that meant everything. We were stoked.

Miss Grant bought all the stuff with her own money, but my God, she had to fight to give poor old Fanny a party! I felt sorry for her, but I couldn't say anything, or we'd all get punished. I could only root and listen hard to Brutus and Miss Grant arguing. Miss Grant cracked me up when she almost slipped and called Brutus "Brutus". Super fast, she went "Bru-I mean, Mrs. Mitchell". I had to stick my head in a book fast!

Brutus said, "Miss Grant, if we give Fanny a party, the other girls will expect that if they disobey the rules and attempt to end their own lives, we will reward them with a nice lovely party. That is hardly an incentive for them to grow up and battle through life's difficulties, is it? Besides, we can't afford birthday parties, something I'm sure you're aware of."

"What a pigface," I whispered into my book.

"Mrs. Mitchell," Miss Grant started in, and she was mad, "you should be working in a prison, where people really HAVE done something wrong. It might, it just MIGHT give you some compassion for these little girls. How you can blame them for having the bad luck to be born ill, or to parents that beat them or tried to screw them every time they turned around is beyond me! You're an absolute WITCH!" And she stomped off.

I jumped up and down and danced around my room singing, "Brutus is a witch, Brutus is a witch!" I LOVED Miss Grant for telling her. And there was something else: that was my first official confirmation that many of the girls at the Child Center had had childhoods like mine. Even Elizabeth, maybe. Her parents had maybe "beaten her or tried to screw her every time she turned around." My stomach went sick: poor Elizabeth! If only I'd known; I would have found them and killed them. At that moment, even though Elizabeth had left and lived far away, I felt very close to her, knowing.

Something must have changed when Miss Grant talked to "higher authorities" as she called them, because pretty soon, we were painting signs and balloons, and it was a blast. All the other girls on my floor looked up to me because I was the oldest by now, so when I told them about Fanny, they were unbelievably great about it. We danced around, painting signs and hanging streamers in the cafeteria. But when Fanny came up to us, all paranoid because every one was acting secretive and giggling a lot, the girls would just hug her and kiss her cheek.

When Fanny walked into the cafeteria on her birthday, she was mopey and depressed because no one had remembered. When the cafeteria lights switched on, so did all the lights all over her face. Fanny might never be beautiful, but her plain, sweet face got glowy pink when she read the huge sign I painted: "HAPPY BIRTHDAY FANNY! WE LOVE YOU!" She collapsed on me and sobbed and sobbed. I'd done something right, really right for a change, and I was damned proud of myself, I must admit.

* * *

After that, things started to loosen up at the Child Center. Miss Grant was allowed to take Fanny and me on picnics every Saturday. There was a beautiful creek near the Child Center, and we'd loll around and sing while trying to catch crayfish. On summer days, the sky was so bright it hurt your eyes, and we'd lie in the burning sun getting lazy and suntanned.

Miss Grant said it was really important that I realize the truth about my mother. MY truth was that I missed my mother madly. I'd idealized her, made her an angel-mother who put candles in her window with my name on them, and sighed lovingly when she thought of me. I wrote her secret letters, BEGGING her to let me come home. I had completely forgotten anything negative about her, and that she hadn't really been a great mother to me. I made her perfect in my mind, because I just wanted a mother and a family; I wanted a home without guards and bars. I'd argue with Miss Grant while quiet little Fanny listened.

"Miss Grant, if my father died or was put in jail," I lectured, "life would be PARADISE at home with my mother."

But Miss Grant said no, and she made me cry, saying things like, "Vanessa, your mother is NOT a normal mother. Normal mothers don't let their husbands DO these things. Vanessa, she BEATS you! Don't you remember telling me, in our sessions? You've got to face it, that it's best for you to stay away from her . . ." and on and on. Fanny's eyes got big, and she slipped her cold little hand under mine.

"Miss Grant, if what you're saying is true, that means I've got NOTHING—no home, no family, so great, I get to live in a prison forever. What good is that? Why should I be alive?" Fanny looked hurt, as if I was rejecting her, but I didn't do anything to comfort her except squeeze her hand and try to look nice at her.

"Vanessa, we'll figure something out, OK?" Miss Grant tried to assure me. And we dropped it there.

Closing in on my eleventh birthday, weekend picnics changed. For one thing, Fanny was gone. She had been adopted out, poofo-swift in the night, to a foster home, which really was great for her. Also for me; I cried a little when she left, probably mostly because it seemed that EVERYONE ended up getting adopted except ME, but really, she'd been too much for me to handle. I couldn't turn my back on her for a MINUTE before she'd be squirting fountain pen ink in her mouth, or some damned thing. It was time some one helped her be happy who was better equipped than I was. So then Miss Grant's fiance, this incredibly handsome man named Glenn, started coming with Miss Grant and me every Saturday. He was unreal-nice; it was great singing along with him and his guitar in the fields. We'd sing all day, every kind of song—especially Elvis Presley songs. Glenn knew every Elvis Presley song, and I learned them all, too, super-fast, just so I could sing. With feeling, even: I knew all about "Heartbreak Hotel." (Sometimes I dreamed that Elvis Presley came to the Child

Center and asked for me, because I alone understood him.)
While we sang, we could watch the clouds rush over the
mountains.

I was furious with Miss Grant when she told me she was
quitting the Child Center so she and Glenn could move to
Canada and live in the woods. "How could you DO this to
me?" I screamed at her. "And why is it that every time some
one loves me a lot and I fall madly in love with them and
change and grow better with them—some goddamned good
guy comes and takes them away from me? God, Miss
Grant—when is the good guy going to come and take ME
away?" That was the most I'd ever sworn or talked back to
anyone in my LIFE, but I was crushed. And Miss Grant
knew my insides completely—and loved me anyway. I felt I
could get away with it. No, that's not it. I just didn't CARE
what happened to me for speaking out: I had RIGHTS, and
I was sick of getting trampeled on.

She felt pretty bad. Glenn, too—he just stood there. I felt
my power, and I lunged at Miss Grant and knelt on the
ground before her. "Take me with you, please, Miss Grant?
I'll DIE without you. I'll chew on toilet paper just like
Fanny did, without you! God, I'll be ALL ALONE in the
whole world!"

But as it turned out, even before Miss Grant left—I
stopped talking to her that day, and whirled my back on
her like an angry brat any time I saw her—I was bustled
out of the Child Center. I spent my eleventh birthday in
California with my mother and my little brother, who I
hadn't seen in three long years. It was "SO LONG,
CHIEF!" to the Child Center. They could shove their
gloomy walls and dumb rules and farty old guards and
shrinks FOREVER up their asses.

* * *

My mother was living in this big pink apartment
building near Los Angeles, called "Hula Gardens". It was

surrounded with palm trees, and had a swimming pool! Ours was a three bedroom apartment, so each of us had our own room. I couldn't believe this was happening; it was Paradise, and TRULY the land of milk and honey. My father had left my mother and married some other lady, so HE wouldn't even be a problem. (PHEW!) I went on a diet immediately so my mother would like me better, and prepared myself mentally for this great, normal life. WRONG.

She'd gotten my letters, so I hoped she realized how much I loved her. Maybe, I reasoned, she would love me, now that she knew how deeply I loved her, but in a cold, terrible way she asked me what sort of trouble I'd gotten into, that I was "no longer benefitting from institutionalized correction." Oh, brother! God, that crushed me. It also flattened the bubbles in my glee from being released. But I was so much stronger than before, and I girded all my strength. I squared my jaw as I stared in the mirror, loving how big the mirror was, and how long and lush my black hair hung. I said to the mirror, "OK, so living with her won't be as great as you thought, but you can still try hard to please her. Because NO ONE, no one in the world, will ever get you back into that awful place. Someday, she WILL love you. Other people love you, so why NOT my own mother?"

I loved walking down the palm-lined streets to Junior High School, and I did very well—well, maybe not in English grammar, but grammar is DUMB. Still., even in grammar, I'd stay up all night, memorize all the rules, take the test, get a B, and proceed to forget every rule. Still, A's and B's at this brand new junior high school was pretty good—I was really proud. Even Johnny, my mother's precious son, got C's and D's. She didn't care, though, because he and she played tennis together while I did homework and cleaned up the apartment. At eight years old, Johnny was deadly with a tennis racket. I had to admit, I'd really missed him at the Child Center.

And the best thing of all was that it was here that I met Scott and Mimi Ramsey. My forever friends who loved me,

then and still. Hula Gardens was filled with college guys
and their girlfriends. Mimi and Scott were older, in their
early twenties. They were the managers of the whole apartment complex, but they were the coolest managers you
ever saw; at the wildest parties, if some jerk wanted to
complain to the manager about the music, Mimi and Scott
were THERE at the party. And Scott would charm the guy,
invite him to the party, and the whole building became one
big, dancing family. When my mother wasn't around, Mimi
and Scott let me go to the parties and listen to the fantastic
rock and roll music. Otherwise, I stayed in their apartment
and babysat their two year old son, Eric, with the door and
windows open so I could hear the music. I loved it, because
Mimi was an outrageous artist, and I'd just sit on the floor
in her apartment and look up at all these wild colored can-
vases. Little Eric was a GREAT kid; I had the best time
being a real child with him—it was my first time around,
really—taking care of him, and playing with all of Mimi's
paints. I mean, she was a famous artist, and she let ME
play with her real paints. She acted as if she thought I was
wonderful, and she always told me how great MY drawings
were. (I'm SURE. I knew she was just being nice, but still,
it felt awfully great.) I RELAXED in their apartment—
something I never did in OUR apartment.

And Mimi always stuck up for me with my mother. Especially one time when my mother put it in her mind, like a
CRAZY lady, that I was a slut. Right! I was eleven, then,
but she was accusing me of all kinds of weird sex stuff. So
one day, I was babysitting Eric—really having fun with
him; we played these great monster games together. Meanwhile, my mother came home to our apartment, and I
wasn't there, so I imagine she decided that I was humping
some college guy upstairs. Mimi returned to her apartment
and gave me a piece of sugarless laxative gum just like
hers. (I think she forgot it was a LAXATIVE—I just asked
for a piece of gum), and I went home, to our apartment. I
was all happy and relaxed, but my mother started beating
the holy shit out of me before I could talk. I breathed in

hard when she punched my stomach, and the gum was yanked right down my throat. I went flying all over that room thinking, "what the hell is going ON?" and also, "I am choking to death."

But then Mimi stormed in and screamed at my mother, "Barbara, what in the hell are you doing?"

My mother screamed back at her. "She is a liar and a SLUT!" Even though I was choking to death, I almost died of embarrassment first.

Mimi was FURIOUS, and said, "dammit, Barbara, she just came from my place, where she's been watching little Eric all day!"

I loved it. My mother looked like a total idiot, but I couldn't stick around to enjoy her foolishness. I don't mean to be gross, but that gum Mimi gave me was intense. I never knew it was laxative gum until Mimi and I reminisced, and she told me. I thought my stomach just got strange because all these events had given me cancer. For a long time after that, I was terribly nervous about ever being far from a rest room.

Mimi and Scott and Eric were great; they became my heroes and my family, too. We would spend all day together, Mimi, Eric and I, painting and singing while Scott went to college. Mimi gave me really cute haircuts; she could also sew, and made beautiful clothes for me. Once, she sewed me a bathing suit that I swear to God made me look like a movie star. "See Vanny," she said, "you have a cute little figure! You just have to show it off with the right style." She was the best thing that ever happened to me. She is more beautiful than any one in the world, with the greenest eyes and the most petite figure. She had long, thick black hair, but she was punk before there was ever punk, and she dyed her hair all the time, any color at all: red, blonde, purple—they all looked fantastic on her. Her clothes were total class, really hip-fashionable and arty, but not super expensive.

When Scott came home, he'd go over my schoolwork with me, and lecture all these intellectual things at me. I never

quite understood everything he talked to me about, but it
felt excellant that he thought I was intelligent enough to
share all these things with me. I pulled my grades up to A's,
just for him, and he made a big fuss over it. He gave me
these philosopher books to read – one by Aristotle, this old
guy from Greece, and also a book of poems by Robert
Frost, an American poet. Aristotle was a little tough to
read, but Scott simplified it, and made it all wonderful.
Aristotle said that every artist and poet's personality was
important; each one of us creates something NEW and
SPECIAL and IMPORTANT because of who we are and
how we see things. That made me feel special, which I know
is why Scott wanted me to read it. Robert Frost wrote
poems that were easy to understand: they were beautiful
enough to make me cry when Scott read them. They
reminded me of beautiful forests, but also of scary dark
parts of my life, and how all my nightmares about the past
and also scary places mashed together sometimes in my
head at night and gave me headaches.

Robert Frost's poems reminded me of Rama and Queen
Shalimar and Ginny Barnes and Miss Grant and Elizabeth
and Fanny. All the places I'd been, and all the "miles to go
before I sleep." Also, Robert Frost understood about the
countryside on beautiful days: crisp, autumn days and
crunchy leaves.

But the very best things about Scott were his insomnia
and his motorcycle. I swear, until I met him, I thought only
Elizabeth Forsey and me couldn't sleep at night. Even poor
old Fanny had slept at night, but she whimpered so much
in her sleep she kept me awake. I'd lie there in our apartment listening to both my mother and my brother snore
away the most relaxing night. It was horrible, because bad
things would come into my mind, gross puke things about
my father etcetera. And though most nights, I would use
Miss Grant's methods and go back to the garden and kill
the slug, sometimes I was not in the mood for battle. One
night, I pulled the curtain back from the window next to
my bed to watch Mimi and Scott's apartment window.

Instant comfort and relief. Scott was awake with the light on, reading at the breakfast table. I watched him for the longest time, feeling happy that a grownup, intelligent person with a beautiful wife and child also couldn't sleep. His face was sunburned, and his squinty blue eyes raced back and forth across the page. He was handsome like Robert Redford, only he didn't have any warts on his face. Well, really, with those squinty eyes, he looked more like Clint Eastwood. The bright lamp on his hair showed off the gold highlights from the sun. I could also see the tiny bald spot Mimi always teased him about. (But she always kissed it after teasing him a lot, so he never seemed to get his feelings hurt too badly.) I stayed there, watching him, afraid if I breathed I'd break the happy golden spell of watching him. All my nightmares must have disintegrated, because the next thing I knew, it was morning, and I was crunched over the windowsill, waking up.

Scott had a Suzuki motorcycle that was unreal. He terrified me with it, but I loved it. "Vanessa!" he shouted at me once, sort of pretend-angry, "get your butt out here! You're going to the library with me to do your homework!" He was so handsome and charming, my mother didn't say anything as I raced out the door with my books. I had the biggest grin on my face.

"Hop on!" Scott shouted.

I was timid and frightened to DEATH, but then we flew off. Scott was wild; we went off the curb and raced over to Loyola College in Westchester. He did five wheelies! I screamed and clutched his back and thought sure I would die, but I LOVED it! Tears streamed out my eyes, we went so fast. I knew we would die, and I dreaded the pain of my head splattering all over the street, but terror and rushy excitement churned around together in my stomach. When we got to Loyola, Scott rode the motorcycle down this HUGE long bunch of steps. I dug my nails into his shirt and screamed to high HELL. And laughed, and screamed some more until my stomach ached. When we got off, my legs were like shaky jello and I walked all wobbly.

"What'sa matter, kid? Can't youwalk? Been hittin' the bottle, or what?" he joked.

I laughed and ran over to him, screaming. "You CREEP!" And I hit him on the chest a few times. Then we went in, and studied in the college library. Every one there was a college person, and the whole room smelled like old books and fog mixed together. I kept smelling it: warm fog old books. I felt warm and safe and happy.

Mimi loved all this extra education Scott was giving me; she'd always ask my mother if I could stay for dinner. Dinner at the Ramseys' was always excellant—sphagetti or barbecued chicken. Or Cheerios. Mimi was like my mother, my sister, my hero, and my best friend rolled into one. "Vanny," she'd say, "it's always so fun to have you over. You're such a smart, pretty girl." She really liked me, just as I was. She always complimented me, and Scott always teased me. Eric sat on my lap and showed me his Monster Mash Bubble Gum Cards.

So things were really great there at the Hula Gardens. We cruised along like that, happy and friendly, for three years. The college kids in the apartment building knew that Mimi and Scott liked me, so they liked me, too. They treated me as if I were their little sister. Once, my brother and I started a huge water balloon fight with all of them. We were deadly with water balloons—especially Johnny; he couldn't miss! "Bombs Away!" He'd yell, then, smasho, they were drenched. One guy, Rod, who lived just over us upstairs, was throwing balloons at us from the balcony upstairs. Johnny hit him plunk in the gut, and Rod went "OH! GOD! I'm HIT!" And I screamed, because he jumped from the second story balcony into the pool and played dead. Pretty soon, every guy and girl in the building was jumping into the pool from the second story balcony. One of them jumped up and grabbed me, and pulled ME into the pool. Johnny jumped right on top of us, and all of us splashed around the pool with our clothes on. (Except my mother, of course, who was at work. Mimi helped us stuff all our clothes in the dryer so my mother would never know.) I wish I could just say THE END HAPPILY EVER AFTER right now. But I can't, because my father left his other wife to return to my mother. That's right, he moved in again, when I was fourteen.

* * *

The thing is, when you know that some one loves you, the way I knew Mimi and Scott loved me, it makes you feel strong. You're not lonely and stupid and helpless anymore. Not so much, anyway. When he moved back in, you better believe I practically moved in with Mimi and Scott. I was there every second I could escape.

I couldn't believe it; my mother acted like she was on her second honeymoon when he came back. He was the same drunk old bum who never worked or even bothered to throw away his empty Jack Daniels bottles, but she giggled and acted gross mushy anyway. She would say things to me like, "go be nice to your father," and I'd give her a dirty look, and she'd say, "well, he IS your FATHER, after all." After a few times of that routine — I still refused to look at him or speak to him — she yelled at me.

"What is your PROBLEM? That was a LONG time ago. God, you think he WANTS you or something? It's not as if you're DESIRABLE." Oh, brother! She had to make everything about ME sound strange and perverted, but she acted as if the really perverted things — like HIM — were normal. So I got slapped a lot, mostly by her, but I didn't care. I refused to talk to him or look at him; the Child Center had toughened me up. He was a bad guy, and I didn't have to put up with him.

Unless he had a knife. He had several knives, and once, he snuck up on me when my mother was gone. I was just getting ready to put on a jumpsuit that Mimi had given me for my fourteenth birthday. I was singing to myself, "Bye Bye Love" by the Everly Brothers, and I started to take off my blouse. Shit! My father jumped out of my closet at me and yanked at my neck with his arm. I kicked and screamed as much as I could; my heart was smashing around inside my chest. Then he pulled this wicked-looking knife on me.

"You try to get out of this, and I'll kill you. You've got a duty to perform, dammit." God, he stunk. Like he'd taken a shower in Jack Daniels. He held onto me hard with one arm at my neck, with the knife wiggling around at my nose while he undid his pants. I planted my elbow, HARD, in his gut, which was like a brick.

"Goddamn you, you little shit!" He never let go of me, he yanked a huge hunk of hair out of my head. He poked the tip of the knife into my neck so I almost suffocated. "You're doing this whether you like it or not, because I am your father, and you will obey me or DIE!"

"I'd rather die," I said. To tell you the truth, I didn't mean it, because I'm a wimp, and I hate pain, and I don't care who knows about it. My voice, my legs, my hands — everything, was shaking. I did NOT want to die.

"Oh, bull SHIT!" He yelled, and smashed me in the face. He ripped his pants down with one arm, and threw me onto his penis. My head was weaving back and forth, and my face was all tight-hot-swollen from being bashed in.

It was the old ice cream cone number all over again. I knelt down, looked at the "Poisonous Slug", and started crying.

"Please . . . please, no . . ." I blubbered, but he grabbed my hair hard, and shoved the knife up to my throat. Barf was coming up to my mouth; I closed my eyes and started to do it to him, all the while feeling both the barf inside my throat and the knife tip pricking my skin, enough that it bled. When he'd ejaculated and was done, he gave me a dollar.

"These are your choices," he said, smiling at me. He held up the knife and the dollar. "You tell ANY ONE, and I'll kill you AND them." Then he fell asleep, and I locked myself in the bathroom and threw up. I cried and I pounded the walls. I hated life and God at the same time, with all my strength.

* * *

"Hey, kid, you run into a wall or something?" Scott asked me in his usual happy smart ass teasing way. I was too bummed to tease him back.

"No." And I walked away.

Scott could never deal well with scenes like that, so he went into Mimi. Mimi walked out where I was sitting. I was in a pissy mood, sitting by the pool.

"Hi, there, Vanny," she said in her usual sparky-cheerful way. Like she was trying to pretend there was nothing wrong, but there obviously was a LOT wrong. My face looked like a rotting piece of meat.

"Vanny, did some one hit you?" She asked.

"No, Mimi, this is my new mod makeup."

"Vanny, did your dad do this, or your mom?"

"I'll get killed if I tell you."

Mimi was good at this kind of stuff. "So don't tell me, Vanny. Just nod your head, yes or no. Your dad?"

I thought about it, and nodded yes.

"Scott is going to talk to him. He'll fix it for you."

"NO!" I yelled. "He said he would KILL me, with a KNIFE, which he almost DID. LOOK!" And I showed her the black and blue spot on my neck where my father had poked the knife into my vein. "He said he would also kill ANY ONE I told. You know, to destroy the evidence."

"Jesus Christ! Scott, would you come here right now and look at what that bastard did to his daughter?" Tiny little Mimi was PISSED.

Scott said he'd take care of everything, and when I saw him talking to my father all charming like they were buddies, it was pretty irritating. I was hoping Scott would cut him up and throw him in the Los Angeles River when it got dark, but all that happened was they had two drinks together. Unfortunately, Scott was really good at beating around the bush. Scott said it would take time "to get his confidence". Maybe there was hope, but I doubted it. My father put on his sweetheart act, and it was bigger than Scott.

I never told Mimi about, you know, the ice cream cone routine, because I didn't ever want her to know I was that weird, or that I did such a gross thing to my father. She treated me as if I were this wonderful normal person who did normal innocent things that fourteen year olds did. Shit, I didn't even do half of them! I never smoked, never drank, never kissed a single boy. Marijuana was just starting to go around the tough-kid circles, but I didn't even know what it was, I was such a little priss Miss! My pure white bobby sox were for real. Well, except for ... No, when my father popped out of closets from time to time and pulled the knife on me, I just did it, collected my dollar, and felt my insides shrivel up with cancerous anguish. Life was utter hell again.

* * *

I tried NEVER to be in that apartment alone if I thought he was there; I was terrified of him. Mimi had to walk in the apartment and go around checking all the closets before I would go in. One time, it was raining and Mimi wasn't home, so I just sat in a lounge chair by the pool while the rain poured on me. I tried to act like it was the most normal thing in the world, to be sitting in the rain getting soaked. It was a lousy grey world I lived in, a world where a kid has to sit in the rain because she's afraid of her sick old man.

Mimi showed up with Eric and some shopping bags. Her hair was really blonde that day, and she wore this outrageous red plastic raincoat with big black and white triangles on it, and these incredibly fashionable black boots. She was like instant sun. Eric, too: he wore a bright yellow, plastic-hooded raincoat.

She walked over to me and didn't even talk to me like I was crazy. She just said, in the sweetest voice, "hi, Vanny, would you like to come in and have some hot chocolate or something?" She was six months pregnant, but she still looked tiny-petite, only with this canteloupe in her tummy. I felt a little better, and even joked around with Eric a little, but it sure wasn't the same as before. I was seriously depressed.

Every one started worrying about me, even my school. I didn't care about school or life or anything, and the principal sent home a letter saying something to the effect of, "We don't know what you're doing to Vanessa, but she's gone from being an energetic straight A student to a depressed D student. If this doesn't change, we will investigate." Something like that. One of the things better back then than now about how they treated kids was that they didn't just assume I was on drugs. This was in the early sixties, just before high schools turned into drug stores.

My father and I swam around in all this hatred toward each other. It ate me up, and my mother knew it, and hated it. Both parents would punch me for not coming home when he told me to, which was always a time of day when my mother was at work—but that was cool. They couldn't throw me around the room all that much anymore, because I had friends all over the apartment building who cared about me; they listened hard to make sure my body never hit the walls. He could only get his penis licked when he used a knife on me; in my mind, that made him the most pathetic worm on earth.

But the old man was shifty. The final confrontation came on a day when I was almost excited about a school dance; Mimi was making me this yellow dress, and we'd been shopping for fabrics. Even I could see that I looked terrific in yellow. We came to my apartment moderately stoked and happy. First Mimi went in, checking all the closets and under the beds. Then I went in, and she said she'd come back after she picked up Eric at nursery school.

I started cleaning up the apartment, humming "Ba-ba-ba, my Barbara Anne" by the Beach Boys, and was almost feeling good. I went in the bathroom with a sponge to clean the toothpaste out of the sink and watched myself in the mirror while I sang. I really exaggerated my mouth on the "oooooowooooooo − oo" part. Mimi had made such a fuss over my "huge, dark eyes" that I'd let her put eye liner on. I have to say I looked pretty good. I barely saw him jump out at me from behind the shower curtain. My father. He had the knife. I screamed, threw the sponge at him, and jumped out of the bathroom. I was insane, hysterical, screaming out of my mind and crying, crying. But too slow.

He caught my shirt and ripped it. I screamed again, and he pulled my hair. Through all my tears and screaming stomach, he put the knife at my throat. He was ten times drunker than usual. I could see it and I knew. He meant it more than ever, this time.

"Come in the bedroom right now, or I'll fuckin' kill you."

"NO! NO! NO! I WON'T, YOU BASTARD!"

He slashed at my face with the knife, and got an eyelid. I pulled away hard, and he ripped another big piece of my shirt. My bra was all exposed, but I ran like crazy and made it out the door. He followed me.

I couldn't see because of all the blood in my eye. I pushed my hand up, and it was oozing blood. I screamed and screamed and cried.

"HELP ME, HELP ME!"

Rod, Brian and Betsy from upstairs rushed out from their apartment. Betsy screamed when she saw me drippy with blood, but Rod and Brian stared at my drunken father, standing there with a knife as if he was going to pass out.

"Call the police! Get an ambulance!" Somebody yelled. Scott and Mimi came running at me.

"You son of a bitch," Scott said to my father. "We're going to put your ass in jail for this!" Mimi walked me away, into the apartment and gently washed my eye. I was shaking, out of control; my teeth were smashing up against each other.

"You're safe, now, Vanny. We will never let him near you

again. There, there—oh, Vanny, look, that's not such a big cut at all! Everything's going to be OK. I SWEAR it. Do you hear me, Vanny?"

I nodded a little, but I didn't believe so easily anymore.

* * *

THE STATS AND A LITTLE HISTORY LESSON

Dear Little Sisters and Brothers,

In the United States, *during an average week*, 5,000 children are sexually abused, *90% of them by someone they know and trust*. Two thousand other children will run away during an average week, *simply to escape the sexual abuse in their homes*. Forty other children will be kidnapped, sexually abused, and killed. All this, in only ONE average week.

There are *600,000* child prostitutes in this country. Some of them were kidnapped, but most of them suffered sexual abuse in their homes, and ran away. They are doing for money what they learned to do at home.

"Even by the most conservative estimates," says Senator Christopher Dodd, "every two minutes, a child is sexually abused in the United States."

One Federally funded study's figures suggest that one out of THREE girls have been or will be sexually abused by the time they are eighteen, and the number of boys sexually abused may be almost as high. 56% of all these sexual abuses are committed by the children's NATURAL FATHERS.

A United States Postal Service investigation concluded

that 80% of child pornography collectors are sexual abusers of children.

The average pedophile (sexual abuser of children) will abuse 70 children.

80% of sexual abusers of children were also sexually abused as children.

70% of ALL PRISONERS in ALL JAILS in the United States were sexually abused as children, says one U.S. Justice Department study.

Friends and relatives who know what I'm working on have said to me, "gee, sexual abuse of children sure is on the rise," or, "boy, there NEVER used to be so much sexual abuse of children." WRONG! Children have been used for sex by grown-ups for THOUSANDS OF YEARS. IT IS NOTHING NEW! It did not just suddenly start happening.

There is a big difference, though, between the Old Days — when grown-ups just did whatever they wanted to, to children — and Now. Now, in the 1980's, women feel strong enough, for the first time EVER, to say, "NO MORE! You guys kept me silent while you did it to me, but MY CHILDREN WILL NOT SUFFER THE WAY I DID!" Good guys — men and women volunteers — have joined in a huge fight to stop the abuse. We are dedicated to teaching our kids and our little sisters TO SAY NO, and to break a six thousand year old cycle.

You can find incest in the Bible. Does anyone out there REALLY BELIEVE that Noah slept and slept, NEVER WAKING UP, while his two daughters raped him? In Ancient Greece — another bit of our historical culture that man is extremely proud of — they did a lot of baby killing. Their Greek mythology is filled with Greek gods raping Greek goddesses, and also of Greek gods flying to Earth to rape mortal women. They're all swine, as far as I'm concerned. Grown men who raped young boys in Greece told each other "it's good for these young boys." Young girls and boys were put in harems, but first they castrated the young boys. (That means they cut off the boys' testicles — their balls.)

Modern man also picked up a lot of great culture-stuff from Ancient Rome. In Rome, if a man raped a woman, do you know what she was supposed to do, if she had any class? KILL HERSELF! Honest, things were no better for women and kids in Rome than they were in Greece.

And you can say, "oh, WELL, they were PAGANS." And I can say, "Oh, yeah? Well from the very holy days of the Italian Renaissance until well into THIS CENTURY, young Italian boys with beautiful voices were castrated so they could sing in the Church choir and sound terrific." If their testicles were cut off, you see, their voices stayed really high and pretty, like girls' voices. Yeah, I know, you're wondering, "wouldn't it have been a lot more humane to just have GIRLS sing the high parts?" No, little sisters and brothers, that would have been just TOO logical. Girls back then were treated like total dirt.

All over the world, throughout our history, women and children have been labelled "the property of men", for men to do with as they liked. Was there ever a time when it wasn't like this, you ask? Yes, there was! It was before the Bible, when God was a woman. Women and children had rights, then, and good jobs. They got respect. Those people weren't much into war, though, so all the macho guys came in and slaughtered them. So, OK, we've been down a few thousand years, but we're coming back! Taking back our power.

And don't anyone try to tell me I'm anti-God, or anti-Christian, or anti-religion. No way. I am anti-child abuse, and anti-rape. Jesus Christ's very favorite word was Love, but for some reason, it got lost in the translation. Ever since Jesus, our whole race has, for the most part, been LOUSY at loving each other. Little sisters and brothers, take a look at any children's Bible, you'll see a picture of Jesus with a bunch of little children. He loves you. Yes,

Jesus wants children to obey their parents, but NOT when it means abuse. Jesus would HATE to see adults abusing children. Using a child for sex is not loving a child enough to think about the CONSEQUENCES to that child. It is selfish, and selfishness is lousy loving. If the person abusing you belongs to a church, and says you must obey, because it is God's will, that person is trying to fool you, himself, and God. And you know something? Not you, him, or especially God gets fooled that easily.

And so child abuse went on, throughout our noble history, into the Victorian Age. Everyone thinks that Victorian English people didn't do anything sexual, but there were a LOT of child sex abuse scandals. There was a LOT of white sex-slave traffic in children. It was no secret, either, but during this same Victorian Age, Sigmund Freud, the Father of Modern Psychiatry, played his dirty games. He was a real jerk, little sisters and brothers, and I'll tell you why: he KNEW how many daddies were doing it to their daughters, and he could have helped them – and us! – right then and there. Do you know what he did instead? He hushed it up. We're talking numbers: EVERY SINGLE ONE OF HIS WOMEN PATIENTS complained of being sexually abused as children, but he hushed it all up. Watergate was NOTHING compared to this coverup!! Old Sigmund falsified his incest cases, all because he was embarrassed that there were so many middle class "gentlemen" who were total perverts. He didn't want these "gentlemen" embarrassed. BUT DID HE HAVE ANY PROBLEM EMBARRASSING THE VICTIMS OF CHILD SEXUAL ABUSE? No, sir. He wrote many fancy documents saying that these women were wackos who simply IMAGINED the abuse because they really WISHED THAT IT HAD HAPPENED!! God. Little sisters, read Freud if you want to find out that all you really want in life is a penis. And I'm serious. (Check it out.) How do I know that Freud really KNEW the truth? Because, ha, ha on you, Herr Ghosto-Freud, your PERSONAL letters, where you CONFESSED the obscene truth about YOUR OWN incest problems, were dug up and published. You're outa' here, Bud.

OK, but Freud was a pretty important guy, back then, and everyone believed him. Things got out of hand, so that ALL the fancy shrinks and doctors and lawyers wanted to keep the truth about child abuse covered up. All these psychiatry people HAD to agree with Freud and THE LIES if they wanted any respect. And the problems created by all this coverup persist until today. You'd better believe it! Until very, very recently, nine times out of ten, the first reaction a molested child met with when she told was "you must have made it up, kid." In the early part of this century, before pennicilin, V.D. – a disease you ONLY get from having sex with someone who has it – was ALL over town. When seven and nine year old kids got it, instead of asking the obvious, like, "hmm, I wonder who's been having sex with this child," doctors would say, "well, I guess she got it off a towel." And if she was pregnant, this, say, twelve year old child? Do you think anyone was gentle to this child who was raped, probably by her own father? No way! This poor child was probably treated like she was the worst slut on earth.

There were *many* jerks that followed Freud. This one guy, John Henry Wigmore, in 1934, wrote a big legal text saying that ANY FEMALE, ESPECIALLY A CHILD, WHO COMPLAINED OF A SEXUAL OFFENSE, WAS LYING. He warned (WARNED! Like, "watch out for those five year olds, 'cuz they're so dangerous," right?) that it was just PART OF WOMEN AND GIRLS' NATURE to falsely accuse "men of good character". May he spend eternity puking. But, folks, we've got some of Wigmore's personal letters, too, where HE ADMITS TO FALSIFYING REPORTS OF GENUINE SEX ABUSE. For example, two girls, seven and nine, accused their fathers of sexual assault. One girl had gonorrhea, (V.D.), and the other girl's vagina was too horribly swollen and inflamed to examine. The good doctor Wigmore ommitted these two pieces of medical evidence, however, and told the court that these two girls were perfect examples of typical children telling their typical lies.

Are you getting sick to your stomach? Do you know what the ACTUAL FIGURES ARE regarding children and lies? Children do NOT make up sexual abuse; several studies concur that, of all children's accusations of sexual abuse, LESS THAN ONE PERCENT WERE UNTRUE. Of the accusations where children came forth, accusing a sexual abuser within the family, and THEN recanted— which means that she said, "oh, I made it up. He didn't really do that"—ALMOST ALL OF THESE kids were forced to recant by someone in their family. Many of the wise judges in these cases said, "well, at last we have the real truth," then sent the kids home to get not only raped again, but also beat up badly enough to need hospitalization. What about in the late 1980's, when children "claiming" they were sexually abused in a San Francisco Day Care Center tested positive for the AIDS virus? You don't "create" AIDS in your head; it's a disease that is always fatal, and you only get it from sexual contact.

This attitude stayed hot and heavy with American psychiatry for such a long time that, in 1975, American psychiatry announced that incest occurs one in every million girls. Now, what if you were one of the women who'd been abused as a child—by your dad, uncle, brother, or by the neighbor? You thought you were one-in-a-million, and it made you feel lonely. You didn't feel you could just talk to anybody about it, because you were such a weirdo. Wouldn't it piss you off when you discovered the truth—that you were really ONE IN FOUR, but everyone had been working their tails off to cover up that fact?

Because we ARE one in four. (Some figures say one-in-three, but most stats say one in four.) These are the eighties, and those are the real numbers. Women and children are taking some power for themselves that they haven't had for SIX THOUSAND YEARS, and we are busting down doors to stop the abuse. We're not going to take it for another minute.

If you were sexually abused, you have lots of sisters and brothers to hug. Some of them are gorgeous and rich and famous. Some of them made it, and some of them didn't. Marilyn Monroe was sexually abused when she was eight or nine. She was gorgeous, but she didn't make it. I wish she were around, so we could all help her make it. Being sexually abused as a child, believe me, can do weird things to your grown-up life. Rod McKuen is a famous man who was abused as a child. He writes beautiful poetry, now. Then there's Oprah Winfrey; she was raped at nine, and she's a champion survivor. She's a gorgeous, rich-and-famous, GREAT woman who helps sisters like US a LOT. Then there's Senator Paula Hawkins, in Florida; she was sexually abused by a family friend when she was five. She's a beautiful lady, AND she's a SENATOR! You betcha' she looks out for child abuse victims, with power and with laws. And then there's me: NOT movie-star gorgeous, not even rich or famous. But happy, FINALLY. And, not only a survivor, but also a lover of life.

If we all work together, then, this gross kind of abuse will never ever be shoved under the carpet again. Sex abuse of children will end, and when it does, honest, the whole world will be a better place.

* * *

Once again, I was the one put in jail, not him. Again, I was the one whose sanity and truthfulness (yes! MY MORALITY QUOTIENT!) was probed and prodded along with my genitals and anus. Only this time, there was a big difference. I knew all the words they threw at me this time, and I wasn't so afraid of them. Best of all, I had witnesses.

"Yes,' I answered, "my father used a knife to force me to do oral copulation on him." I looked the attorney straight in the eye while my mother glared at me.

This time in court, Rod, Brian, Betsy, Mimi and Scott stuck up for me, and testified about both my parents beat-

ing me up. Scott even talked out of control, telling every
one about my straight A's in school, and what a great artist
I was. He went on and on while my mother rolled her eyes.
Looking back, I must say that Scott did pour it on a little
thick.

Scott spoke desperately – as if I were on trial for murder,
or as if he were in a movie. "I wish the people in this room,"
he began, then paused, looking at everyone's faces, "could
see her with my young son, Eric. When nothing in the
world can get Eric to sleep, Vanessa comes and sings lulla-
byes that would tear your heart out. They come from her
gut. I mean, she is *good*." Scott's eyes are always watery, so
I don't know if he'd made himself emotional – very likely –
but he looked moved. He'd definitely affected everyone in
that room. Even my social worker dabbed her eyes with a
Kleenex.

I was SO embarrassed; he made me sound like Miss
America! (I kind of loved it.) Then the judge – all crabby as
he got something out of his eye – got impatient and said,
"please try to answer only the questions you are asked, Mr.
Ramsey."

Rod, Brian, and Betsy were much straighter; they simply
told the court about my father that day, with the knife and
the ripped blouse.

They called my mother to the witness stand. At first she
looked nervous. Then she warmed up and told the court
about my D's, and how I never minded, and how I've been
seeing shrinks. She reminded the court that I'd been institutionalized, ("Emotionally Disturbed"), etcetera. She told
the court she loved me very much, and she couldn't understand why I wanted to tell lies to turn every one against her
and her husband.

"Yes, my husband has a bad temper – it's worse when he's
drunk, but those awful other things Vanessa says he does:
they're filthy, absolute lies!" She made herself sound like
the ultimate Ivory Soap Mom, so it was pretty funny what
occurred during court recess. I was standing outside the
courtroom with my assigned social worker sitting behind

me, and my mother walked up to me without a word and smacked me hard across the face. My social worker popped up from behind me and said, I SAW that, Mrs. Morelli." The great thing was, the Judge himself walked by. He was in a big hurry until he caught our lovely mother-daughter act. Then he stopped; he saw the whole thing.

"So did I," he said coolly.

"You BLEW that one, Mother." I said. It was the only time in my life I ever smart-assed her, and it felt fantastic.

* * *

As much as my father desperately needed to be locked in jail, it would never happen; there was absolutely no medical evidence (the ice-cream-cone number leaves no physical marks), and there was no witness who SAW him sexually abuse me. Slicing his kid's eyelid was a total "ACCIDENT", he said, and between my father's charm and his defense attorney, Justice didn't stand a chance. So I would stay at the "Detention Center", "until" the Judge said, "we can find an excellant foster home for you, Vanessa. You need a place where you are safe. Mr. and Mrs. Ramsey have offered to keep you, . . .

I had to interrupt. "Oh, yes, your honor, PLEASE CAN'T I JUST GO WITH THEM, PLEASE?" I was crying hysterically; "Detention Center" sounded too much like "Nazi Gas Chamber". Mimi started crying, too. The Judge, I must admit, was a really kind man trying to just "do his job" impersonally. All the hysterics were making him tense.

"Vanessa, the Ramseys' apartment is practically next door to these people. No. I'm sorry. For your own safety, you'll have to go farther than that from them."

I could feel all the love in the room coming from Scott and Mimi, but I still could not ask the questions burning inside me, like, "what about HIM?" (Sob, convulsion), "Why can't you just LOCK HIM up for a change?"

The Judge must have read my mind. His voice got quiet, sad, and kinder. "Vanessa, it takes time. And there are certain PROBLEMS." He gave my mother a Mega-dirt look. "You are not being punished, young lady. We are trying to protect you. We MUST keep you away from these so-called parents of yours. The court has decided to terminate their rights as parents, which means you will never be subjected to their brutality again." He took a deep breath when I didn't jump up and down with glee. "You've been through a lot, but it will be better for you in the long run that we're doing it this way. Court dismissed."

But in this Detention Center, they made absolutely no distinction between hoodlum juvenile delinquents and kids with kinky fathers. Keeping in mind that I was a goody-goody prude virgin, imagine how amazed I was by these tough chicks all muddy-headed with dope and killing people. They wore beehive hairdos teased up sky high. They didn't even try to hide the razor blades embedded in their hair. They were into sniffing spray paint and robbing liquor stores, and really bizarre sex acts. (I do not feel the need to elaborate; it was pure hell, and I don't care to remember much about the place.) It was like a weird voodoo dream, being there. I sucked in my breath, and held it for two months, trying to be invisible and not get beat up too much. Mimi and Scott, I believed, would not allow me to stay here for long. But then, that thought terrified me worse, because Ginny Barnes had once said that she would not let me stay locked up for long.

* * *

Dear Little Sisters:

I just had to remind you, right here and now, that they no longer lock up victims of sex/child abuse with criminals. It took everyone awhile to figure it out, but they finally did: WE ARE NOT CRIMINALS, AND WE NEED A

DIFFERENT KIND OF PLACE. If you are in danger in your parents' home, they HAVE to get you out of there, but the place they put you will be SO much nicer. My horror story happened in the early sixties. YOU WILL NOT HAVE TO GO TO THIS KIND OF PLACE, and that's a blessing, because the place stunk. The really sad thing is that even this Mega-Bad juvy hall was better than living in a place where my sick-drunk father jumped out of closets wanting you-know-what.

I tried to get involved with school at this place, which took major bravery. Young, tough women beat on me whenever they were in the mood—whenever I didn't melt into the wall. None of the other girls—or teachers, for that matter—gave a damn about school, so my struggles to be perked-up interested made me more than a little conspicuous. I spent an awful lot of time during my loner-meals drawing Richard Chamberlain, who was then acting as Dr. Kildare on television. I always drew him in a silver Corvette Stingray. I'd never told anyone that he'd sent me an autographed, black and white photograph of himself, signed, "To Vanessa, Love, Richard Chamberlain". I took it everywhere, hidden in my school books. I imagined he would drive his Corvette, smashing into one of my classes right through the window, and rev up his Stingray right next to my desk. He'd smile with those incredibly white teeth and say, casually, "Vanessa . . . Doctor's orders. Hop in!"

All the teachers were tough warden-types; unlike the Child Center situation, maybe they had to be for their own survival. God, I remember having trouble in the bathroom in between classes. (One of the problems with not having a normal mom is that you never do learn how to put in tampons right.) So I reached the classroom three seconds after the bell started ringing, and this crew cut Marine-type told me to go to the principal.

I walked into the principal's office shaking and sweating. The principal was one of those greasy-haired men with dan-

druff all over their eyelashes who spend every minute of
their lives trying to impress people with how tough and
hard they are. He pointed his finger at me really hard and
talked to me as if I were a year's worth of dust.

"Now, look! We KNOW what you are, and why you're
here, so DON'T think you can get away with that kind of
shit here!"

He hadn't taken a goddamned minute to look at my file,
and see what exactly my "crimes" were. But that was the
basic attitude this Detention Center had toward every single girl in the place: we were ROTTEN TO THE CORE in
their minds. It was HELL, and the only thing I can say in
their defense is that they were grossly overcrowded, and
suffered from massive shortages of staff and funds. Back
then, there was absolutely no place for girls my age to go
who hadn't done anything wrong except be born to a
shithead sicko father, which is really no one's fault. It's
better now—there ARE places to go, people to talk to.
Some politicians want to cut back funds for kids like us,
but I don't want to talk politics here and now. Suffice it to
say that, in my opinion, the idea of cutting back funds for
abused children SUCKS.

* * *

The guy who called himself a shrink at the Detention
Center pissed me off so much that he improved my life. His
name was Mr. Dean—of absolutely NO relation to Jimmy
Dean, another of my fantasy idols. (Of course, when I imagined JIMMY driving through the window right up to my
desk at school, HE drove a souped-up '57 Chevy. An Apple
Green one.) This Mr. Dean had serious problems. He
thought he knew everything, and I mean EVERYTHING.
He sat in his desk so that he blended in perfectly with all
the black splatter paintings mashed together on the wall
behind him. He wore humungus black glasses that totally
magnified his wormy yellow eyes. He thought his head was

a million dollar crystal ball, but it was merely your basic Acne Metropolis. (How DOES one get zits on the top of one's head?) I had to see him three times a week after school at the Detention Center.

Every time I walked in, he looked me up and down, past all my chubby little lumps and bumps, like, "what a worthless little turd." I felt so goddamned lonely when he did that, and I always started sweating. Better than crying, I guess. It went something like this:

"Hello, Vanessa," Mr. Dean would say, looking me over, then checking his wristwatch.

"Hello."

"How are you feeling today?"

"Like I want to get out of this place." One good thing was that I didn't have to be nice to him, or make up polite things to say like, "I want to sing opera, and give joy to the world, and I want to feed starving children in China." In talking to other women who were sexually abused as children, I now realize that I LUCKED OUT, getting Mr. Dean, beause THEIR shrinks kept trying to tell them the sex abuse never happened—that they IMAGINED it because they WISHED IT HAD HAPPENED. Yuck. OR, when my friends kept trying to bring it up, like, "hey, shrink, this thing that happened to me when I was a kid REALLY BOTHERED ME," the shrink would change the subject totally: "let's do ink splats." But not Mr. Dean. His was a different approach.

"Vanessa, what are your plans for the future?" Mr. Dean was big on Future.

"I'd like to live in a Foster Home with reasonable people like Mimi and Scott Ramsey until I can go to college and become an interior decorator, or some kind of artist that gets paid."

"What are your feelings toward men?" He asked, as if NOTHING about my future CAREER plans or living-arrangement-dreams was important. "Are you repulsed by men? Wouldn't you rather make love to a woman than a man? Or would you rather get even with your father, make him pay for what he did to you–by making ALL men pay?"

That was his gig, and he was really stuck on it. Every time I saw him, basically what we talked about–what HE talked about–was that I absolutely must admit my desires as either a lesbian or a prostitute. Now, as an adult, I see that this was his BIG THEORY that he was working to confirm–maybe as part of a thesis. Actually, Mr. Dean was ahead of his time; number one, he BELIEVED that kids were NOT lying about sexual abuse, and number two, he was one of the first guys doing compassionate studies of prostitutes. He later told me that something like 70–80% of all the prostitutes (hundreds) he'd interviewed had been sexually abused as children in their own homes. Twenty years later, other studies and their conclusions come close to Mr. Dean's. OK, but he could see nothing else.

Now, if lesbianism or prostitution had been my desires, I would have been happy to discuss them. But sex was the last thing on my mind; I needed COMFORT. I needed to talk about the GODDAMNED UNFAIRNESS OF LIFE that was chewing up my insides. And I sure as hell didn't appreciate some one TELLING me what I was destined to become. God, he was a pain. He actually asked me once "did you ever once enjoy making love with your father?" HOW COULD HE HAVE USED THOSE WORDS?

Back then, I was horribly wimpy, and terrified of all authority figures, but when he asked that question, all the power of a lifetime's worth of choked rage–like a hydroelectric dam busting open!–surged up inside me. For one minute, I didn't give a goddamn what happened to me. I changed; I wasn't the normal, wimpy Vanessa. I sprang out of my chair and kicked it hard behind me. I jumped hard and fast into his yellow acne face and grabbed his stupid little polyester shirt.

"You fucking FASCIST! I may be a little dirt clod that everybody likes to squish into the ground, but there's a limit to what I'll take, and you are IT." I shoved him, hard, back into his chair, and turned to leave as if I was still hot, but my terror had returned. My knees were NOT THERE, and it was very hard to walk with dignity without my knees. But somehow I persevered with my tough-guy act, and said over my shoulder—to scare him, really, "if you want to get off on people's sex talk, go do it with some one else." I'm still proud of that one. That made him sound cheap, as if all he was was a little man in a porno shop, paying a quarter to look at the naked lady in the window. I suspect that tore him up, and I'm glad about it. And I slammed the door, scared beyond imagination that I'd get locked up in the state penitentiary for LIFE for what I'd just done.

Absolutely nothing happened to me for blowing up. The next time I had to go see Mr. Dean, practically peeing in my pants I was so scared, he acted as if nothing in the world had occurred. He did quit telling me that I'd end up a hooker or a lesbian, though, and—most amazing of all—he actually started letting me tell him how I FELT about things, HERE and NOW. I'm sorry, Freud and Jung, but sex was NOT the major focus of my life at that time. Justice, and life's lack of it—coupled with my desperate loneliness—were the things that busied my mind.

He, in short, RESPECTED me for exploding—he acted as if he did, anyway. Maybe he'd been trying to get me to explode all along. Anyway, I learned a lot from him. I learned that if I demanded that people treat me with respect, it would happen more often. I could never love this Mr. Dean, but he became my ally. I could say anything on earth to him that I felt like saying, and, if he never gave me comfort or gentleness, maybe he gave me strength: toughened me up for the real world. He thought so highly of himself, that, in showing me respect, I think he felt he was doing me the highest honor of all.

* * *

Dear Little Sisters,

There are some fantastically GREAT men shrinks out there. One male shrink, the greatest of all, saved my life. Sometimes, if a girl has been abused by a man, or if a boy has been abused by a woman, it's healthy for them to have therapists of the opposite sex: you can "work out" the problems with the abuser more easily. I had serious problems with both parents, so both my "Best Woman Therapist" AND my "Best Man Therapist" were essential in helping me. But BE CAREFUL. Just as there are the greatest therapists and shrinks, both male and female, there are also some scary-bad ones. There's still a little strangeness in SOME men (and women) shrinks' minds; they have dumb attitudes that can hurt you, like, "did you ENCOURAGE this sex abuser?" If you get a male (or female) shrink who IN ANY WAY acts like YOU MUST HAVE DONE SOMETHING to get this pervert sex abuser feeling sexy, flip this person off. Tell him what a stupid idiot he is, and get a new shrink. HE'S wrong, not you. I HOPE I don't also have to tell you what to do if a male or female shrink EVER wants you to have sex with them. And pay attention to this: in one survey, 70% of male therapists said they knew colleagues who screwed their patients. WATCH OUT FOR THAT! If a shrink, or priest, or ANYONE you go to for help wants to screw you "to make things better"–ha!– give it to them good and hard, little sisters: with every bit of pent-up rage you've got, POWER-KNEE THEM IN THE NUTS! !

So, anyway, one day, in his office, I couldn't help it. I started laughing right in the middle of Mr. Dean congratulating himself. He was delighted with how correctly he'd diagnosed Bad Betty, one of the toughest inmates, as a victim of sexual abuse. She'd been locked up as a runaway-drug-abuser-prostitute, at sixteen. Most of those young women ARE victims of sex abuse, as many as eighty per cent in some studies: Why the HELL do you think they run away? Because their homes are just like HAPPY DAYS? Where do you think the first place a twelve or thirteen year old girl gets the idea that she exists primarily for someone else's sexual needs? Grow up, people! Is this really so hard to figure out? But it took Bad Betty a long time to admit to what her Daddy did to her, because she was so convinced it was ALL HER FAULT he did it. That was why she thought she was so bad. That's why she ACTED so bad; she thought she was dirt, so she acted dirty. Now, I know, and you know, that Mr. Dean had no right to mention such confidential things to me about another patient. He didn't mean to: it just slipped out. He wanted ME to respect HIM, and he was trying to win my respect by showing me that he'd helped Bad Betty. But I started laughing. Something wonderful had happened.

"Uh, Vanessa, what is so funny?" Mr. Dean asked. He was smiling.

"Mr. Dean, I'm sorry. It's just that, well, I just figured out that if someone like you can like yourself so very much, and want respect from me, it isn't at all unreasonable for me to like myself, and want respect." We both smiled, maybe for different reasons. I was strong with Mr. Dean, and I gave him a hard time—which he deserved—but I honestly think it was Mr. Dean who helped Mimi and Scott get me out of there.

The first possible visitors' day, Mimi and Scott came to see me. Scott slapped me on the back as he always did, and pointed to Mimi.

"Would you look at your good friend, here? You ever see anything so fat in your life? I swear, she's going to have the kid right here—either that or fall over backwards. Whoa, girl!" He pretended to hold her up by standing against her back with his back. "Lean FORWARD, MIMI!" He grunted and groaned as if she were a drunk elephant, which was pretty comical, because soaking wet and nine months' pregnant, I'm sure Mimi weighed all of a hundred pounds.

"Oh, Scott, would you grow up? You're scaring Vanny." Mimi laughed and kissed me, and pinched my cheek as always.

"It's no big deal," Scott continued. He always joked

around a lot when he was tense, and this Detention place with the razor blade beehive ladies would make ANY one tense. Three of them shuffled past us, looking slime-vicious-sexy as if they would first rape Scott, then cut Mimi's baby right out of her stomach. Scott made the funniest monster-eyeball face when they'd passed, but they scared the shit out of him. He cracked me up! I lost MOUNTAINS of tension, laughing at his monster-eyeball face. Mimi was frightened—"ssh, Vanny, they'll come back, and slice us up!" So Scott kept talking, fast and funny. "You breast fed Eric in phone booths, Mimi, for Christ's sake! SUPERMOM!"

I laughed; that one really got me. God, it was good to see them. "Are you guys getting me out of here?" I asked them. "Please, oh please?"

Mimi grinned really big, so you could see all the teeth in her tiny mouth. "As a matter of fact we are, cutie. How would you like to live in Beverly Hills?"

"WHAT?" I asked, really disappointed. My voice sank, because now it sounded like a big joke. "Very funny. You sound just like Scott, Mimi. Maybe you've been hanging out with him too long."

Scott changed his plastic face to "Serious". "It's the truth, smart ass. We're signing the papers in an hour if Mimi here can keep from dropping her load. I talked my parents into taking you in. If it works, and you like them, they'll be your official foster parents—and they really DO live in Beverly Hills, so THERE." And he stuck his tongue way out at me.

It was REAL! I grabbed him. "God, are you KIDDING? NO! Scott, I never knew you were RICH! How can ... I am SURE!" I was delerious. HA! Beverly Hills. My God! Scott's parents! "God, I'll be your Foster Sister! I don't believe this! Mimi, I'll be your foster sister-in-law, and your baby's foster aunt! Thank you so much, you guys! I LOVE you!" I kissed both of them a million times. Scott pretended he hated it, but I knew he loved being a good guy. It was Beverly Hills for Vanessa Morelli!

* * *

So maybe now you think I should just write "the end happily ever after," huh? WRONG. Rich people, I mean some of them, can be strange and weird, even if they are kind and nice and mean well. Each foster home—every home, for that matter, has its own strange rules. Rich people, I discovered, are not necessarily very happy. So Beverly Hills wasn't Paradise, but my God, it was better than ANYPLACE except Mimi and Scott's apartment, or maybe Ginny Barnes' house, or Moravia, that I had ever been.

The hardest thing about going to Scott's parents' house was wanting very badly for Scott's parents not to hate Scott for sticking them with me. I wanted his folks to be HAPPY they had me there. That was a tremendous burden to suffer: I would DIE if Scott and Mimi got in trouble because of me.

The first dose of Culture Shock set in when we parked the car in front of a high, grassy mountain. At the top of the mountain stood a massive grey mansion.

"There?" I asked, suddenly frightened. "People LIVE in places like that?" It looked so grand, but also imposing. What if there was a gorgeous-haughty Bitch Queen living there, like the jealous queen in Snow White, who never took off her tiara? She'd send me to the dungeon for picking up the wrong fork. I already knew that they gave you ten forks at dinner, in mansions like that. My parents were smack-in-the-middle Middle Class. We'd been to restaurants that had three forks and two spoong sitting beside the plates—I'd gloried in those restaurants, but I wasn't quite ready for this much of a jump upward.

I puffed and puffed, getting up the long, long stairway that led up the mountain to the front door. The entrance was GONE WITH THE WIND amazing, I didn't care how dumb I looked, gawking at the immense, winding staircase. It was noble. The ceiling was thirty feet high, and a chande-

lier as big as Seattle hung from a long brass chain. Two
gilded Louis XIV chairs upholstered in exquisite tapestry
(I knew what they were, because my mother had taught me
about fine things) sat, a little lonely in this grand entrance
hall. The floor of the hall was made of emerald tiles, as were
all the winding stairs leading up, up, up to some dark, cold
place.

"The Emerald Staircase!" I gasped. Dead, murdered people might lay beneath my feet! I moved from the hallway,
quickly, but, I hoped, in a way so that no one could be
suspicious. I entered the ornate Louis XIV living room on
my right.

Gleaming in the corner, and reddish brown as a chestnut
horse prancing in a field, rested a grand piano. In my imagination, I saw myself sitting grandly, spreading my taffeta
gown behind me on the piano stool, and played Mozart. But
actually, "Heart and Soul" was all I knew. I played shyly,
that day, alone in that magnificent room with some wild
dreams in my heart. On all the walls around me hung for-
mal portraits of the family. There was Scotty's portrait! He
was younger, but SO handsome, even with his flat-top hair-
cut. I'd never seen him look so solemn and dignified. I
closed my eyes, and imagined that someday I, too, would
be solemnly posing in my black taffeta gown, looking dignified and lovely, my thick black hair streaming down my
shoulders. I would be on these walls, someday: a grand
young woman. Was this really happening? Where WAS
everyone? The house was so dark and quiet, I was losing
my nerve.

Reality tremor number sixty five was that Warm and
Friendly, my fantasy friends, were in no way part of my
welcome to the Ramsey Castle. When do the real and the
fantasy ever match, is what I'd like to know. I mean, in my
fantasies, Scott's dad looked just like Scott, and cracked
jokes and was gentle and kind and pretend-gruff at the
same time. Whoo, boy: Reality-Tremor Major. If he was
just pretending to be gruff, Mr. Ramsey Sr. deserved an
Oscar! He was just like the mansion he lived in – huge and

dark and cold. We had eyes like a huge, suffering, angry moose, and when he looked at you, you knew from his look you bothered the hell out of him. When he was in the house, the entire mansion felt tense and tight. His initial greeting to me, according to his own people, was "classic Bart Ramsey."

"You Vanessa?" He shouted at me. I jumped; he had this incredibly deep, loud voice that echoed all over the emerald tile hall.

"Yes, Sir."

"I don't want any GUFF out of you," he growled. For the rest of the time I stayed in his house, he never said another word to me. He turned away from me, and walked up the long flight of movie-mansion emerald stairs in the dark. He walked slowly and heavily, as if he carried a trunkload filled with life's heaviest CRUD. He'd scared the shit out of me with his welcome – I wanted to run – and yet, as I watched him trudge up those glamorous stairs, I felt sad for him. He wasn't happy in his castle; he felt awful. Cheez, if *he* couldn't be happy here, how could I?

Tears clouded up my eyes, but Mimi squeezed my hand hard. I couldn't believe it; she was giggling. "Tsk! Vanny, he was only JOKING!"

"Joking?" I laughed-cried, nervously. "Gee. Funny guy." I doubted I could ever get used to my foster father's sense of humor.

"You'll get used to him! He's funny like that with every one. Eric thinks he's a riot."

I gave her a dirty look, and she smiled sympathetically. "Wait till you meet Scott's mom."

She wasn't a lot warmer, but at least she wasn't mean. She didn't want me there, though; that was obvious, because right in front of me she offered me my own apartment at one of the apartment buildings she and her husband owned. Scott was a little embarrassed – it's always easy to see, because he blushes like crazy – but he kept his power while he talked to her. "Mom, Vanessa could use some FAMILY after all the crap she's been through. We can't just stick her all alone in an empty apartment." (He almost said "shit" and not "crap", but he caught himself in time.)

Mrs. Ramsey Sr. cleared her throat. Now SHE was embarrassed. "Oh! OH, WELL, if that's the case, of course, we'll be glad to have her. She can stay upstairs, with Beth."

"Sure," Mimi chimed in, squeezing my hand as if to say "everything is going to be wonderful starting now." But her voice sounded a little forced when she said, "Bethy will LOVE having a big sister!"

"That's great!" Scott said, relaxing. He looked over at me, wanting me to tell him with my eyes what a great job he did. I wasn't so sure yet, so I looked down, at this tough-looking little cat who lifted its tail and was about to spray all over me. I jumped up fast, and the cat sprayed from beneath its lifted tail all over the kitchen cabinet. Mimi was embarrassed, but Scott thought it was hilarious.

"There, you see, Vanessa? The official house welcome. Pisser's done that to every guest we've ever had!"

I started to laugh, until it was obvious that Mrs. Ramsey did NOT think it was funny. She jumped over to see if Pisser was injured by this remark. ("Pisser" is what every one except Mrs. Ramsey called the cat—she called it "Speck" after the speck of black paint on its nose.) She didn't seem the least bit concerned that all this drippy stuff was running down the bottom cabinet, but they had a couple maids, so I guess she didn't need to. God, I couldn't help thinking that if my parents had even allowed a cat in their house, if it had done that, it would be dead in one minute!

"Poor little Speck," Mrs. Ramsey cooed to Pisser. "Don't you listen to him." She turned to us. "He gets excited. He just needs to go outside.'"

All of a sudden, the window in the room next to us exploded; glass shattered for what seemed like hours. Mrs. Ramsey's mouth froze in a horrified "0". Scott moved quickly.

"Holy SHIT!" He yelled, and ran out of the room. Mimi

and Mrs. Ramsey followed Scott, and I followed them, feeling panicked and awkward and lonely.

Two scruffy brown-haired, Norman Rockwell-type kids stood giggling in the patio. The younger one, Kelly, held a baseball bat. He grinned wide, showing enormous dimples and looking alarmingly like Alfred E. Newman of MAD Magazine.

"Whoops," he said, grinning wider.

But the rest of us were all frozen, and staring up at what I presumed (correctly) to be Mr. Ramsey Sr's bedroom. Waiting, I guess, for bullets or axes to fly. Nothing.

Mrs. Ramsey sighed deeply. "Thank GOD. Your father must be taking a nap." And with that, she walked inside. I was astounded: not a word about the gorgeous bay window that was ruined. I would have been massacred for putting the tiniest crack in such a window. Learning the rules here would either be really easy—as in, maybe there WERE none, except "don't wake up the old man", and apparently, he was a pretty hard napper—or really strange. And that was a profound lesson to me: each change of scenery in life comes with its own personal package of rules.

That was my introduction to Kelly and Beth. Beth was ten, Kelly was eight. Beth reminded me of some of the girls at the Child Center in Seattle: skinny, no self esteem, and beat upon. She wouldn't have struck others that way, giggling with her brother and pretending to be tough, but I'd seen enough brutalized young girls to recognize them in any disguise. My heart relaxed, for I saw in Beth some one I could take care of—some one who would love me. Kelly decided immediately that I would be a great new person to terrorize; as soon as I turned away from him, he threw a hard, giant dirt clod at me. What a beginning: in a half hour, I'd been yelled at, pissed on, and dirt-bombed. I begged Mimi and Scott to at least see me through my first dinner at the Ramsey's house.

Scott didn't want to—which told me something—but Mimi talked him into it. "C'mon, honey, it's her first night in a house filled with strangers. Your dad'll come down from his nap all grouchy and horrible – c'mon, let's help her out."

I gulped hard. The maids had cleaned away both Pisser's mess and all the glass bits from the dining room. We sat at a long table. I sat between Beth and Mimi, but, unluckily, I was at the head of the table. By the way everyone walked way around the chair as if it were irradiated, I could figure out easily enough who would be sitting at the other end, directly opposite me. I could hear Mr. Ramsey coming down the hall toward the dining room, because all the tiny crystal pieces in the chandeliers shook and tinkled. He looked bad when he entered: absolutely the angry, suffering moose, only as if some one had shot him in the eyes. They were amazingly bloodshot. This man did not wake up from his naps gracefully.

He looked right through me to the closed shade that someone thought might completely cover up the broken window incident. I think the shattered jagged edges' shadows gave it all away. He knew, EVERYTHING, but he didn't say a word. He didn't give a damn about the window, but the attempt at coverup irritated and depressed him. He'd get even, maybe, I thought. If there had been any jolly words before his entrance, there certainly wouldn't be, now. Kelly sat on one side of him, and Mrs. Ramsey sat on the other side. Kelly stared at his food, as if he were too busy scheming to eat. He never picked up his fork.

None of this disturbed Mrs. Ramsey; she cheerfully passed beautiful china plates filled with mashed potatoes, vegetables, and meat. Pools of melted butter sloshed over all the potatoes and vegetables.

"What're you LOOKING at?" Mr. Ramsey growled at Kelly. "Pick up your fork and eat."

Kelly picked up his fork, and slyly waited. While Mr. Ramsey busied himself with cutting his potatoes and steak into equal numbers of squares, Kelly lifted food onto his fork. I watched Kelly pass food from the fork onto his hand, then the hand under the tablecloth where Elvis, the family poodle, waited quietly. That worked twice, (I was a nervous wreck), but then the old man started watching Kelly.

"Marion," he said to Mrs. Ramsey, "please give Kelly two forkfulls of vegetables."

She did. Major silence and tension in the room.

"Now. If we have to sit here until nine o'clock tonight, you're going to eat every single one of those vegetables."

Kelly was an unbelievably stubborn kid. If I hadn't been so timid, I would've said, "Kelly, they really are NOT that bad! Your mom put so much butter on them, you can easily pretend they're pancakes, you know? They'll slide right down!" But no one said anything. We ate our dinners silently. Beth and Mimi, on either side of me, ate with their faces down, as if their plates contained an absorbing design. I did the same. Very attractive plates. We then waited with Mr. Ramsey and watched Kelly. The room grew black as twilight faded and sank, but no one moved to turn on the lights, so we sat in the dark. Kelly would not lift his fork and eat. By now, all the butter had congealed on our plates. In the silent room, we heard a strange popping noise. It was Mimi—her water broke.

"Um, honeeee. It's time."

Scott jumped up. "Jesus Christ! She's gonna have the kid right here! Thanks for the dinner, Mom. We gotta run. Holy shit—crap—excuse me. Mom, call the doctor . . .". Mrs. Ramsey jumped up, in a panic.

"Marion, you will sit down RIGHT NOW. Mimi, Scott, both of you. Sit DOWN." Mr. Ramsey meant it. I couldn't believe this was happening; Scott, Mimi, and Mrs. Ramsey sat down in the dark and once again started to watch Kelly watch his cold-congealed-fat-vegetables.

"Dad, Jesus Christ, would you knock it off? My wife is gonna' have a goddamned BABY!" Scott was more panicky than I had ever seen him.

Mr. Ramsey was stone calm. "Having a baby is the most natural thing in the world. Your grandmother was born quite easily in her home, on her parents' bed. I have no worries. But Kelly here could starve to death if he doesn't eat. So we'll all just have to wait."

Mimi started to sweat. Pains, probably; little groans started to come out of her. It was all getting to her. She started to giggle uncontrollably. "I can't—oh, God! That was a good one—I cannot believe this is happening to me." Her forehead was sweaty. She giggled (her creepy giggling was GETTING to me), then breathed in sharply—a super contraction pain. Then she talked mean, with her teeth clenched together. "Kelly, would you just stuff your goddamned vegetables in your goddamned mouth so I can get to the hospital and HAVE THIS BABY?"

Kelly gave her the most angelic grin in the world, picked up every piece of food on his plate, and stuffed his cheeks. In a flash, every single one of us shoved the chair out from under us, and ran in a hundred directions. I, for one, ran to the bathroom and breathed deeply, then puked really fast. Except Mr. Ramsey, who got up very slowly, ignored all of our panic, and trudged upstairs in his same, heavily burdened way. I could hear that same, slow trudge up the stairs, which were fairly close to the bathroom. He had utterly no interest in the approaching birth.

When I returned to the kitchen, Kelly ran right to the trash and spit out all the food he'd lodged in his cheeks. "Yick!" he said, and grinned at me. (He'd waited—to do it in front of me?) "Don't tell my dad, OK?" He begged. God, he was cute! He shrugged his shoulders. "I had to do something! Mimi has babies fast."

Two hours later, in the Emergency Room, Jeffrey Scott Ramsey was born. Mrs. Ramsey snuck into the television room to tell Beth and Kelly and me. Behind her head in the door was the most handsome Surfer Boy in the world. He was yelling at Mrs. Ramsey in the rudest way; if I had ever yelled anything like that at my mother, I'd be dog scraps fast. The handsome rude Surfer Boy was holding a huge steak up with his fork while Mrs. Ramsey quietly announced about Jeffrey.

"Mother, what IS this? Do you call this MEAT? It's WELL DONE!"

Mrs. Ramsey turned to him. "Albert, Mimi just had a baby boy in the Emergency Room."

He was not overly thrilled. "Oh, so that's just GREAT. So I don't get any dinner."

"Albert, it's pink, for God's sake! You can still eat it."

He was furious. "It's not FIT to eat!" And he stormed out.

Kelly and Beth laughed. "That's Albert. Our brother. He only eats his steak if it's blood red."

Mrs. Ramsey sighed, and said, rather cheerfully, "well, I'd better go fix your brother another piece of steak."

"Elvis'll eat it!" Kelly called. "Go have some steak, Elvis" he called as he pushed Elvis out the door. Kelly giggled. He was enjoying a wonderful evening.

I turned to Beth, who was clearly traumatized by everything that had happened. "Is it always like this around here?" I asked her, hoping for a straight answer.

She thought for a moment, and sighed. "Sort of. Yeah."

"Hey!" Kelly yelled, jumping on the couch and throwing four expensive, Oriental brocade pillows at me. "Albert's probably got the lock off his door. Let's go in his room and steal comic books while he eats!"

Jesus, would this kid ever stop?

Beth's eyes grew, she was excited-terrified by the thought. "God, Kelly, he would KILL us! No WAY! You can, not me!"

"You're boring. I don't know how I ever manage to have any fun around here," Kelly said, and shuffled out, really depressed.

I was left alone with Beth, who was agitated. "Albert's gonna' KILL him."

"Beth, how old is Albert?"

"He's sixteen and a half."

God! Perfect! I was fifteen; back then, "Older Men" were cool. Albert may have given a bad first impression, but no one who looked THAT dreamy could be ALL BAD. He had a perfect tan, was built-to-the-hilt, and had gigantic surf bumps on his knees and ankles. (Surf bumps, far beyond Cool, were absolutely esoteric.) His hair was surfer-shaggy, and just-right bleached by the sun and salt. Contrary to everything Mr. Dean-the-shrink said, I was fully capable of falling in love at first sight, and with a guy. Even if he could be a real jerk sometimes. My hormones ran the show.

* * *

Kelly rushed in with a pile of SUPERMAN and DONALD DUCK comic books. I got queasy in the stomach, seeing instantly that I had to do something to get away from Kelly, or I'd never do well with Albert. Beth was delighted.

"GOD, Kelly, you got all the SUPERBOY ones—my FAVORITE! You'll have to put them back, after I read them, but I can read fast."

"No way. YOU put them back."

"But I told you not to take them!"

"But you love them, and now you'll read them. I didn't want to READ them. So it's your fault."

Everyone sighed. Kelly was just stealing for the sake of hassling his brother. Beth was depressed. "OK, then, forget it. I WON'T read them. Go put them back, please? Before he kills us."

"That sounds boring." He dropped the huge pile on the floor, and went back to jumping up and down on the couch. He looked at me. "Hey, DUFFY! You want to have a pillow fight?"

I was trying to be a good sport, even though I didn't like my new name. "Duffy"—where did he get it?— was better than what he called Beth: Poop. Albert was simply "Bumps". "Sure, Kelly! Let's have a pillow fight!"

We whacked each other hard with all the pillows. Beth joined in half-heartedly, and screamed at us when we slid across the pile of comics. A couple of the comic books' covers ripped off.

"God, you guys! You're ruining Albert's comic books!"

Not very bright, Beth. Albert suddenly appeared at the door, plate of food still in hand. Probably THE most embarrassing moment of my adolescence. I was on the couch with Kelly, giggling and squealing while he belted me with a pillow. Not very mature, Vanessa.

"Very funny, Kelly," Albert said, and belted Kelly HARD. Albert still had a plate in his hand, piled high with food; I couldn't believe you could beat some one up and hold a plate full of food at the same time. He started pummelling Kelly, who was crying and swinging at the same time. I was scared he'd really kill Kelly, so I yelled really loud.

"Hey, guy, Would you cut it out? He's a lot smaller than you—your comics are there, dammit! Why don't you go pick on some one your own size!" I know—not very original, but I will always hate violence, especially against the weak and helpless. I had to stop him beating on Kelly, but, frankly, I also hated what I was doing: forever eliminating my chances with the first Surf God I'd ever known in person. I didn't care—he was really a jerk to hit such a little kid so hard.

Albert squinted his eyes and looked at me as if I were the most alien new bacteria just recently discovered. "Who are *you?*" he asked; he must have really been floored, because a fork stuffed with food tumbled off his plate and onto the Persian carpet. He continued to squint at me.

I smoothed my skirt down toward my knees. "I'm Vanessa." It did not register at all. "Vanessa Morelli. Pleased to meet you.' Nothing. "I'm, um, living here—as, like, a foster child."

"You're kidding." This was all news to Albert. He turned to Beth. "Is this true?"

Beth laughed, embarrassed. "Yes, I guess so. Well, I mean, nobody told me anything, but she ate dinner with us, and I think she's going to sleep in my room, with me—'like a big sister,' is what Mimi told me." God. Like I was a stray dog, or something.

"Nobody tells me ANYTHING." He bent over and picked

up all his comics. He looked hurt. I started to feel his loneliness, his sense of alienation in that house, but then he went and spoiled those soft feelings by smashing Kelly on his way out.

"You come in my room again, and I'll KILL you!"

Kelly finished crying the second the door slammed. "Thanks a lot, Beth."

Beth started crying. She felt guilty as hell. "I TOLD you not to go in his room."

"He never would've known it if you hadn't yelled."

Beth was suffering; she sobbed while she looked at her smashed-up brother. Kelly had succeeded in making her feel that it was her fault. That was too close to feelings pushed onto me all my life. I, the intruder, had to step in.

"Kelly," I said really softly, "you know, you stole about two hundred comic books. Albert certainly would've found out, sooner or later."

"Shut up, DUFFY! You're not family," Kelly spit at me. I left the room, incredibly hurt by that small bit of truth. I crept into bed and cried myself to sleep. My first half day at the Ramsey house had exhausted and bewildered me. I can't say it wasn't a dream, but I think maybe an hour later, Beth sat on my bed beside me, and patted my shoulder with her bony little hand.

"It's OK. Vanessa. You can be MY big sister, ANY day."

* * *

Dear Little Sisters and Brothers,

THE LAW SAYS that children have the right to be raised by their parents free from substantial harm. In all states, it is AGAINST THE LAW for parents to beat you. It is AGAINST THE LAW, in all states, for adults to molest or sexually abuse children. It is AGAINST THE LAW, in all states, for parents to starve their kids, or to not give them any clothes. KIDS HAVE RIGHTS.

Don't forget about The Child Abuse Reporting Law. It's in effect in all states, and says that if your teacher, doctor, or football coach thinks you're being abused (or, if you TELL them you're being abused), they HAVE to report it. It's a good way to get the ball rolling while you are SAFELY out of the house. All the child welfare people will then step in to see that you don't get beat up for telling.

A child who says she or he has been abused is entitled to a lawyer.

If parents really neglect or abuse their children, the court can "terminate parental rights" – that means, they tell your folks to go take a walk. You are then free to get adopted, by much nicer people. That's what happened to me. In some states, such as Indiana and Missouri, for example, the state has to really try to re-educate the parents on how to be good parents before they totally give up on the parents.

The magic words in most state laws are, " . . . if it is found to be in the child's best interests." The courts really do want kids to be free from abuse. You can help them by demanding they do a good job.

If you are old enough to really TALK to your lawyer, MAKE YOUR LAWYER LISTEN TO YOU! In my days, kids didn't have lawyers. You've gained POWER. Don't just sit there quietly. Tell your lawyer how you really FEEL about everything. Be strong. Demand your rights.

Most likely, you won't have to sit in on the court thing. But then again, you might. And it's a bitch! Be strong, and be tough, little sisters and brothers; it is hell. The first thing you must do is: demand to know whether or not your county has a "Child's Legal Advocate" system, and if they do, hassle them until they assign one to you. An advocate is a human being who speaks English. You need her! When the creepy lawyers ask you all these questions in legalese-garble language, the child advocate turns to you and speaks real English that you understand. Usually, she even talks in a nice voice! So do everything you can to get one of them.

The main thing is, DON'T LET THEM BULLY YOU!

Don't let them tear you apart, so you change what you say. They will try to trick you; they will try to get you to change the truth, just for THEIR sakes. Tell the truth, and STICK TO IT, no matter WHAT they try to do to you! If they try to make you into a bad person, as if you're some kind of mega-slut, SHUT THEM DOWN, and don't let them win. THEY are the people with problems, NOT YOU. You are not on trial. You are NOT a bad person. When it starts to get to you, BE STRONG, and take three deep breaths. Answer in a strong voice, yes or no. The truth, the truth, the truth. It never changes.

God, I read about one trial in which a fifteen year old girl's natural father had been raping her for years. Her lawyer asked her to tell the court who it was who'd been raping her, and could she point to him.

"My father," she said, and pointed to her father in the courtroom.

"Objection!" Her father's attorney yelled, and they spent ALL DAY arguing whether or not he was really her father. Had blood tests been done? Could the babies have gotten mixed up at the hospital, the day the girl was born? They put her mother on the stand. Are you SURE he is the natural father? Are you SURE you didn't have an affair with someone else? The craziest thing about this particular trial is that this man had already CONFESSED to raping the girl, who he considered to be his daughter! GET SERIOUS, PEOPLE! This is a bullshit travesty of what the law is supposed to be all about. But, you know? Reading about it made me stronger, because this young woman stayed tough, and stuck to the truth. She won, and God bless her, if she didn't also announce to that lawyer, RIGHT on the witness stand, that he was irritating the hell out of her. She stayed strong, largely for herself, but also because SHE WANTS HER FATHER TO GET THE PSYCHIATRIC HELP THAT HE NEEDS. She cares about her father. She doesn't want him to go to jail, but she DOES want him to admit that he did wrong, so they can all HEAL, and get on with life. THAT, you dumbshit lawyers, is a mature person who understands what is really important: healing, not power games. They put her through not one, but TWO trials. The first trial shook her badly, but she took power for herself, and was stronger for the second one. She'll make it.

Hey, little sisters and brothers! Did you know that you can SUE your parents for all the child abusing they did to you as a kid, the minute you turn eighteen? YOU CAN! It's a new law. It's a hassle, and, unless your parents are worth some really big bucks, I don't reccomend it. It's probably not worth the heartache, but still, THAT'S a POWER that you now have! And I want you to know about it. Likewise, if you get sent to a foster home, and you get abused there, the law says you can sue the shit out of them. They deserve it.

So those are the laws that pertain to you. What about THEM, the guys – and some women/some mothers – who abused you? What kind of jail sentences are in store for them? Incidentally, about women abusers: Current statistics say that 1% of all sexual abuse is committed by women – mostly, mothers abusing their kids. Recently, those numbers have started rising, either because more kids are reporting, or because more single-parent, stressed-out, lonely mothers are abusing. As yet, it is unclear exactly what is going on. But the numbers are rising.

Every state writes the whole thing up differently; Mississippi's statute provision, for example, reads, "death or life imprisonment" for sexual abuse of children. Montana's reads, "minimum two years, maximum twenty years." But what the books SAY and what the courts DO are two different things. Nobody, it seems, ever gets the maximum sentence. In Montana, for example, (and you might have seen this one on Phil Donahue), there was a deacon in the Church up there who had five daughters. He raped every single one of them over a period of many, many years. (When the audience jumped on his wife, saying, "where were you," she said, "when your two year old daughter has a vaginal infection, WHO STOPS TO THINK IT MIGHT

BE BECAUSE YOUR HUSBAND IS RAPING HER?")
Now, wouldn't you say that raping five of your daughters
warrants the maximum sentence? But, hey, his good buddies, the fellow deacons in the Church, stuck up for him to
the end, and called the five year old girls sluts. In a state
where stealing a sheep can get you ten years in the slammer, this guy got TWO YEARS.

So, again, it's different in each case, and in each state.
From all that I've read, I'd say two years is pretty average.
BUT, if the guy ADMITS HIS GUILT, AND IS WILL-
ING TO GO THROUGH A SEX ABUSE THERAPY
PROGRAM, and he really GOES to it, and he works to heal
all the problems in the family that brought about the whole
mess in the first place, the courts might allow him to keep
his job. In that case, he'll only spend nights and weekends
in the slammer for a couple years.

The main thing to remember, little sisters, is that YOU
did not send your father to jail. YOU are IN NO WAY the
cause of his problems. HE SENT HIMSELF THERE, by
doing what he did. So don't feel guilty; two years is not so
long for him to pay, for screwing up your life. And the
important thing is that 99% of the time, once their big
dirty secret is out, the incestual abusers DO stop sexually
abusing their children.

* * *

The first thing Mrs. Ramsey had to do, she said, was
buy me some clothes. I'd moved into her house with one
outfit, which I slept in that first night. We drove through
downtown Beverly Hills, where I was amazed by all the
limousines and Rolls Royces, to Saks Fifth Avenue. It's the
only store I'd ever been where a man dressed as a Burger-
meister opens the door for you. His smile was enormous
when he bent over. I think he was from that African tribe
where everyone is over seven feet tall.

"Good day, ladies!"

The only building I had ever seen like Saks Fifth Avenue was the White House. And I'd only seen pictures of the White House; this was in person! The tall, tall ceilings were detailed with sculpted flowers, and curves, and there were marble statues, and huge bouquets of fresh flowers, everywhere! I couldn't close my mouth.

"This is the most beautiful building I have ever seen!" I told Mrs. Ramsey.

But she was in a hurry; she was always in a hurry. "Now. Let's get you into some nice new clothes."

"HERE? You're going to buy me clothes from HERE?"

"Is that all right?" She was beginning to feel awkward. I don't think she'd spent too much time around middle class kids.

So we went to the teenage section, and I tried to be calm while Mrs. Ramsey piled dresses and skirts and pants and blouses on the door to my dressing room. Also a beautiful camel hair coat, one like my mother had wanted all her life, but could never afford. It made me sad, looking at this long, beautiful coat. Maybe without me around, my mother would be able to afford one, now.

Mrs. Ramsey cleared her throat from outside the dressing room and said I had "a full figure—you might, er, need one of these"—and she threw about five different-sized bras into my dressing room. I was getting the Lonelies again, a bad case of them. The bras were very difficult to hook together, and I was in the dressing room for what seemed hours while the rather nice sales lady asked about a hundred times: "Is there anything I can get you?" I hated her guts, because she kept opening the door on me when I was half dressed, so I finally barricaded the door with the chair in the dressing room.

I finally came out, dressed in the bra (which no one could see, but it did make my boobs look perky and firm), and a really beautiful brown pantsuit. Mrs. Ramsey's eyes went from irritated-bored-shitless to really excited-happy when she saw me. I must admit, the suit was really flattering.

"Wow!" She said. "THAT brings out your best features. We'll take it!"

I laughed. God, I wanted her to like me! I wanted her to be happy she was stuck with me. I mean, if she could love a stray cat that pissed all over everything, why not a stray girl who didn't?

We picked up two nightgowns on the way out, but we were already carrying so many bags that the saleslady called a "porter" with a huge cart to carry all our bags down. The shoe department was on the first floor, though, so we had to stop there. We picked up a pair of heels, and a pair of flats "for casual wear," Mrs. Ramsey said. Also a pair of tennis shoes that would've cost one tenth the price at the dime store where my mother had always bought our shoes.

We were both exhausted, and we stopped in a coffee shop. Mrs. Ramsey grinned and said, "how would you like a chocolate malt?" She was the most wonderful lady on earth when she was warm like this. We fidgeted for words to say until the burgers and malts came. All I could think of to say was "thank you Mrs. Ramsey, SOOO much. If I can ever pay you back,.." and on and on. I probably thanked her ten times. Then she cleared her throat. "Now. It's very, very important that Mr. Ramsey doesn't know about any of these clothes we bought today. You must hide them from him so that he never knows."

Was she KIDDING? The entire trunk AND back seat of her huge Lincoln Continental were crammed with huge bags. God, suddenly my stomach started churning around.

"But, Mrs. Ramsey, what if he SEES me in them?"

"Oh, don't worry. He won't notice. If he does, just say, I don't know, say that you found them."

"But how will we get all these hundreds of bags upstairs into my room?"

"No problem. We'll all work together while he's taking a nap."

She was bored and cold again, so I didn't ask the one BIG question: what happens if he DOES catch me taking all these bags up to the room? Nor did I feel I could comfortably ask the other questions: What will he DO to me? Why did we BUY all this shit if it's his money and he doesn't want to spend it? Being rich in Beverly Hills, I learned, was strange: there was no such thing as unsullied joy. Each potentially great time had to cost something big. I also started feeling sorry for Mr. Ramsey, again.

* * *

So we drove up the half-mile long driveway to the house, while hot and cold flashes raced up and down my skin. I was positive Mr. Ramsey would be watching out the window, and would SEE all the bags from Saks Fifth Avenue. He would Kill me first, then Mrs. Ramsey, then Mimi and Scott and Eric and Jeffrey. But all we found at the top of the driveway was Kelly, Beth, and Elvis-the-dog. They were throwing around a big softball—without the bat, thank God. Kelly grinned at us and then threw the softball right at the windshield. I ducked, hard. Mrs. Ramsey yelled at him.

"Don't DO that."

"Did you get me anything, Mom?" he asked, looking in her purse. He pulled out a pack of ROLOS candy. "Oh, boy! Thanks, Mom!"

"Beth, is your father taking a nap?"

Beth looked scared. "Yes. He came home in a really BAD MOOD. He was mad that you weren't home, so he yelled at us for about ten minutes, and went upstairs. I took his ice water up, and took off his socks and shoes while he laid down on the bed. I think he's taking a nap now, because he started snoring while I was taking off his shoes."

Mrs. Ramsey's face read "FEAR". "Oh, my GOD. Here, Beth, you and Vanessa get these bags up to your room. QUIETLY, so your father knows nothing about them. BE CAREFUL. I'm going upstairs and pretend I've been there all along."

Guilt attack: I had put the old man in a BAD MOOD,

and his wife was in huge trouble. She would hate me forever. It was all my fault. I didn't even want the clothes, at
that point.

But Beth gave me a compassionate look that said, "hey!
We're sisters, it'll be OK." She was really a scrawny, sad-
looking girl, but she could light up with a big freckly smile
when she wanted to be kind.

"C'mon, Vanessa, let's get your things upstairs. It'll be
OK, honest. My dad sleeps for hours after a bad mood."

So we loaded ourselves with bags, until I could only see
Beth's skinny red stretch pants underneath a piled-high
load of white bags. I wished like hell that Elvis would quit
barking at us, but then Kelly ran up and started throwing
the soft ball at our bags. Hard. Beth screamed.

"WOULD YOU QUIT IT!"

Kelly laughed, and mimicked her—with absolute PER-
FECTION, I must admit. "Would you quit it?" When Beth
only pouted her response, he was bored. "What's in the
bag?" He asked, threatening to bomb it with the softball
again.

"None of your business," Beth said. I was getting tense;
we were right beneath Mr. Ramsey's bedroom window.

I spoke up. "Clothes, Kelly, nothing but clothes. Girl's
clothes, for school and stuff. Do you think you could help
us?"

"No, I'm afraid not. Clothes are very boring, and if I
touch girl's clothes, I'll get cooties, really bad. Sorry." And
he whammed the softball right at Beth's load, so all the
bags fell to the ground. Which made Elvis yip like crazy.
Beth started crying, Kelly laughed and ran away, and I
seriously considered shooting myself. First, though, I had
to comfort Beth, who was grossly depressed. I also spent
tremendous self control to keep myself from strangling the
barking poodle.

"Hey, Bethy, it's OK. We'll just pick up the bags and start
over. Everything's going to be fine. Your brother's just
being a typical dumb old brother, nothing else. All brothers
are like that."

"But he's so MEAN to me," she sobbed. "Why?"

I wanted to say, "do you have a week, kid? I could tell you all about mean people, and how there sometimes ISN'T any 'why'," but instead, we just loaded all the torn-up bags into our outstretched arms, and trudged upstairs. Once in our room, we were safe. We breathed deeply, and enjoyed some real happiness.

Bethy lit up. She could go from total despair to lit-up perky, surprisingly fast. "Show me what you got."

I giggled. "I was hoping you'd ask." And I tried on every single outfit for her, turning and twirling like a high style fashion model. I felt gorgeous, watching her watch me.

"You look BEAUTIFUL in that," or, "Oh! That is REALLY beautiful," she murmured over every new ensemble. She said it as if she were praying, as if she couldn't picture anything more miraculous than the beauty of being fifteen. She made me feel as if I were a miracle – a grown-up miracle. Suddenly, though, her face blanched. "It's my Dad!" She whispered. We dove on the bags, and shoved them madly under the beds. We were on the floor panting when Mr. Ramsey opened the door and said "Dinner" as if it were a filthy swear word. I jumped, I would never get used to that deep, low growl of his.

* * *

The next thing Mrs. Ramsey had to do, she said, was get me into "a good" school. The Ramsey's were devout Catholics, so of course I would be sent to a Holy Mary kind of Catholic high school. Everyone wore strange brown and yellow uniforms, so that no one could tell if you were rich or poor just by the clothes you wore. I was in no way prepared for that place! Mrs. Ramsey and I walked down this long hallway that was lined with all these huge white holy statues: Mary and Jesus, Joseph, St. Theresa "the Little Flower" (I read the inscriptions on each one, wondering who in the hell all these weird-eyebally people were). The school

principal was a nun; I'd never seen one close up. She wore
this starched pure white cardboard all around her face, and
a long black robe. Frankly, she needed some lipstick or
mascara—something. Her face looked as if it had never
seen the sunlight. But she had big white teeth and really
clean-looking blue eyes; once I ignored her lack of color, I
liked the kind way she looked at me: as if I truly were a
pure, innocent child of God. For one split moment, I was
caught in a spell—the nun's spell—and I would've done anything; I would have joined instantly, become a little white
cardboard nun. It was giving me the creeps, though, this
moment, and I had to look away. I got the feeling she would
do anything for Mrs. Ramsey.

Mrs. Ramsey talked, and I couldn't believe what came
out of her mouth. Scott Ramsey Words, all of them. Jesus.
I wanted to die.

"She's brilliant, Sister," Mrs. Ramsey started. "Her IQ is
so high, it could not be measured. Her numbers sailed right
off the charts, to quote my son." If Scott had walked in the
room just then, I would've punched him. That was definitely his kind of talk. I snuck a look at the nun, who managed to keep a straight face through this whole crazy bullshit story. For just a moment—before sinking into deep
depression—I smiled to think of how all these nuns would
take it when little genius Vanessa flubbed it up on all the
tests. Maybe they'd think I'd been possessed, or
something.

Mrs. Ramsey signed the check, and I was enrolled for the
school year, which started the following week. Mrs. Ramsey was relieved to know that she could order my school
uniforms and saddle shoes over the phone. They were conveniently delivered during one of Mr. Ramsey's naps. I buried my face in them, not really believing how GOOD brand
new wool and cotton uniforms could smell. I was excited: if
the school was half as much of a high as the way the uniforms smelled, I'd love it.

From day one at Holy Mary High School, I was Miss
MEGA-MISFIT. These girls had studied Catholic versions

of life since they were baptized: they knew what a rosary was; they knew about Benediction and confession. Jesus, Mary, and Joseph – whoever they are – didn't do a damned thing for me. I was lost! Nothing had prepared me for all these Bible chapter numbers; they didn't make any sense. They're not in ANY logical order! The Lonelies burrowed into my uniform, and itched like hell. But instead of screaming for help at the Ramsey house, (I'm sure Beth knew how to look up all those chapters), I pretended I was doing great in all my classes. I figured if the Ramseys found out I was dumb at school, they'd throw me out and kill Scott for lying.

One night, I was up studying well past one in the morning; I had a massive Religion History test the next morning. Even though the history part of it was different from any other history I'd ever learned, I could just memorize it, and try not to get it confused with other versions of history I'd read, i.e., the ones with Aristotle and Plato in them. ("Pagan", the nuns called that version of history.) It was the Bible chapter numerical order that was busting my brain. I decided to take an Oreo-cookies-and-milk break. I crept down the huge, dark, spooky-as-anything staircase.

Why did I not turn on the light? We were not allowed to turn on lights in the house unless we were reading. Mr. Ramsey always reminded us that "electricity costs money", or "you don't need to SEE each other to talk", or "if you can't see in the dark, you should eat more carrots". So I always pretended I was practicing for if I ever go blind, and groped along the walls with my hands.

However, when I got to the dining room on my way to the kitchen, ten baby chandeliers blazed, in Open Rebellion. Albert was studying at the long rosewood dining room table. Hundreds of his books and about ten empty cereal bowls were spread from one end to the other of the long, gleaming table. I was frightened for him, at what his father would do to him if he caught him with all these lights on. I was also in awe, of his beauty – the shape of his nose was Roman-godlike – and his studiousness. I'd never seen any one study so intensely before. Beth had told me that Albert was number one in his school, and now, watching the way he hunched over his books, I instantly understood all the committment that required. I would've been intimidated, except for Albert's screaming loneliness.

"Hello," I said as I passed.

He looked up squinting, as if I were a curious-looking insect he'd never seen before. He said nothing. Offended, I continued to the kitchen, poured some milk, and sat down with the entire crystal cookie jar of Oreo cookies. I became wholly absorbed in tearing the cookies apart, then rolling up the white cream filling into perfect round balls.

"What do you think you're doing?" It was Albert, but he sounded a great deal like his old man.

I jumped, but recovered enough to grow irritated and strong. Albert was never going to treat ME the way he treated Beth and Kelly. My life was lonely and frustrating enough; the last thing I needed was another villain to terrorize me. "None of your business," I sassed him. It felt wonderful.

"Oh. I see. Do you plan to, uh, leave any of those for any one else?"

"Maybe. What's it to you?"

"What are you doing up this late?"

"Same as you. Studying. You're not the only person in the world who has finals, you know."

"Oh, is that so? And I'm sure you'll get an A just like me, huh?"

It was obvious he liked me. Everything bad in my life melted. I kept my sassy tone of voice. "Quite possibly an A+. I don't know if You've heard, but on my IQ test, my scores were so high, they sailed right off the page."

We both laughed. Albert probably had heard that one before. "That's right. You're a friend of Scott's. Must've been a very special IQ test. If you're so smart, let's see you spell antidisestablishmentarianism."

"I'm sure. That is utterly useless information, but go ahead, Albert. Impress me."

He did. He spelled it with absolute perfection—well, I assumed at the time that it was perfect, because he spelled it without hesitation, rapid-fire. God. He was gorgeous and smart and lonely. I was hooked.

We never heard the old man creep up on us. He must've been wearing moccasins like the Indians wear in the forest up in Washington; my mother said they could sneak up and steal a child at a picnic right from under its mother's nose, they were so quiet. ("So you'd better be good," she'd taunt, "or I'll let them take you.") Because there were no weary trudging steps, this time. Suddenly, he was just THERE, looking huge and bald and ugly-mean, with giant, red bug-eyes. I think his ears were smoking, the way a toaster smokes when it's not quite working right.

"What the HELL do you think you're doing?" He spoke only to Albert, but I felt like a total ass, with all my white, rolled-up Oreo filling balls in a line on the tablecloth. Experienced as I was with the bad-ass-father-routine, I had a feeling where this scene was headed. Mr. Ramsey's blood pressure was rising; he was getting himself more and more worked up. His voice made my ears scream, and the freezing shaking in my gut was spreading through my whole body. In my mind were the words that would not come out of my mouth: "But Mr. Ramsey, we weren't DOING anything. I'm sorry if we woke you, but we haven't done ANYTHING WRONG." His voice swelled like an ugly wave at riptide.

"You leave on every goddamned light in the house, you mess up every bowl and plate with your goddamned cereal, . . ."

"I was studying, Dad," Albert interrupted.

Mr. Ramsey boxed Albert in the head. Not hard, but still, I cringed, expecting to get it next. No one paid any attention to me.

"Studying, HELL! You're a goddamned BUM!" He boxed Albert in the head again, and shoved him up against the wall. I started crying, and hating myself for having no power to stop what was happening. Albert was yelling back at Mr. Ramsey when I fled upstairs.

"I WAS studying! You're just hassling me, for no good reason!" Albert yelled. He was crying. THUMP! He got smacked again. I cringed at the top of the stairs, with Beth, who had wakened. She cried. Beth's body crumpled in despair, and I held her while she sobbed. Life's injustice made her SO SAD, whereas I just felt bitter and old. I muttered over and over: "life is shit." And then, "someday, I'm going to have power over bullies like this. And me and all the NICE people are going to get together and shut you fuckers down."

"Vanessa, it's all my fault!" Beth sobbed all over me. "I hated Albert for beating me up, today. He hit me so hard, and he locked me in the closet because I'm so ugly, that I PRAYED TO GOD that someone would beat him up! Now I take it back! God, God, please make it stop!" She was hysterical.

Everything downstairs was suddenly quiet. Mr. Ramsey and Albert were talking quietly about history and electric bills. They made some jokes we couldn't hear, and laughed together. I rubbed Bethy's back. It was just a little creepy, as it made all the Catholic Mysteries that much more powerful. For Beth, however, it was matter-of-fact, so I didn't let on that I was BLOWN OUT.

"See what a good job you did, Bethy? Your prayers really pack a whollop! Quick, let's get back to bed."

* * *

I hated myself; it had all been my fault. Albert would hate me now, too. Good. I deserved it. I wished I were dead.

When I saw Albert again the next day, he pretended as if nothing had happened; he didn't even look any different. His father didn't hit him hard, the way mine used to hit me. He was even almost nice to me. We became allies, in a way.

At least, I understood him and his trials better than his surfer girlfriends did, or his friends at school who maybe had friendlier homes. If there was such a thing. I mean, of COURSE there were wonderful, happy homes out there: Leave it to Beaver homes, Father Knows Best homes, and I Love Lucy homes. Mimi and Scott homes. Ginny Barnes' home. I simply wasn't lucky enough to LIVE in one.

Albert was in the kitchen when I walked in after school. Mimi, Scott, and Eric were there with Jeffrey, who at four months, was wearing bright red overalls. Albert teased Scott.

"He doesn't seem very intelligent. Maybe he's retarded. Look at him, moving his lips like a fish. God, Scott, he just looks DUMB. Maybe you can still take him back."

Mimi laughed. "Tsk! Shut up, Albert!" She cooed to Jeffrey. "Just ignore him, Jeffrey. He looked just like you when he was a baby, only you won't turn out so nasty and awful when you're bigger."

They brought joy into that house; I breathed it like a choking person, realizing, now that it was here, how desperately empty of joy the house had been. Christmas vacation started in two days, on Friday: the good part of finals. Where, normally, Christmas had been just another wonderful thing the rest of the world enjoyed and I was denied, Christmas around Mimi, Scott and Eric was festive. They WERE Christmas in that dark old mansion. Eric sucked on a candy cane and wore an elf's cap. Mimi's hair was red again, and she wore a bright green miniskirt with red tights. They'd just been to Bullock's department store to see Santa, and Eric was beside-himself excited after his discussion with Santa. Albert pretended to be bored by all of it, but he wasn't. He was also breathing them, in the way a suffocating man in a collapsed mine would take his first breath of air when he was set free. He never pushed VERY hard for Scott and Mimi to move their car so he could get out of the driveway and go surfing.

"Look what we made!" Kelly yelled, running into the kitchen. He was dripping with silver spray paint as he held

up a silver spray-painted pine cone. Beth followed, holding
a red and a green spray-painted pine cone. These kids were
painted messes; their hair, their faces, and hands were total
red-green-silver. Their Holy Mary Grammar School uniforms were ruined with spray paint, but their faces glowed
with pride.

"Aren't they beautiful?" Beth asked, not quite sure why
every one looked so dismayed.

Albert laughed a smart-alec, "boy, will you get beat"
laugh. Dread started coming up biley in my throat.

"Yes, Beth and Kelly, they really are beautiful." I had to
say it.

Scott's voice got tense-practical. "You better get the hell
out of those clothes and wash up before the old man sees
that mess."

The back door slammed hard. "Oh-oh. Too late," Scott
said quietly, and every one of us in the kitchen started
sweating. The room flashed hot and close.

Mr. Ramsey walked up behind Beth, who was quaking,
and Kelly, who was still grinning. (Wasn't there anything
that scared this kid?) "I want to see the two of you in my
room. NOW." He turned with mounting high blood pressure
to his wife. "Marion, are you aware that the entire laundry
room has been spray painted silver, red, and green?" He
kicked Kelly lightly in the baggy seat of his pants. "I said
GET UP THERE!"

Beth, shaking, looked up at her father. "Dad, it's MY
fault. I bought the paint with my allowance, and I MADE
Kelly help me. I'm really sorry if we got things a little
messy, but I should be the only one to get the spanking."

Wow. Beth had done what I couldn't do the night
before—wimpy little Beth. I was impressed. Mr. Ramsey
softened; you could see it.

"You'll get a spanking all right. Kelly, you're a very lucky
boy. Now get upstairs, both of you." And with that, he left
the room, in his weary, unhappy-heavy way.

The rest of us exhaled loudly, together, but no one talked.
We listened to Mr. Ramsey's heavy trudge upstairs. We

listened to the bedroom door slam. We then listened to see if children's bodies were being thrown against the wall, but all was quiet. Finally, Albert turned to me.

"Remember that; next time."

Again the guilt swelled up in me. "I will, Albert. I swear it."

"So!" Mimi said, all cheerful again. "There's an awful lot of snow up at Mammoth, right now. How would you like to come skiing with us, Albert and Vanny?"

Albert played cool, but not me! "YEAH! GREAT!" Unsaid: "get me OUT OF HERE, MAN! QUICK!"

Mrs. Ramsey was solemn. "I think that would be the best thing in the world, right now. Mr. Ramsey is just not feeling well." I think Mrs. Ramsey had planned this amazing Winter Wonderland dream-come-true. I was ecstatic, at all levels: to be AWAY from the gloom, to be with Mimi, Scott, and Eric. (I didn't love Jeffrey, yet—it seemed as if Scott and Mimi didn't care so much about me any more. Not that I didn't COMPLETELY understand, but still . . .). AND to be with Albert—it was too wonderful to be true!

Scott and Mimi stayed for dinner that night, which helped me get through the awful moment when Beth and Kelly walked into the dining room. Kelly walked in first, grinning. "I only got two swats—not even hard ones! Beth got five, but they weren't any big deal," he announced. Beth's face was all splotchy from crying. Mr. Ramsey was worn out. His body was beat. It was all he could do to pick up his fork; he took long rests in between bites. He didn't have the energy to even feebly attempt to stop Kelly from feeding Elvis. I thought to myself, "he should be in a hospital, he's so sick—or is he just OLD? Man, if this is what happens to men when they get old and rich, I think I don't want to ever marry such a rich guy." I wished I could have helped him get well. Surely everyone else could see that he would be nicer if he felt better.

Dinner was almost pleasant. Mimi suggested that all of us go to pick up a Christmas tree that night and decorate it. Kelly agreed. "Hey, yeah! With lots of tinsel, OK?" The old

man generally did not allow talking at the table, but he
never objected, that night. Had he felt better, he might
even have said something nice. Instead, he just gave tiny
Jeffrey an odd look when the baby started gurgling from
his little carrier—as if to say, "who is this?" I think he'd
forgotten Jeffrey was born.

"He's talking to you, Bart," Mimi joked with her father-in-
law.

"Well, tell him to shut up," Mr. Ramsey growled, but he
must've been joking, because Mrs. Ramsey laughed, as did
Scott and Mimi. I could not understand the jokes that went
that way. Ever. Eric laughed the hardest. He was crazy
about his grandpa!

"Hear that, Jeffrey? Better do what your grouchy ole'
grandpa says," Mimi joked.

"Yeah, Jeffrey, or he'll WHUP you with his cowboy belt,"
Eric chimed in.

I shut my eyes hard when Eric said that; he was DEAD,
I thought. But Mr. Ramsey looked up at Eric, who was still
wearing his little elf hat, and almost grinned.

"Where'd you get that hat?" He growled, really mean.

"Santa gave it to me, Grandpa." Eric loved his grandpa,
without any fear.

"Santa must be a faggot."

Eric giggled, and Albert made a funny scrunched-up face
at Kelly while Kelly was drinking his milk. When Albert
mouthed the word "faggot" at Kelly, Kelly giggled wildly
and spit up his milk, all over the table. All over Mr. Ramsey's dinner. Kelly became immediately penitent, even
though you could see his insides still shaking with laughter.

"Albert MADE me, Dad," was Kelly's immediate
defense.

You could see that if Mr. Ramsey had had the strength,
he would have trashed Albert for making Kelly spit up. But
Albert was too far away, so he just gave Albert a filthy
look, and continued to eat around the spit-up milk on his
plate. We finished the meal in total silence.

This place, I decided, was worse for my digestion than

any institution or other place I'd ever lived. No wonder I was losing weight! Every meal with Mr. Ramsey was bile-producing. I didn't have bulimia, folks, it just came, "with the territory," as they say.

We had a great time buying the tree that night. Kelly, Beth, and Eric ran wild in the Christmas tree lot, knocking trees over, while Albert, Scott, Mimi and I discussed branches and silvertips as if our lives hung on them. Mrs. Ramsey had snuck a fat wad of money into Scott's palm (for a TREE — I couldn't believe it!), and we ended up buying a movie star tree: the most perfectly shaped, twelve foot tree on earth. It cost seventy five dollars! That's about TWO HUNDRED AND FIFTY DOLLARS in today's money. It was absurdly unnecessary for Scott to give me the overly familiar caution: "Don't EVER tell Bart how much this tree cost." I would never get used to the money that rich people threw around.

We came home and put on some Christmas records, and decorated the tree. Mimi made some hot buttered rum, and Kelly and Eric threw tinsel balls at each other. In those days, tinsel was made of metal, and you could squish it into hard little balls that really hurt when they hit. Poor Eric was crying in no time.

I couldn't WAIT for friday to come and go, so we could be on the road to THE SNOW to go skiing. Mrs. Ramsey gave Mimi a Saks credit card so that Mimi and I could go buy all these fashionable ski clothes. We had a blast, but I could've gone in ragged old potato sacks and been just as happy. I prayed all day for an avalanche that would keep us snowed in for months.

* * *

The snow trip was wonderful, even if it was too short. I loved the sharp, clean air of the mountains, and the huge empty white meadows. All the pine trees had clumps of snow on their branches, but in the cold sunlight, they came

"ka-THUMP!"—ing off. Albert and I were like caged pup-
pies suddenly set free; it seemed we would NEVER tire of
smashing each other with snowballs. Mimi and Scott and
Eric joined in; we played football in the snow, we wrestled,
we tried to bury each other in snow. I showed Eric how to
make angels in the snow, and all of us then made a monster
parade of angels.

"Mom, look at this angel! Mom, come look at this one!"
Eric yelled after every one. He must've made a hundred
angels, while Mimi, holding Jeffrey—who basically spent
the whole ski trip blinking at the total whiteness of it all—
tried hard to be enthusiastic about all one hundred of
them.

"That's a really great one, Eric! . . . Oh, boy, Eric, you
really made a pretty one, there!..Just super, Eric!"

Albert was bored. "So when do we ski, Scott? I thought
this was supposed to be a ski trip."

I could've died then and there, I was so happy, so when he
said that, I had to smash him hard with the most monstrous snowball. THUNK! "GROW UP, Albert" I yelled,
then squealed when he chased me. He stuffed my mouth
with snow. "YUM, YUM!" I laughed.

Scott tackled him, and they rolled over and over in the
snow. Eric screamed, "get him, Dad!" and we all laughed
and cheered when Scott stuffed a ton of snow down
Albert's pants.

"To answer your question, smart ass," Scott said to
Albert—who looked really uncomfortable—"tomorrow we'll
hit the slopes."

I was a hopeless skier; Eric was a thousand times better,
but Mimi, Eric and I had a great time snow plowing down
the bunny hills while Scott and Albert raced down the
moguls. THIS was it; THIS was what I'd always wanted,
and I closed my eyes a few times that day and smiled at the
sun. I breathed it in deeply and tried to freeze it, this amazingly free and happy feeling. We felt like a family, a really
happy family, playing in the snow. I wasn't out of my mind
for dreaming of this all my life; it DID exist. Ginny Barnes'

family had it, so I had seen it, but even before Ginny Barnes, I'd known—or maybe just dreamed—it COULD exist.

After the second day skiing, there was to be a big dance at the ski lodge. Jeffrey and Eric were exhausted early that night, so Mimi and Scott elected to miss the dance. Mimi could see how badly I wanted to go—I wanted to do everything except sleep on this incredible holiday—so she approached Albert.

"Oh, man?" He protested. "Are you kidding?"

But Scott casually walked him into the other room of our cabin, and talked to him quietly. Albert came out looking like the ultimate martyr.

"So let's go. What're you standing around for?"

I leaped into the air. "Whooo—weeey! All RIGHT!" I ran around the room putting on Mimi's earrings and throwing on my beautiful new "Apres Ski" sweater from Switzerland. We were out the door before any one could change their mind. Albert rolled his eyes; he was being a pain in the ass—clearly letting me know this was the last thing in the world he wanted to be doing—but I didn't care in the least. I saw him tap his feet at the dance; the band was really good. The lodge was filled with high school and college kids, many of them dancing up a storm. The music got me wild in a hurry; I bounced around madly, standing in place.

A really cute guy walked up to me, but he was looking at Albert, my "date". He didn't want to get hit, maybe. What the hell? I thought; I'm so happy, the music is so good, what do I care if I make a total fool of myself?

"You wanna' dance?" I asked him, scared silly.

He looked at Albert again. "Is it OK?" But Albert ignored him.

"He's my COUSIN!" I screamed above the music. "Let's go!"

And I found that I could dance; it was my first time out on any floor, but I took over. Bass guitar pumped life from my legs to my heart, and the banging of the drums sent me flying all over. I had never felt more alive in my life. I usually flunked my P.E. classes, but suddenly, on the dance floor, my body leapt around like a charged-up Olympic athlete. And the guys didn't seem to want it to end: they were clapping for me, hooting, and changing partners. All these cute guys flashed in front of me as I spun around, but really, I was dancing, flying, alone. Cinderella must've been a true story, because I know exactly how she felt. I hope the music was as good for her.

Hot steamy vapor whooshed up from the neck of my sweater, I was so hot, but I didn't want to take the sweater off, because then the guys would see all my perspiration. They'd be grossed out. No, I would've sweated to death happily inside that sweater, but, luckily, the band took a break. I found Albert.

"Vanessa, is it warm enough in here for you?" Albert asked.

"Whoooo! I'm havin' a GREAT time!"

"You sure dance better than you ski," he said. That's probably the nicest thing he ever said to me.

"Hey, thanks, Albert. Really. And thanks for bringing me."

"It's a pretty good band." Then he shuffled his feet around. "Where'd you learn to dance?"

"Right here! Tonight! I never danced before in my life!"

"Sure."

"Swear to God."

"Then I could probably dance much better than you."

"Albert, why does every goddamned thing in the world have to be a competitive thing with you?"

"Because it does."

"Fine. You go ahead and dance better, because I don't care. I'm just having a good time, OK? So let's go!"

And we danced together, laughing and showing off. Albert must've really studied me, because he was doing the same steps I was; we were great together! We danced together for hours, until the band finally stopped for the night.

The entire ride home, Albert was explaining to me why he

was the superior dancer. I laughed and laughed; my whole face was one big grin.

"Vanessa, it's clearly obvious! You jump around without any style, like a horse with hiccups, while I dance with the grace that you can only get on a surfboard. I'm sorry, it's just the obvious facts. You have to face them."

"Albert, you crack me up! I mean, you are just too much!"

I hope like hell that Albert could see that my Lonely-Alien feelings never went away, the way I could see that his Lonely-Alien feelings never went away. He wasn't a total jerk, he had a lot of soft spots he was afraid would get trampled on if people knew about them. So he made himself into a funny "character", an actor who played all kinds of obnoxious parts that no one could ever completely figure out.

The avalanche I prayed to Jesus Mary and Joseph for never came, and so we had to drive back to the Ramseys' for Christmas Eve. I cried walking from the silent winter forest and our cabin to the car. This had been the happiest week of my life. I'd been silly and high with JOY, and no one had beat on me once for it. Joy was allowed, here.

"Thank you, Mimi and Scott, so much!" I hugged them both while I cried. "I've just been so happy here!"

Albert was really cynical when he said, "come on, Vanessa, don't you want to go home and join in all the festivities of Christmas Eve at my parents' house?" He didn't want to go home, either.

* * *

But Christmas was pretty good—the best, in fact, I'd had in my life. (Christmases in the institutions only made us girls feel dreary and unloved—not that the authorities didn't try to spruce them up a bit, but still . . . for me, the idea of Christmas had always represented all the warm, loving things in life that I didn't have.) I was shocked to see how our gorgeous Christmas tree had been brutalized in our absence, by Elvis, Pisser, and Kelly. Poor Bethy started crying every time she looked at it. But still, Christmas Eve dinner was great, and every one drank and got rosy, happy faces. We each opened one small present at the dinner table. Beth and I each got a broken pen and pencil set. Kelly got a pair of socks—to which he said, "socks! I didn't want socks! I HATE socks!"

Mr. Ramsey opened a present of cheese from Mimi and Scott, and exclaimed, "God, I hate cheese! What're you trying to do, kill me?"

Mimi said, (I think she was a little tipsy), "hey, that's great, Bart! We'll just take it back, if you don't mind. We're a little broke this week."

I laughed, and got a really dirty look from both Mr. and Mrs. Ramsey. But then Mr. Ramsey rose, saying, "Marion, it's bedtime. Kids, you, too—Christmas morning tomorrow."

Kelly threw a stormy pouty fit. "God, can't I stay and watch them open all those presents hiding in the closet? Mimi got a big blue sweater, and I played with Eric's GoMobile, it's pretty dumb . . ."

Every one in the room except Mr. Ramsey freaked when he said all that, but Mrs. Ramsey kissed him hard on the mouth. She was whispering something in Kelly's ear. I watched Mr. Ramsey; none of this was big news to him. He was immersed in his own exhaustion. When Mrs. Ramsey finally got Kelly to stand up and walk toward his room, there was a gigantic pair of red lipstick lips on Kelly's cheeks. Everyone laughed at that.

Mrs. Ramsey hugged everyone except me, but, oh, well. She talked in my ear. I could smell the Port on her breath; it was sweet, and perfumey when she said, "I want you to have a very Merry Christmas." That was the nicest she ever was to me. It felt wonderful. As she turned to go, she said to Mimi and Scott—in a truly secret agent voice, "you'll take care of everything, won't you?"

"Sure, Mom," Scott assured her.

And we all stood listening to the heavy plod, plod, plod of weary Mr. Ramsey's steps climbing up and into the bedroom. I was so sorry for him, that his body wouldn't even allow him to be well for Christmas.

"OK, guys, let's have Christmas!" Scott said, and he and Mimi went and got about a hundred (no exaggeration) wrapped Christmas packages and passed them out. I was dumbfounded; there were FIVE huge boxes with my name on them, "from Mr. and Mrs. Ramsey." Expensive sweaters, a coat, a skirt – I couldn't believe this! The broken pen and pencil set was about the usual I'd ever gotten at Christmas, though it had really been strange watching the Ramseys' real live kids get them. I certainly hadn't expected anything else. Getting a hug from Mrs. Ramsey would have been the best present she could have given me.

"Mimi, what's the story here?" I asked.

"Oh, nothing. Bart's kind of a scrooge, so Marion gives us a 'Secret Christmas'. Bart really likes doing the Santa Claus bit with the younger kids, but when you start to get too old for Santa around here, he figures you can go out and 'buy your own damned Christmas'." She mimicked his deep voice really well. "He knows about all the presents in the closet, of course, but he pretends not to know. Poor old Marion has to sneak out of the bedroom at all hours of the night to wrap the damned things. It's just the way they do things around here. Pretty strange, huh?"

Pretty strange. All the triple intrigue was starting to get to me. Something was tweaking, inside me; it was only a matter of time before I climbed out of my regular, silent-observer character and tried on something new.

* * *

A Note to my dear little sisters and brothers who have run away:

Dear Little Sisters and brothers,

The Old Way was that abused kids who ran away believed they were bad people. Then, they were treated as if they were running away because they were hoodlums. The Old Way was dumb, and wrong.

If you have run away because you are tired of the abuse at home, you are not a bad person. You are running away to survive. However, you must run to a place where people will be GOOD to you, and will help you set up a REAL life for yourself. You deserve it. The main thing is that you GET OFF THE STREET. The street will ruin you.

The first thing you must do when you run away is call the RUNAWAY HOTLINE in your area. It's on the very inside cover of your telephone book. If there is no runaway hotline, then call the EMERGENCY SHELTER for women and children. Go there. They will LISTEN to you, and help you get your life back together. They will let you stay for free, overnight, where it is safe and you won't get raped. (That's the LAST thing you need at this point!)

If you live in a big city, and you don't have a car, and you're just sort of wandering around, go to a big hospital. Ask if they have an EMERGENCY CRISIS CENTER. Most of them do, or they know where you can go. If you live way out in the boonies, you can call 1-800-4-A-CHILD. They'll tell you where there's a place in your area you can go. You might need some bus money. Hitchiking is a really BAD idea. DON'T. I don't need to tell you that there are bad people out there in the world. They don't care how sad your story is. They'll rob you and rape you anyway. If you live way, WAY out in the boonies, and there's no phone booth, and you don't have a dime, go to the Church Pastor. Even the tiniest towns have a lot of churches, so if the first pastor doesn't treat you nice, go to another one.

If you just hang out on the street, people might come up to you ACTING like they want to help you, but, really, most of them will only look at you in terms of how much money they can make off you. They want you to buy their drugs, they want you to be their prostitute, or they want your parents to pay them big money to get you back.

DON'T TELL ANYONE ON THE STREET THAT YOU
HAVE RUN AWAY! Tell a professional counselor, at an
emergency shelter, or a priest or minister, or a hospital
counselor, but don't tell any other stranger. The counselor
will try to HELP you. Counselors don't even think you're
bad if you come in drunk, or full of drugs. They'll still be
nice to you, and give you a place to stay. They'll try to help
you fix your life, so get your bones in there!

* * *

School started again, and I slumped into depression
again: all their weird religious rules about life seemed
bizarre and ridiculous at the same time, but everyone in the
place took them so seriously. I mean, you can't touch the
host with your teeth, the Virgin Mary made it with the
Holy Spirit, and only Catholics can go to heaven. Patent
leather shoes were a sin. Everyone in the school assumed I
was a Catholic, and I kept my mouth shut about it, feeling
guilty as hell because God knew everything. On the one
hand, I didn't want people to know I was the odd man out,
but on the other hand, this stuff was weird, and I didn't
want any part of it. On the other OTHER hand, the Ramsey mansion had special nooks BUILT INTO THE
WALLS for their Virgin Mary and Sacred Heart statues.
They were hooked; when Kelly knocked the porcelain halo
off the Virgin Mary with a basketball, Beth prostrated herself on the ground with her arms outstretched and
shrieked, "Forgive him, Father! He knows not what he
does!" So I crammed all my "pagan" feelings into the secret
aching part of my gut I'd stuffed all the other hordes of
secret aching feelings.

Looking back, I should have just shined it. Religion Class
was the only really gross one that poured all that Dogma
out in Dogma Buckets. Art Class was great, and History
was OK when it wasn't religious history. Religious History
angered me: it was wicked and heinous to slaughter Chris-

tians, but you could become a SAINT if you chopped
enough heads off the Moors. Every religion does it; the Old
Testament is Bloodbath City, with Israelites raping and
slaughtering people, do you know why? Israelites cut up
people for dancing around a golden calf! And they call this
murder HOLY. No wonder we're all so screwed up! Let's
hear it for man's stinking wars and POWER TRIPS! (And
do you know who never plays the war games, but who
always gets raped, as a matter of course? The women; they
get carted away to become the winners' sex slaves. THIS
SHOULD TELL YOU SOMETHING ABOUT WHERE
MEN GOT THE IDEA THAT IT'S OK TO TREAT
GIRLS AND WOMEN ROTTEN. IT'S ALL THERE, IN
THE HOLY BIBLE.)

So in my terrified-stomach way, I was always paranoid
that someone would "Find Out". I worked hard at getting
my little Chapel Veil on right, and mumbling the Rosary
really fast. I never learned the real words, but it didn't
matter—the cool people rattled them off too fast for me to
glean what they were saying. When I tried "Hey Mary, full
of grace. . . .nowry our deafAmen," it worked fine.

At the Ramsey house, people were starting to figure out
what to me seemed pretty obvious: Mr. Ramsey's health
was SHOT. He felt lousy, and the pile of pills he took every
morning at breakfast suddenly mushroomed. Some new
blue and red and pink ones added great colors to the lot,
but he stared at them with utter disgust before he put them
in his mouth. Picking up all the pills exhausted him, and
sometimes he'd stare at me inbetween swallows, as if to
say, disgustedly, "don't ever let this happen to you. Don't
ever get old." I felt sorry for him, even if his Bad Moods did
get a hundred times worse. More than ever, I felt that I was
in the way: an outsider that they didn't need or want to
have around. (Unfortunately, Kelly and Beth also felt that
way about themselves.)

One day, Kelly and I were in the TV room watching some
boring after-school program, and Kelly started rocking vio-
lently back and forth in Mr. Ramsey's chair.

"Hey, Duffy, wanna' see something fantastic?" He asked me, all excited.

"I don't know, Kelly. Will it get us in trouble?"

"No way! My dad's taking a nap. Watch."

And he rocked and rocked until the whole chair did a big loop in the air and came down back side up. It *was* pretty amazing: a high-tech chair before its time. Kelly had gone completely upside down for a few seconds.

"WOW!" I said. I was pretty impressed.

"Help me do it again."

So I set it up for him about five times, and watched him go loop-de-loop around and down.

"You do it," he generously offered.

"Sure, Kelly, I'll try it. It looks fun. Are you sure Mr. Ramsey is taking a nap?"

"Of course!"

So I got in the chair, rocked back and forth and back and forth until WHOOSH! God, I went totally upside-down! It was hilarious! I laughed and laughed when I found myself upside-down, my uniform up over my head, and this chair lying on top of me.

But Kelly was silent, and when I pulled my uniform down to my knees, I was looking up up up at Mr. Ramsey's sour old face and bloodshot eyes. I wasn't his kid, so he couldn't hit me, but I'll tell you: getting hit would've been a hell of a lot better than getting looked at like that. God! I felt like the worst criminal on earth; I felt as if I'd set fire to his whole empire. Looking back, it was just a goddamned chair that you couldn't break unless you used cherry bombs. Feeling instantly nauseous with guilt and dread, I got up and set the chair back properly.

"I'm sorry, Sir. It won't happen again." And I stood there with my head hung to my waist—it felt that low. He just stood there, hands on his hips, I think trying to keep his blood pressure from exploding Out his eyeballs. They were all red and bulging. Then he turned around and started to walk out. Kelly made the DUMB mistake of grinning at me—too soon.

WHACK! Kelly got it in the side of his head. "What the HELL do you think is so funny? Huh? Get upstairs! NOW, or I'll GIVE you something to take that smirk off your face!"

Kelly ran fast, beyond his father's reach, up to his room. It was the second time somebody else got hit (I felt) because of me. God DAMMIT, I swore to myself. "He's going to hit ME next time, or I'll smash his face."

* * *

One day, the most amazing thing happened: Mimi brought a letter to the Ramseys' house for me – from Elizabeth! I couldn't believe it: I stared and stared at her name on the return address. She lived in the Valley, near Los Angeles, only about a half hour from the Ramseys' house. God! What would it be like to see her? She'd be so different, it'd be strange.

She was eighteen, and living in a rented house with two other girls who were going to college. God, Elizabeth was in COLLEGE!

"... In the evenings, I work in this really great cafe, singing, if you can believe it. I LOVE it, Lady Vanessa, and, I don't know, it just reminded me of you, and of all our made-up songs – the only GOOD memory I have of that place. When I turned eighteen, I was allowed to get information from The Child Center. They told me your real parents took you back, (weird???), so that's how I got your address out here. Sure is better weather down here, huh? Hope everything is going well with you.

Love, Elizabeth"

She'd sent the letter to my mother's apartment, and my mother had given it to Mimi, without even opening it. God, I thought, that was really, really nice of Mom. (I'd been creating idealized pictures of her again—suggesting, maybe, that I felt insecure in Beverly Hills?) I walked around feeling nervous and goosey-strange about the possibility of seeing Elizabeth again. Someone with whom I didn't have to fake that my past life was normal, that my present life was normal, or that Catholic rules were normal. I started immediately making up funny patent leather shoe stories, and funny Confessional stories, to tell Elizabeth. What would it be like after almost six years? And what would she say if she knew I was living in BEVERLY HILLS?

One especially stinko Friday when I knew I faced total flunking out of Holy Mary High School, I came home crying, I was so happy it was Friday. When I walked up the long driveway, loaded down with all the books I would need to memorize in order NOT to flunk out, Kelly and Beth were playing King of the Mountain on the lawn, beating the shit out of each other and covering their uniforms with grass stains. Beth wiped her tears when she saw me, and I wiped mine. She and Kelly ran wildly over to me, crazy-joyous.

"Mom and Dad are gone for the whole weekend! You're our only babysitter! YAY!" And Kelly started throwing dirt clods at me. I looked at Beth, not really concerned with the thudding dirt clods all over my uniform. They were appropriate to my mood.

"Bethy, your folks are GONE? For the whole weekend? What am I supposed to FEED you?"

"Anything!" She grinned. "We don't care!"

"Get Albert, your LOVER, to take us to Ship's Coffee Shop for hamburgers!" Kelly suggested.

"Don't you EVER say that, you hear?" I yelled at Kelly. I jumped on him, and started rolling down the big grass hill with him. Now I felt great. Dirty and covered with grass stains, I wanted to know. "What did he say, what did he say? TELL ME, you little munchkin! Did he say anything?" I was pretend-choking him, and Kelly loved it.

"You love Albert, you love Albert," he sang at me. My

face was bright red, and my hair tangly with dirt clods, when Albert showed up behind us. "Hi, Bumps!" Kelly yelled up at Albert. He SAID "Duffy LOVES you," but I had my hand over his mouth, so it was all garbled mush. Beth distracted Albert to talk about food. One of the very few things Beth and Albert had in common was their constant hunger for food.

"Albert, can you take us for hamburgers at Ship's? PLEASE? There's no food in the house!" Beth pleaded.

"What about for me? Didn't they leave me any steak?"

"Nothing. They just took off for the weekend."

"That is really great."

"I have some money, Albert," I said. "I could buy all of us some hamburgers at Ship's."

So he went for it, but "NOT with those two. We can bring their burgers back. I'm not going ANYWHERE with them."

"We can wait in the car," Beth offered. She was starving.

"Hey, yeah!" Kelly added.

"God, Albert, that's so mean, making them wait in the car. I'll take care of them, don't worry. They'll be good," I offered.

We had a great time at Ship's, even though Kelly did embarrass us by putting ketchup in the salt and pepper shakers, and mustard in his chocolate malt. Albert ate six hamburgers, and skinny little Beth ate three. Where she put it, I'll never know. Kelly ate half of one, which is more than any non-sugar item I'd ever seen him eat. Basically, Ship's was wonderful, until one of Albert's surfer girlfriends walked by. Albert shoved the three of us under the table.

We giggled madly under the table; it cracked me up to think of the messy table full of plates, ketchup and mustard, and only Albert sitting there trying to impress this really cute girl. (Well, I imagine she was really cute, the way Albert was acting. She had tan, pretty legs – I slapped Kelly when he looked up her skirt – and her sandals were beautiful Bernardos.) "I'm sure she's STUPID," I consoled

myself, hating her guts. She talked like Connie Stevens; her
fake, breathy voice really bothered me.

"Albert, your table is so messy." She giggled. "Are you
going to Sunset to surf, tomorrow?"

"Always," he answered with his mouth full. I could hear
the food sloshing around in his mouth. Gross.

"See you there," Cute-Feet-Fake-Voice said, and walked
away.

We climbed back up to our seats and laughed our heads
off at poor Albert; his face was tomato-red! He was suffering, and we enjoyed it. lae deserved every bit of the teasing
we gave him. I was pissed!

* * *

The next day, while Albert was no doubt show-off-
surfing for Miss Cute Feet, I was bored, restless, and
depressed. It was Saturday, and I SHOULD have been
studying, but it was hopeless. I wanted FUN. But doing
what, and with whom? I had no Holy Mary friends, which
was entirely by my design: I was too paranoid they'd find
me out. At school, therefore, I merely recited the Ramseys'
prestigious address and stuck my nose in the air: better
they think I'm the grossest heiress-snob than discover that
I wasn't a real Catholic, or—worse—about my past, which,
SURELY, was loaded with mortal sins. Besides, I was
stuck watching Kelly and Beth rip up the expensive pillows
they were using to beat each other. Elizabeth. I really
needed to see Elizabeth. She had loved me enough to find
me, after all these years. I ran to the phone.

"Elizabeth? Elizabeth, it's ME! Vanessa!"

She squealed. I squealed. "Elizabeth, I-I'm coming over. I
HAVE to see you! Give me the directions. I'm in, um,
Beverly Hills."

I wrote the directions down. I went into the TV room,
and gasped. Kelly and Beth were emptying the bookcase of
all the rare, expensive books that had pure gold in the

pages and on the covers. They were playing frisbie with them. One book's golden side seam actually ripped. I could NEVER leave these two alone. They'd absolutely destroy the place!

"C'mon, kids, we're going for a ride!"

"Great! In what?" Kelly asked.

"In your dad's souped up T-Bird, that's what!" And I held up the keys like a happy criminal.

Beth's face went green. "Vanessa, he'll KILL you!"

"Oh, Beth, don't be such a NINNY. Your dad's never going to know. Tsk, Jesus!" But she'd acted as my true conscience—the secret aching part of my stomach that was saying, "you are out of your mind to be pulling this."

Kelly went for it. "I'll drive, if you don't know how."

"I know how to drive, silly!"

But not well, it turned out, and both kids were dead silent as I fumbled around trying to get the damned T-Bird down the long driveway. They remained silent throughout the entire drive to the valley. I tried to act gay, zipping down the electric windows and hanging one arm casually out the window. I turned the radio up really loud, and sang along with the Rolling Stones, (" . . . no satis-FACK-shun") to show them how much fun we were having. Still, they sat like tortured children, fantasizing, I imagine, the heavy steel blade of the guillotine upon their delicate necks.

Elizabeth was gorgeous; God, it was good to see her! She was tall and thin, but HEALTHY thin. Her limpy blonde hair was blunt cut. She looked happy.

"Lay-dee Vanessa, my GOD! Are you the same chubby girl I used to play with when I was a kid? Jesus, what a BOD! WOW! You look just like Sophia Loren!"

"Get OFF it, Elizabeth!" I teased her, loving every word.

Elizabeth laughed, and looked down at the long, sad faces on Kelly and Beth. "And who are these guys—your brother and sister?"

"Sort of—they're my foster brother and sister."

"Ah-HA. Didn't work out with your folks, huh?"

"Ah, no. My dad came back. So, . . ."

Elizabeth's eyes – still exactly the same, almost-invisible Malamut eyes – stared straight into mine, and read the rest of the sentence. She still loved me. That was the most I'd ever verbalized about my past to her – those four words, but she understood. Everything. She was sad for a long moment, but then she smiled softly.

"So how's Beverly Hills?"

"Did you see the T-Bird out there?"

"THAT'S YOURS?"

"Not exactly. C'mon, let's go for a spin!" And Elizabeth bounced around in the seat, singing along beautifully with the radio. She and I sang harmony with "Run For Your Life" by the Beatles, which finally got a smile out of Beth. When they played a "double header" off the Beatles' RUB-BER SOUL album – "Michelle, my belle, . . ." she sang along with us. It was GREAT, and when we stopped at Tony's Drive-in for burgers, even Kelly thought it was fun.

Elizabeth was incredibly ALIVE; she loved her foster parents a lot, that was clear. "They come by once a week to watch me sing at the Yellow Cafe," she said. "God, Vanessa, you should COME, you could sing a DUET with me – wouldn't that be GREAT?"

"God, could I really?" I went right back to feeling mushy adoration for her. Boy, would I love to sing with her – ONSTAGE. We could sing, . . . oh, the dreams I started dreaming!

We decided it was time to go; Beth kept clearing her throat and saying "they're supposed to be back, you know, this evening." When we pulled around the corner to the Ramseys' house, we saw it: Marion's car, resting in its dark space at the top of the hill. They were home. We were busted. We sat in the car, doomed to death row, quietly discussing our lack of options.

"I guess we'll leave the car down here, on the street. We'd only make it worse if I smashed something on the way up the damned driveway."

"At least he can't blame this one on me," Kelly said. He

grinned. "Guess it's a good thing I didn't drive—but I bet I could've driven better than YOU, Duffy!"

"No, Kelly, that's right," I said. "It's not your fault."

Beth suffered; her face was white, and her knees shook. Tears rolled down her face.

Mrs. Ramsey met us at the door. "Um, I think you'd better go in the TV room, Vanessa, and wait. Kids, upstairs. Your father wants to see you."

"But, Mrs. Ramsey, no! That's not fair! It was ALL my fault. They didn't even WANT to go! I just thought I shouldn't leave them alone! Please, let ME go see him!"

"Vanessa, the kids aren't in trouble. Mr. Ramsey is very calm about all of this. Now you just wait right here."

But Kelly and Beth didn't believe it for a minute. Their faces screamed, "We are about to be slaughtered! Unfair!"

I would kill him if he even yelled at them. But he never did. All was very very quiet, and when the kids came out, you could see they were relieved. Until they looked at me, down at the bottom of the stairs. Only for a moment, they looked down the long stairway at me, and then they went to their rooms. I snuck back into the TV room and waited for something to happen. Nothing ever did happen, except there was no dinner, and when I finally did go upstairs into Beth's and my room, all my things were packed. Beth was crying.

"Bethy, what happened?"

"My dad says you're a bad influence on us," Beth cried. "So you have to leave—tomorrow."

* * *

And that was the end of my stay at the Ramseys' house. Mrs. Ramsey came in the next morning, all nervous.

I wanted very much to say SOMETHING to SOMEONE about it. "Mrs. Ramsey, I'm SO sorry about yesterday. I've caused you so much trouble, and. . ."

But she didn't want to hear it; she wanted everything OVER with. "Yes, well, Mr. Ramsey feels that it would be best for the children if you lived in a better foster home. My husband is ill, you know, and, . . . SO! We've found an excellant home for you. You'll be MUCH closer to the beach!" . . . She cleared her throat. "We'll leave in an hour."

I never had the chance to say goodbye to Beth, Kelly, or Albert. Mr. Ramsey was off to work without a word to me, and the kids had gone to school. I was shuffled off – a high security risk, I guess! – to my next home. The worst part of it all was that, as far as I knew, I'd never see Mimi or Scott and the boys again. I'd let them down, and they would hate me forever.

I never said a word during the drive. If there'd been a kitchen knife in the glove compartment – I checked – I would've killed myself. Mrs. Ramsey was trying hard to be cheerful, about the weather and about this foster home I was going to. She cleared her throat during my non-responses.

"They have two other foster daughters, just about your age", . . . I heard her say, but all I wanted was to jump out the door onto the freeway. I couldn't, though; Mrs. Ramsey controlled the "door lock".

She stopped in front of a beautiful little home with blooming roses along the walkway. Mrs. Ramsey walked fast just ahead of me, carrying my two big suitcases. I caught up with her.

"Mrs. Ramsey, I know it's been a hassle for you, and I'll never say 'I'm sorry' enough so you know how much I mean it – but I sure thank you for everything you've done for me. For the house and clothes and letting me live with Kelly and Beth and Albert. I'll come back when I'm grown, so you'll both HAVE TO listen to me say everything you won't let me say now."

She cleared her throat. "I think you're going to be very happy here, and we want you to be happy."

"Could you please say goodbye to Beth and Kelly and Alfred for me? And thank Mr. Ramsey for everything –

really? Because I know I could never have gotten out of the Detention Center without him: I know it was Mr. Ramsey who said I could come to your house. Could you please tell him a hundred times I'm sorry?"

"I certainly will."

"And could you please tell Mimi and Scott and Eric and Jeffrey I love them?"

"I will."

The front door to the house opened, and Mrs. Ramsey disappeared with Mr. Johnson into the living room, while Mrs. Johnson and I went into the kitchen. I didn't see Mrs. Ramsey again, not for many, many years.

* * *

Mrs. Johnson was a stout, gentle blonde woman in her fifties. She didn't seem to mind that I was not thrilled about being here. That all I did, in fact, was sulk. Lia and Karen, the other two foster daughters, were kind and gentle, and left me alone. All I could think about was yesterday—twenty years ago and the other side of the tracks—and the heinous criminal act I'd committed with the T-Bird.

The Johnsons were really good people. They were financially stressed, so they appreciated the extra income the state gave them for taking in foster kids. Each of them reminded me that "you're our sixty-fifth foster daughter, and all the others turned out pretty good! You're not as pretty as Karen, and I doubt you're as smart as Lia, but we're sure you're a good kid. You've had some bad luck, getting the God-given parents you got, but now, you're in a good home, and you're going to be all right." Amazing: I heard this same speech twice, once from each of them. They had it wired.

When I first moved in, I was lucky: I had my own room to brood in. I could immerse myself in honest self-pity without feeling guilty for depressing someone else. Lia was almost eighteen, and so would be leaving soon – the checks from the state quit when foster kids reached eighteen. She was a quiet, smart young woman who wanted very badly to be on her own and get rich. She had long dark hair, and she wore glasses that made her dark eyes jump out at you. Karen had just turned seventeen. She was a petite, gorgeous, strawberry blonde who intended to use her looks to get a "really rich husband who won't give me any shit." Handsome guys often parked outside the house hoping to talk to Karen, but when she calculated their net worth – "it's a nice Chevy, but it needs new tires"–they usually didn't measure up.

But as nice as everyone was to me, I trudged around in my own crate of thick black mud, not giving a damn. The trip with Mr. Ramsey's T-Bird was the one and only time in my life I'd ever done anything truly rebellious and criminal, but there was no epiphany in it. No reward. And self hatred was eating me alive.

I no longer felt the pressure to fake it at Holy Mary High School. Mrs. Ramsey had paid for the whole year, and had swallowed my act that I loved the place. I gather that she and the Johnsons had discussed my feelings about the place, because Mrs. Johnson quoted Mrs. Ramsey afterwards: "by all means let her finish out the year there". I imagine, too, that they somehow figured I wouldn't mind the two hour busride to get there. So I sat, lumpy-proton-style, in the classes and simply didn't give a shit.

Finally the Johnsons, God bless them, filled out all the necessary applications to get me into a Mental Health Outpatient Clinic. Because there I met Jesse, one shrink in my life besides Miss Grant who helped me a LOT. Jesse had long brown hair–he was the first "longhair" I ever knew – and wore faded blue jeans to the clinic every day. His whole attitude was exactly that casual. For the first time in my life, someone was working hard to get me to RELAX, and he was relaxed the whole time he was working on it.

My first day at the clinic, I walked in with my back aching from all the hunching and moping I'd been doing. I was still wearing my uniform after school at Holy Mary. Jesse had his sandals up on the desk when I entered, and he smiled, a really welcome smile at me. A friendly, crooked smile.

"Honest, Vanessa, things aren't that bad."

No answer. Sullen face. Sigh.

"Or are they?"

I shrugged my shoulders.

"Well, whatever has happened, I swear, Vanessa, I don't think you're a bad person at all."

"Oh, yeah? You don't even know me."

"Did you kill anyone?"

"No." Sulk.

"Hit anyone with a crow bar, or rob an old woman?"

I laughed. "You're close—I took my foster father's T-Bird for a spin when he wasn't home."

He smiled, then leaned closer to me, as if speaking "confidentially". "Sounds like a good time to me." He leaned back in his chair, clasping his hands behind his head. "A souped up T-Bird can be a lot of temptation for someone who has a Learner's Permit. That's pretty normal behavior—maybe a TINY bit wicked. Were you in a wreck? Was any one hurt?"

"No, not at all. I just got caught. But you don't understand—it's the worst thing I've ever done in my whole LIFE, and when I did it, POW! They threw me out of their home within a DAY."

"Maybe that's what you really wanted, Vanessa. For them to be that strict, you must have figured out the penalty before you took the T-Bird. Were you happy there?"

"Yes!—and no. Sort of. Sometimes," I said, fumbling around with the pleats in my uniform. I was confused, now. "I mean, I was so GRATEFUL—God, this rich family in Beverly Hills who were my heroes' parents. I wanted so much for them to like me, but I always felt gloomy and tense in my stomach—just like at my real parents' house. The Ramseys never wanted me. They were STUCK with me. Their son PUSHED me on them, and . . ."

I stopped. That's the most I'd ever said to anyone about my real feelings, in years. I felt insanely free, and, you know, saying all of it aloud ("I took the T-Bird for a spin . . .") made it sound NOT SO CRIMINAL after all! Probably, Jesse was right: eventually, maybe I COULD learn to live with myself, and with what I'd done. Probably he was also right that I HAD wanted to leave the Ramseys' house.

"So, Vanessa," Jesse said, in this really calm, soothing voice, "that makes you damned brave: you risked a lot to change a situation that was not good for you. I'm impressed," he assured me, and he smiled his funny, comfortable smile that made me feel great. I went home exhilarated and thought about all the things Jesse had said. I had to admit to myself that the Ramseys' house HAD been Heavy Duty Tension City, and that maybe I DID do the T-Bird number to escape, and maybe it WASN'T really the worst crime anyone had ever committed. Jesse said that maybe I could like myself someday; maybe he was right. What if he WAS right? WOULDN'T that be SOME-THING? To LIKE myself. Wow!

I stopped in the living room where Mrs. Johnson was doing needlepoint after dinner. "Thanks a lot, Mrs. Johnson, for getting me into that clinic. I'm starting to feel better already. I mean, about getting kicked out of the Ramseys' house and everything."

Mrs. Johnson looked up sharply from her needlepoint. "Honey, you weren't 'kicked out'!" NO, no, Vanessa, Mrs. Ramsey wrote to us months ago, asking when we'd have some space, on account of Barbara, who was moving out. I'm sure I told you about Barbara. She was by far the smartest, prettiest girl we've ever had. Straight A's. Anyway, Mr. Ramsey is a very sick man, and poor Mrs. Ramsey simply has her hands full with the three children she still has left at home. That's all, child! No, no—if he weren't sick, you'd still be absolutely welcome in the Ramseys' home. Mrs. Ramsey says you're a very smart young lady who's always been on perfect behavior in their home. Probably not as smart as our Lia, I'll bet, but Mrs. Ramsey just feels you need a place where you can get more attention, that's all."

Wow, what a revelation! I wasn't branded forever as a criminal, and the Ramseys had started right around Thanksgiving to get rid of me. The car trip had nothing to do with it. Best of all, I wasn't forever branded as a T-Bird thief. Mrs. Ramsey never told them. Gee, it would have been nice if she'd told *me* some of this. But, "I see," was all I said, walking slowly to my room.

I started feeling better immediately. I even spent a few moments contemplating "Barbara", "by far the smartest, prettiest girl" the Johnsons ever had. "Straight A's." She had my mother's name, and she sounded as perfect as my mother. I would never in a million years try to compete or live up to their precious Barbara, and I hoped like hell she was better at picking husbands than my mother had been.

* * *

"But, Jesse, Holy Mary high school costs a fortune, and I'm flunking out!" I told him. Since he was so bent on thinking I was OK, I wanted to see how many terrible things about me he could take before he changed his mind.

"Oh, come on, Vanessa, do you think Mrs. Ramsey thinks for one minute about the tuition? She paid it back in September of last year! Do you really think she stays up nights wondering how her ex-foster child might be abusing the privilege? Really. From everything you've told me about her, I'd bet you five bucks she spends most of her time thinking of her crazy kids and her sick husband. So quit with that guilt. You don't need it. You got A's at your other school, remember? It's just that you can't handle all the mortal-sin-and-Virgin-Mary stuff. God, who could?"

"But I can't stop thinking about the T-bird, and Mimi and Scott—you know, they haven't tried ONCE to contact me. They hate me. They always will."

"I doubt it. But maybe so. Vanessa, you did what you had to do, to survive!"

God, he made me sound like such a Crusader! "Do you think I'll end up a fag or a hooker?" I asked him. "My last shrink said I would."

Jesse laughed. "Jesus . . . some pretty interesting things come from the mouths of shrinks, don't they? I wonder why he said that. Do you have any desire to be either of those? I mean, you can if you want to—neither one would hurt anybody. Well, I think you, Vanessa, might not respect yourself too much if you were a prostitute. That wouldn't be good. I think prostitutes have a hard life, telling themselves they're OK even though all of society doesn't think they're OK. But, hey, if the lifestyle were what you really wanted, I'd respect that."

I laughed. "I don't think so. I don't think they're such BAD things, either. I mean, I'm pretty sure Lia at the house is—a fag, I mean. Not that she 'goes after me' or anything . . . But I think I like guys. Still, one never kissed me or anything—I mean, I'm almost sixteen and a half, and I haven't even been kissed by a guy. Does that mean I'm . . . ?"

His voice was soft. "No. When the right time comes, you'll be nervous, just like every other person in the world is. And, knowing you, Vanessa, it won't happen until you've met just the right person, and it'll be great."

Well, needless to say, I wished it were HIM, the way he smiled at me so kindly, so comfortably. But I knew enough about shrinking to know that it was "very natural" for a patient to fall in love with their shrink. One time Mr. Dean had reminded me: "Vanessa, if you're in love with me, I want you to know that it is a very normal and healthy response to the work we do in here." I had answered him very plainly: "Mr. Dean, I don't even LIKE you," to which he had responded, "that is also a normal and healthy response." Yuck. So, anyway, I never made a fool of myself, daydreaming about Jesse or anything like that; I just liked him. He was a great guy.

* * *

For the first time in my life, I was free to talk with other girls who'd been beaten and molested as children. This freedom made the whole world smaller and warmer. I WASN'T the only one it had happened to. Well, sure, Miss Grant had TOLD me that, but when I'd asked her, "did it ever happen to YOU, Miss Grant?", of course, she said no. And, I also learned, I sure as hell didn't get it the worst. It was hard to believe, but some guys were ten times sicker than my father!

At first, I only listened. Lia and Karen and I would listen to records in the den, and they would talk. They were old, wise, and tough—another world beyond my total innocence. Karen smoked, something that in those days only "fast women" did, and she talked hard and streetwise, the way prostitutes in movies did: not really BAD, but everything came out sexy.

Karen lay on the couch, smoking. She was wearing my Apres Ski sweater the Ramseys had given me. (Everyone's clothes were fair game in that house.) "So, Vanessa—God, that's a sexy name!—why are YOU living in the Johnson's house? You get raped every day, like Lia, or raped sometimes and beaten up sometimes, like me?"

Just like that. For the first time EVER, among my peers: words about unspeakable acts, with words I'd never in my life used. They'd whooshed right out with a puff of cigarette smoke. Both—the words and the smoke—made me dizzy.

"Um, I can't really talk about it. But, um, well, both. I mean, my mom had a bad temper. She didn't beat me too bad, but my dad, he, um, had a drinking problem . . ."

"Your real father?" Karen interrrupted.

"Yes."

"He hit you AND . . . ?" Lia asked, more gently than Karen asked things.

"Yes. And . . ."

"Did he rape you, like my stepfather did to me?" Lia prodded.

"No, but . . ." I WANTED to, but COULDN'T say it.

"It's not your fault, hon," Karen puffed. She was getting agitated. "My uncle, too. Had some real problems. Couldn't get it up. So he played around with me, a little six year old girl. The pig! My daddy's brother. When I told my dad, he just beat on me. Parents are great, aren't they?"

"You don't have to ever tell us," Lia said, "but it is better if you get it out of your head, and it comes out easiest from your mouth. It doesn't hurt so much, once it's out. It sort of evaporates a little. I got raped every single day for four years, back in Kansas, until I couldn't take it. I ran away, out to California. I've been here ever since—five years now. WE got lucky, Vanessa—most kids end up on the streets, in really bad shape."

"He didn't rape me," I started. I now felt it was my duty, after hearing their worst secrets so fast, that way. "But it was related to that. Something really gross," I blurted out. "Oral." I started crying, and hating myself for crying. I couldn't stop, though. I felt dumb and dirty. I wished I could be cool, the way they were about it.

Karen got up and hugged me hard, pounding my back as if she were burping a baby. "It's OK, girl! We KNOW. Life's going to start getting good, for all of us. The Johnsons are pretty easy to live with—compared to, you know. Oh, you'll get pretty sick of hearing how much smarter and prettier Barbara was, and how Lia is the smartest, and has the prettiest eyes, but still. It's better than the streets, you know? And definitely better than what came before." They were great; they made wonderful "older sisters", because they knew all my worst dirt—and they didn't judge me badly for it. When I told them about the T-Bird, they laughed and laughed, as if it were the grandest escapade on earth.

"And you feel GUILTY for THAT?" Karen laughed. "Jesus. They probably don't even REMEMBER, by now.

Hell, their own kids'll probably do TEN times worse stuff
when they hit fifteen. Relax, girl!"

I did, a little. Months rolled along comfortably, and
pretty soon I was spending my last day at Holy Mary High
School. Farewell, farewell; may I never feel guilty about
patent leather shoes or eating meat on Friday again. When
I pulled my work out of the art lockers, I was amazed: I'd
done a huge amount of projects! Sister Theresa smiled at
me and stopped to talk while I was admiring my own water
color paintings.

"I hate to see you go, Vanessa," she said, smiling down at
one piece that I called "Tortured Sun". "You probably have
more talent than any art student I've ever had."

That blew my socks off! I WANTED to say, "Why, then,
bitch, didn't you tell me that back when I was shrivelling
up? All you told me THEN was that my uniform was hiked
up too high." But I didn't; the praise was too interesting. I
mumbled, "gosh, Sister, thank you SOOO much."

At the Johnsons' house, we gave Lia a little farewell
party. She was moving nearby, into an apartment with a
couple other girls while she went to UCLA. She'd won a full
scholarship in Economics. I'd miss Lia; she inspired me
with both her brains and her unwavering approach to
achieving goals. She was headed up the ladder to the top of
international banking, and absolutely nothing would ever
divert her attention. She liked women, and I admired the
matter-of-fact way she spoke about it, years before glamorous people started "coming out of the closets" in droves.

She and Karen and I were sitting in the den one night
listening to the new Beatles' REVOLVER album. We sang
loudly together at the "Good Day Sunshine" chorus. We
peeked out the curtains periodically at the brand new Tri-
umph Sprite parked out in front: another hopeful for
Karen.

"Karen," I teased her, "couldn't you give this poor guy a
break? Throw him a scarf or something?"

'Are you aware, Karen," Lia said, "that his folks have set
up a $100,000. trust fund for him to use when he turns

twenty one?" (Lia worked part time at the Bank of America.)

Karen raised her eyebrows. That caught her interest! She smiled. "So go get him, Lia."

Lia snorted. "I never want ANYTHING to do with men. You know that. They're all the same, every one of them: nothing but massive egos and hungry dicks."

My eyes bugged, because a), I'd never heard ANYONE talk that way about guys, and b) I was pretty sure I knew what she meant about, who she liked instead of men. Karen was casual about it.

"True, maybe. But there aren't that many rich women around, you know."

"No," Lia answered, "but I will at some point BE the richest woman either of you have ever met. And then I'll find a nice, pretty lady to share it all with."

"God," I said, wide-eyed, "I believe you!"

They rolled their eyes at each other, the way they often did when confronted with "Vanessa's innocence". Neither of them could believe how innocent I was. They'd often tease me, saying, "come on. You're not REALLY that dumb and innocent, are you?" and I'd laugh back, "I'm afraid so!" – even though I didn't really enjoy my dumb innocence all that much.

For a year, then, it was just Karen and me at the Johnsons' house. Karen, it seemed, was always on a date, generally wearing something of mine that Mrs. Ramsey had given me. Mr. and Mrs. Johnson were a real Ozzie and Harriett type couple; Mrs. Johnson baked cookies, and Mr. Johnson worked as a handyman. They were kind, and they never hassled us much. Except, of course, for the comments: "gee, you sure don't get many good dates the way gorgeous Karen does, do you?" Their rule was simple: "stay out of trouble, please, but if you find trouble, we'll do what we can." It was comfortable, living there. We were allowed to laugh at the dinner table. We could dance in the den to music turned all the way up, if we liked, between 3:30 and 5:00, after school. After that, we had to turn it down. I usually danced alone, perfecting my dance steps for the weekend school dances. I must say, I was asked to dance quite a lot, with guys who were good, "platonic" friends.

Except for Richard. Richard was a tall, gentle senior, very goody-goody like me, who danced great and was too shy to try to stick his hand down my blouse. Soon, we were dancing with each other exclusively. He started driving me home from school in his brand new Porsche every day. As I explained to Jesse, "I sort of don't want anything else to happen with Richard, because he seems too wonderful to be true, and I don't think I ever want to find out he's not. But on the other hand, . . ." I smiled and looked at Jesse funny (hell, I could say anything to Jesse, but STILL . . .) "well, I mean, I wouldn't mind it if he'd try a little more than he does. I don't know—maybe I have too many hormones."

"No, Vanessa," Jesse said, and smiled. "You are feeling what is exactly normal for a seventeen and a half year old woman to feel about a young man she likes a lot."

"Thanks, Jess."

Eventually, Richard did ask me on a date. "Do you, I mean, um, Vanessa, would you like to go . . ."

"Yes, Richard—anything! I'd love it!" Boy, I felt idiotic when it came out that way, so desperately! We dated every chance we could, after that. And kissed—made out—a great deal.

When Christmas came, Mrs. Johnson made the whole house shiny red and green with Christmas ornaments she'd made through the years. Karen and I had a great time, making long haired, guitar-playing gingerbread men. When she saw them, Mrs. Johnson actually said, "my, do they have girls now who play the guitar?" Talk about dumb innocence! But it was OK on her. Karen and I giggled and roared, then patted Mrs. Johnson on the shoulders, as if to say, "it's OK, go ahead and keep your blinders on. But in case you'd like to know, these are the sixties."

When I was seventeen and a half, and Karen was just turning eighteen, Karen walked into my room and casually announced, "Vanessa, it really is time for you to get laid."

Frankly, I agreed with her.

* * *

One of the great things about being crazy for Richard was that Richard's best friend was David — Rich David, whom Karen was "going all the way" with. So it worked out nicely, going on double dates sometimes with Karen and David. It was a little embarrassing, however, because all Karen and David ever did was steam up the windows making out in the back seat, while Richard and I talked nervously and drove.

"So!" I'd yell to the back seat, without turning around, "you folks comfortable back there?"

The slobbering noises were really gross. Richard and I decided it was more fun just the two of us — "less pressure", as Richard said. But I had this hormone problem that Jesse said was so damned normal. I WANTED that — I wanted to really really be positive that I was indeed "Normal". In those days, "Normal" could ONLY mean "Heterosexual". You know? Man, woman, normal stuff that normal people do. I'd seen Natalie Wood freak out and go crazy and get locked up in an insane assylum, all because she didn't go all the way with Warren Beatty in "Love In The Grass". I was terrified it might happen to me. So I jumped on poor old Richard when he asked me one night, "listen, Vanessa, we've been going together all year, and, um, I mean, would you be offended if I asked you to come to my parents' cabin in the snow for New Year's Eve? My, um, parents won't be there, and, um, well, David really wants to go up there, too — with Karen. You know. But, you know, if you don't want to, I really understand. I mean, I love you an awful lot, Vanessa."

Poor Richard! He was shaking; no guy would shake like that, I figured, unless it was his first time, too. I tried to comfort him.

"Sure, Richard! I'd love to go! God, I LOVE the snow.

Tell you right now, though, I'm not going near the ski slopes. I STINK. I'll just stay in the lodge by the fireplace, you know what I mean? No problem!" Boy, I sound dumb, I thought to myself: like a hairy, eager ANIMAL.

The next day, I told Jesse, "Richard and I have decided to lose our virginity on New Year's Day, the second after midnight. I'm going to start 1967 a whole different person."

"Good luck to you, Vanessa. I guess we both will be starting something new," Jesse said. He smiled his same comfortable old smile. He wore the same old jeans, but he'd grown a beard, and his hair was down past his shoulders. He looked tired, as if he'd been up a hundred nights thinking weighty thoughts. "I've thought and thought about it, Vanessa, and I cannot in any way feel good about going to a war I don't believe in. I could never kill people—never. So, uh, I'll be going to jail New Year's Day."

I started crying. "Jess, couldn't you at least run to Canada? Lots of people are doing that. Jail, Jesse—you don't KNOW how bad it is. Please!"

"No. I have to stay in this country, because I love this country—wrong and foolish as it is, sometimes. My not going has to MEAN something, Vanessa, besides just running away. If enough of us are willing to sacrifice, maybe the killing will stop."

"But, God, Jess. Jail! How long . . ." Shit, it seemed too unreal. All my worst Detention Center nightmares flashed in front of me.

"Will you visit me, old buddy?"

"Give me the address, right now. You need *me*, for a change, Jesse, and after all you've given me, I swear I won't let you down."

"You remember to respect yourself, OK? And you make damned sure everybody else does too, you promise?"

"I promise," I said, crying a lot. He picked a few tears off my face with his fingertip, kissed his fingertip, and made the "Peace" sign with his two fingers. I held my two fingers up in an answering "Peace" sign.

"Peace."

I learned a great deal about courage and conviction, that day, lessons that have seen me through amazing trials.

* * *

So Karen and I set off for the snow, telling the Johnsons the first lie I'd ever told them: that Richard's parents had invited us, and that of course they would be chaperoning us. I was doing well at Lincoln High School – all A's and B's – so they felt I deserved a vacation.

"I'm sure that would be fine," Mrs. Johnson said. She trusted me. Guilt settled in – dandruff and guilt, together on my shoulders.

The ski cabin was absolutely glamorous; the sparkling knotty pine smelled rich and sharp. Karen and David were in bed before Richard and I finished putting the eggs in the fridge. Well, what did we expect? We decided to go for a walk in the snow along the lakeshore.

"Why do you think they call it Lake Arrowhead? It doesn't look like an arrowhead to me," Richard said. He was nervous.

"Sure it does, silly – only all the houses around it distract you from seeing the shape," I explained. I was beginning to think this whole thing was a dumb idea. Maybe Richard and I would end up walking around all night, rather than face you-know-what.

"Vanessa? How old were you when your parents died?" he asked me. That was his assumption – that I was an orphan. I must admit, I never worked very hard at trying to change his ideas, neither about my parents, nor about my "sick relatives in Beverly Hills" that I'd lived with before the Johnsons. That was stretching it, but still, it wasn't a TOTAL lie.

"Um, well, eight, I guess."

"That's so sad. Did you live in an orphanage?"

"Yes. In Seattle, Washington."

"I'd, um, like to be your family, Vanessa. I'd, um, like you

to meet my family, you know, after we get back and
everything."

God, he was so serious! And gentle. I had to like the guy,
if partly because he was even dorkier and straighter than I
was. "Sure, Richard. I'd like to meet them." I was terrified
of meeting them. Richard was dorky and straight and
DUMB—how smart could a guy be who was this crazy
about me?— so he believed I was an orphan with rich relatives in Beverly Hills. What if his parents asked all the
questions that opened up the naked realities? Despite all
the work I'd done with Miss Grant and with Jesse, I hadn't
quite lost that feeling that I was different-BECAUSE, people could TELL I'd been sexually abused.

We killed time and kept away from the cabin in every
possible way until we were both dead exhausted and it was
midnight.

"Happy New Year, Vanessa!" he said quietly, and hugged
me hard. I fell over, so we were lying on top of each other.

"Happy New Year, Richard!"

We kissed until the spit started freezing on our faces.
Then we went back to the Porsche. When Richard fell
asleep in my lap in the Porsche, I nudged him awake. He
looked horribly uncomfortable.

"Richard? Richard, let's go inside. I'm freezing to death!
We don't HAVE to DO anything, you know."

He nodded and smiled a cute, sleepy smile. "OK."

We went into Richard's room, which was more than
small-and-cozy. I mean, there was nothing else to do in
there except get in bed, because that's all there was to the
whole room.

And I'll tell you: I was lucky as hell that it was Richard
who was the first, because his terror of the whole thing
made me strong. I was so busy helping him through it, I
didn't have time to think about the ugliest part of my
past—my father forcing sex on me. It wasn't related. I'm
not saying it wasn't there at all, that foul odor from the
past—it was. A little. It was a faint odor; helping Richard
get through his first time, and my truly wanting a good,

happy sexual experience with him, blotted out most of it. There was some physical pain—there is, maybe (?) for everyone, the first time—I'm no sex doctor, so I can't say for sure—but Karen had prepared me for it.

"For, um, girls like us," Karen had said, referring to sexually abused kids, "there's the psychological thing—which you can get over—but I think the physical pain is there for everyone the first time. But, you know, nothing, could, um, hurt the way it did, back then, as a tiny child. So it's not a big deal pain like before. Richard's so sweet, Vanessa, you'll be OK—just make him go slow."

"It's OK, Richard," I assured him. "Karen says it's supposed to hurt a little bit."

Richard kissed me all over the face. "I never want to hurt you."

I thanked God that I had somehow let myself be worthy of kind, wonderful Richard. The gratitude, and God, and Richard's wonderfulness all swelled up inside of me, in a pure, heady passion. Swollen life-at-its-ripest surged through us, until there were no thoughts, no controls. Nothing but this surge.

* * *

Dear Little Sisters and Brothers,

I don't want to pretend that normal adult sexual relations with someone you care for is an automatic, easy thing. It isn't. The bad, nightmare things that happened in the past never quite leave you forever. Sorry. I wish they did. Maybe someday, some genius will find a way to erase it—ALL the ugly stuff—from your mind forever.

In the meantime, please, do what Jesse told me to do: respect yourself, and make sure every single person in your life respects you also. Each one of you is a very special person with something special to share, so, please, love yourself enough to wait for someone GOOD, who really loves you. You deserve something great, something really special. When you want something to happen, OK, let it happen, ON YOUR TERMS – and not a moment before. I wouldn't just say this to abused kids; I'd say this – and probably will say this – to my daughters, when they're older. Don't let ANYONE push you to do anything, EVER.

Even though it's hard at times, you CAN separate the bad sex stuff from the beautiful sex stuff. With someone you love, and absolutely trust. With someone who loves you with a big, full heart, and is gentle, slow, and patient. And then, honest, it can be incredibly great. You feel like a beautiful, flying bird, a whole lot freer than before. Love is the miracle that makes it happen, the freedom and the flight.

Respect yourself, then, and make sure everyone else around you respects you, too, OK? And for EVERYONE'S sake, especially your own, USE BIRTH CONTROL! !

* * *

There was one problem: swear to God, I knew nothing about birth control. The next morning, Karen finally emerged and joined me in the bathroom. While we did each other's hair, she asked me.

"So. How was it?"

I blushed. "Good," I smiled. I was SO embarrassed.

"What did you use?"

"Use?" I asked.

"Use, Vanessa – I mean, did he use a rubber, or . . ."

I hated being so dumb, but I couldn't fake it on this. I had NO idea what she was talking about. "a rubber WHAT?" I honestly wanted to know.

"Oh, Jesus. Vanessa, please tell me you're kidding." She looked at my blank face and knew. "You're not. Oh, great. Vanessa, I don't mean to sound strange, but, like, do you even know where babies come from? I mean, you and I get our periods on exactly the same day, hon, and what I'm saying is, you may be in really serious trouble. I mean, I hope you and Richard really love each other a LOT!"

She was pissed, ranting and raving all the way to her room. She hated herself for not teaching me the basics of birth control, and she hated me for being SO STUPID.

When my period was three weeks late, I, too, started to panic. They didn't have those nifty little home pregnancy test kits back then – they still killed rabbits, I think, to find out – so Karen said I had to go to the free clinic. For a pregnancy test. She picked me up at the Art Shop where I worked after school, and drove me there.

When the nurse told me to take off "everything from the waist down," I knew: that meant a gynecological exam, which I would die rather than go through. THAT, the cold steel exam, brought back the horrible nightmares fast. Lying there on the table, the ugly crud from the past swarmed around my face so I couldn't breathe. The other cold steel exams, performed on a tiny, frightened girl. "I see no signs of penetration or sperm," they had said, while they prodded my insides. I started to scream, then caught my breath. I was here again, but I was ten years older. I didn't know what was then and what was now: "now, if you could just slide your fanny down here further," a doctor-hard voice was saying from behind a sheet. Just like before, when I was eight, I closed my knees tightly and whimpered. No, no, no, I argued with myself: no one will ever humiliate me that way again. This is different: you're OK, you're strong, these people can't hurt you. Do it – just do it. It's now, not then. Shove that stuff out of your mind the way Miss Grant and Jesse always tell you to.

"Could you please try to relax?" The doctor voice pleaded. "Take some very deep breaths: in, out. In, out. In, out. That's it. In, Out. That's very good."

And I lost myself in the breaths: in, out, in, out. I made them loud and harsh, so the breath and the noise covered my face and made me invisible. All the breaths turned bright green, and swallowed me. As I used to do when I

was young, I removed myself from my body. I thought of
Elizabeth. I'd been too ashamed to call her as I'd promised
to after the snow trip. Elizabeth had made it—really succeeded in only ONE foster home, while I'd bounced all over
Southern California. If she knew I'd gotten pregnant my
very first time in the sack, wow, she'd realize I was a thoroughly hopeless loser. But then I thought to myself, "heck,
maybe I should punish myself for my stupidity—call Elizabeth, and watch her hate my guts when I tell her how
stupid I was." She'd wanted me to sing with her.

"OK, you can get dressed now, and wait outside. I'll call
you."

Karen waited in the hip waiting room with the Jimi Hendrix posters all over the walls. She suffered. "It's all my
fault, Vanessa. I got you into this, just because David and I
wanted to stay in the cabin. I feel like such a jerk."

"Karen, don't be weird. I wanted to go. It's not your fault
I'm so DUMB about those things."

She smiled—a smile that said, "yeah, you're pretty dumb
all right," but I was awfully glad she didn't SAY it.

I was pregnant, the doctor said. "Do you have any idea
what you'd like to do about this?"

"No, sir." I was numb, in a fog. Do you have any good,
lethal sleeping pills? I wanted to ask him. But I kept quiet.

His voice went soft. "Well, you have some time to think it
over. We're here when you decide."

Karen had no trouble reading the verdict on my face.
"You should probably tell Richard, don't you think?"

"God, Karen, I don't want to tell ANYONE. Karen, I
can't have a baby! I'll BEAT the kid. I'll HURT it! Do you
know what the statistics are? Have all your shrinks been
bitchin' enough to tell YOU the way they told ME? Almost
all battered kids grow up and beat on their kids, you
know—I'm sure you've heard."

Karen knew. "I know," she said quietly. "I was hoping I'd
be sterile so I never ever made a kid go through what I had
to go through. But you know," she said, "Jesse would tell
you that all those statistics don't mean a thing."

"You're right. Today's my visiting day. I haven't missed one yet. I should go visit Jesse this minute. Can you give me a ride to the bus stop?"

* * *

I don't want to make myself sound like a saint or anything, but it took all the bravery in my whole body to go inside that jail once a week. I couldn't quiet the illogical, foolish idea that they would make me stay there forever. Once inside—SLAM! They'd lock the gates, and I'd be stuck there. And it didn't matter how many times I took the number 57 bus to get there, the queasy feeling always took over.

I looked incredibly innocent compared with the other women who waited to see their men. I'd brought Jesse some Van de Kamp's chocolate chip cookies (his favorite); they wouldn't let you take in anything homemade, or any package that'd been opened. I had to fill out a form that included questions like, "have you ever been incarcerated?" I struggled with that one, and decided to "lie"—not tell them about the Child Center or the Detention Center. They'd get the wrong idea, and at that point, I surely didn't want to discuss my troubled childhood with prison wardens. The guilt and paranoia the little lie produced was nothing compared with the terror that I'd be locked up if they knew my ugly past. GODDAMN MY PARENTS AND THE WHOLE ENTIRE WORLD FOR MAKING ME FEEL GUILTY FOR WHAT THEY DID TO ME!!!

The jail was in a beautiful countryside setting, way out in the boonies. Once through the pretty minor checkpoints, a woman guard inspected the cookies intensely—but with a smile on her face. I went into a curtained room, and she passed her hand lightly here and there. Unenjoyable, but she was friendly and gentle, and she made it fairly easy. I was ushered to an outside, fenced-in area that was bordered with picnic tables. It was a big grassy park, with children playing, and inmates hugging their women. There was no sign of any bad-assed looking guards waiting for the wrong kind of eye-blink or anything. I relaxed a bit, especially when I saw Jesse, who looked exactly the same as always. He gave me the old comfortable crooked smile; he always looked glad to see me.

"My faithful friend. Peace."

"Jesse, how ARE you? Really? Is it—I mean, you know, you won't get stabbed or anything? I'm so WORRIED about you."

"I'm fine, old girl. How 'bout you? Kill any rabbits today?"

"Jesse, YES! What am I going to do?"

"Have you talked to Richard?"

"I came straight here."

He smiled. "Do you want to be a mother?"

"God, NO! I'll beat it—you know what the statistics are: battered children all end up as child abusers. And what if that's also true about, you know, the other kind of abuse, you know, if I turn into a pervert or something? I'd kill myself before I'd do that to a kid!" I started crying all over Jesse's blue work shirt.

"Hey, hey, Vanessa, listen to me!" He made me look at him. "Remember what we do with statistics? Out the window! You could never, EVER beat a child, especially if you were stronger than the anger. And you ARE—you are one tough person—also a GOOD person. No. You would never do that. Or the other kind of abuse. Don't even think that, not for a minute."

"Yeah, well, what if I did—I really don't want to find out."

"Are you going to tell Richard?"

"I guess so . . ." I laughed. "So long, Richard! Oh, well—it was nice while it lasted."

"You might be surprised by his reaction, you know."

"Bets? Five dollars says he dumps me."

"Five dollars says he doesn't, Vanessa."

"Hey! What's a foxy lady like you doing with a faggot

like him? He looks like a woman, can't you see that?" A jerky redneck-type bad guy was hassling us, and looking for a fight. I was frightened, mostly for Jesse; what would this guy do to him after I left?

"It's OK, Vanessa," Jesse said quietly. I couldn't believe it; he smiled at the guy! Jesse took this "Peace" stuff too seriously for me, but if it got him beat up, he never mentioned it. I promised him I wouldn't worry too much about him, and left when the announcement came that visitors' hours were over.

* * *

"Will you marry me, Vanessa? I love. you, and, well, I just want you to know that—you know, it meant everything to me, what we did. Please?"

OK, so I owed Jesse five dollars. I didn't especially want to get married, and I DIDN'T want to be a mother, but the fact that someone WANTED to marry me really astounded me. Like the rest of the world, I have this problem with self esteem. Only it might be a touch harder for abused children to gain self esteem. Hell, I might never get another offer like this, I reasoned, at the ripe old age of seventeen and a half. So I said yes.

Karen, who'd moved out of the Johnsons' house and into an apartment with David (very risque at the time—they had separate phones so that David's folks would never find out), dragged her guilt with her whenever we got together.

"God, Vanessa, let me at least make your wedding dress," she said. She was a brilliant seamstress—which reminded me a lot of Mimi—and her exotic wedding dress designs excited me.

But nothing else did. I liked Richard well enough, but that was all. On the other hand, I figured, someone with my background maybe never could be all-out crazy in love with a man, even though physically, I had the hormonal "thing" for them—men, I mean.

For two weeks, Karen-the-martyr sewed up a storm: baby clothes, a wedding trousseau, etcetera, etcetera. I had to go through with it, now! But I couldn't. I bought Karen a hope chest instead.

Suddenly, without talking to Jesse, Karen, Richard, or the Johnsons, I returned to the free clinic. "Excuse me," I said at the reception desk, "but I'd like to find out about having an abortion."

"How old are you?"

"Um, seventeen and a half."

"We'll need your parents' consent."

I had to tell Mrs. Johnson—who had, after all, always said, "you can come to me about ANYTHING."

* * *

By then, there were two younger girls living at the Johnsons' house—Vicky and Carol. Vicky and Carol would've been a handful anyway, as they really liked smoking hashish all day—something the Johnsons had never experienced and were in no way prepared for. But what Vicky and Carol really couldn't stand was listening to the Johnsons harrangue at them about how much better Vanessa's grades were, and how much cuter Vanessa's boyfriend was. Amazing: I had moved up the ladder to where *I* was the favored one. Instead of hearing about how superior my competitors were, I heard about ME—MY superiority! Funny, it hadn't bothered me that much, hearing how much better than I Barbara, Lia, and Karen were; I'd agreed with the Johnsons, that everyone was better than I. But the younger girls were PISSED, and hated my guts. They hated my miniskirts, my shaved legs, my nail polish, and mostly, the fact that I didn't take drugs: I was OUT OF IT, folks!

So, yes, I did feel some justice inside—perhaps I had been bothered by their act—when I got to tell Mrs. Johnson that goody goody Vanessa with the best grades and richest boyfriend had gotten knocked up. AND wanted the unthinkable (in those days): an abortion. That's something people went to sleazy back alleys in Mexico to do—and die, many of them.

She took it pretty well, except I felt a little badly that she blamed herself. "I guess I never told you the facts of life. Vanessa, we've TRIED to give you a good home, keep you out of trouble, but that young man, Richard, thinks he's so great just because his family's well-to-do. Shame on him for taking advantage of you!"

"He didn't, Mrs. Johnson. He asked me to marry him."

Her eyes lit up. Richard was instantly a white knight again. "He DID?" She couldn't believe it, either. What her voice IMPLIED was, "imagine! A girl with YOUR background, nabbing a rich handsome young man like HIM."

And, I must admit, I greatly enjoyed announcing: "But I'm not 1 ready for marriage. I want an abortion." Would she, could she love me, after that blow to her equilibrium? "They say I need a parent's consent, so that's why I've come to talk to you."

She was great about it. She stared at the kitchen table a lot, trying to sort it all out, but then she was calm.

"We've been through this problem before—with Barbara."

Wow! I was blown out. Goddess BARBARA—the first Great One I'd been hopelessly stacked up against—had gotten knocked up? Amazing!

Mrs. Johnson continued. "I'm afraid you need your natural mother's consent on this one. Foster Parents don't count, here."

The kitchen table started spinning. I hadn't seen my mother in the three and a half years since she smacked my face in the courtroom. I couldn't believe it: *she* was the person entrusted with my welfare here? But I had made a choice, a decision, and by God, I was going to stick with it. With sweating hands, and shaking voice, I called my mother. Twice. The first time, my father answered, in his thick, boozy, "charming" voice. Gross. I hung up immedi-

ately, and sat staring at the phone. Sweat bunched up in
my palms, and squirted onto the phone receiver. "I have got
to do this," I said, and I picked up the phone again. This
time, she answered, in the same cold, efficient voice she'd
always used on the phone. I mimicked that cold efficiency
of hers.

"Hello, Mother, this is Vanessa. I have to see you,
ALONE. As soon as possible."

She breathed sharply. "I see . . . All right. Where?"

"Can you get down here, to the beach, to Reuben's?" I
asked. Reuben's was an excellant restaurant; Richard had
taken me there a few times. The prices were outrageous,
which was very important to me. My mother respected
money. I could almost see her on the other end of the phone,
raising her eyebrows. "My treat," I added. I was making
pretty good money at the Art Shop, as Weekend Store
Manager.

"Fine."

And we set it up for the next day. I was nervous as hell,
but you know? I realized—maybe for the first time—that
Jesse was right: I WAS tough. I WAS strong. I'd be OK.

* * *

I was early, and waited outside Reubans'. I was clean,
tidy, and dressed like a young sophisticate. I was also thin
and gorgeous, my friends told me. You bet your sweet,
sweet booties I was hoping for her approval! Shrinks tell
me that you never grow out of that desire for approval. Too
bad, because usually, it can NEVER come big enough to
make up for all the years it never came. Usually, in fact, it
never comes. Period.

She was exactly the same: crisply dressed in a light yellow suit, not a single, short grey hair out of place. Her feet
clop-clopped purposefully, without a waiver. Suddenly, I
felt like a slob. She looked at me as if she'd just seen me
yesterday—and as if I looked exactly the same as I had,

yesterday. The lady showed no surprise. All that getting gorgeous, the last three years – for nothing.

"Hello, Mother."

"Shall we go in, or did you want to speak to me outside Reubans'?"

We went in, I with my legs now limpy-wimpy. She could reduce me, in a flash, to peanut-size. The three and a half years' worth of intensive work I'd done with Jesse to build myself up had crumbled to dust, too rapidly. It was unfair. She is a master at that. (Does she even realize it?) What I really wanted to do was cry. Of course, I couldn't.

"So," my mother, ever the businesswoman, said. "Are you pregnant, or what?"

I smiled. The foolish fantasy of the loving mother-daughter reunion was forever shattered. Might as well get down to business. Thank God a cocktail waitress appeared. Mother ordered a Vodka Tonic, and then, even though I was underage and had never touched booze in my life, Mother turned to me and said, "what will you have, Vanessa?"

"Vodka Tonic will be fine," I said in my most sophisticated voice. I felt like a total criminal, but the waitress never blinked an eye. Mother turned to me when the waitress had gone. I had to speak, but, unfortunately, my "mature sophisticated voice" had shrunk a bit. "Um, well, yes, as a matter of fact I am pregnant." I stared at the absorbing design on the silverware and started rolling up my cocktail napkin. I felt nauseous – whether morning sickness or trauma, I can't say. I continued staring down. Down, down: hoping to find China and disappear into it. This was really stupid, getting together with her this way. What had I expected – a motherly hug, or something? A comforting, "Oh, honey, it happens! But don't worry, I still love you!" Yes! Not expected, maybe, but fantasized. Dreamed. Hoped. Very dumb.

The cocktails came, and I gulped a couple gulps of mine: the first alcohol ever to touch my lips. I gagged; I swear, if I'd been with ANYONE ELSE, I would have spit it up instantly. (It would have been a BLAST to spit up if, say, Kelly had been there.) Instead, I just closed my eyes and swallowed hard. What a shitty rite of passage this was turning out to be!

My mother smiled. "Well, I am glad to see you haven't added alcohol to your list of bad habits. It's probably for the best . . . what do you intend to do—and, what do you expect me to do about it? Do you have any idea who the father might be?"

That's it, Mom. Put me down. Make me into a total slut. As always. "Mother, he's the first and only one. It was our first and only time. He's asked me to marry him, and he's from a VERY wealthy family." (Take that, Bitch!)

"I see. Well, congratulations. Would there be any point in my trying to talk you out of it?"

"I want an abortion."

"A wise decision." She took a huge—but ladylike, with the uplifted pinkie—swig of her drink. Her second drink. Funny—she never used to drink. Either she'd changed, or this was an unusual day. I noted that the raised pinkie she held up while she drank was trembling. It was the first time I ever saw my mother lose it, if "lose it" is what you could call a trembling pinkie. For her, it WAS: trembling simply wasn't one of my mother's normal characteristics. Something had gotten to her, and that made me feel a little more substantial. Appreciating this, I tried another swig of my drink; enough people drank this stuff that there had to be something to it. The second drink went down much easier. Anaesthetizingly so.

"Vanessa, look. No one needs to tell me what an inept mother I was to you. No one needs to try to make me feel guilty—including you. I do, thank you, feel guilty at times. And sorry. Very sorry. About everything. Does that make you feel victorious? I don't apologize very often."

I couldn't believe this was happening. I think I was drunk. I felt drunk, with my head whirling around. This was the nicest she had ever been to me. Through everything, across the miles and years, I'd fantasized and prayed that she'd apologize someday. She took another big swallow, and kept talking.

"But I'll tell you something. Something I've never told anyone. I tried like hell to abort you, because you ruined everything for me. Every one of my big dreams and plans – shot to hell. For FIVE LONG MONTHS, I tried every hospital, and every sleazy-sounding doctor's name. For nothing. No one would touch it. No abortion. It was ILLEGAL. I tried everything, including punching my stomach a lot, but you persisted. I wanted to BE something, Vanessa. NOT a mother. Did that give me any right to hate you? No. Any normal woman would've maybe learned to go with the program and love her kid. But I'm not normal. I hated your guts for taking all my big dreams away from me. I chose a man who's not the greatest, but don't think I'll ever admit that again outside this restaurant. I made my choice, and I'll stick with it to the end. It's a terrible excuse, and I know it, but there it is."

"God, Mom," I said. My voice sounded whiny-drunk. "I'm really sorry." For what, being born? But I FELT sorry. For her.

"But now I've got it – my big dream, Vanessa. I'm moving to Singapore to manage Shell Oil, if you can believe that. Finally, all the work has paid off. Still . . . there will always be guilt in my luggage, for what you had to endure with me while I hated you. DON'T do that to some little kid."

My mouth was moving, but my head spun in a slightly vommity daze. I was a little glad to hear that she felt guilty, and exhuberantly joyous that she had apologized, but I didn't want her to know it. So I played her game: Efficiency. "I need your signature before they'll let me have the abortion. I don't think I want to get married right now. I think I'll just live with Richard when I turn eighteen. Is that OK with you?" My voice was a little girl's voice.

She shrugged, an I-don't-give-a-damn-what-you-do shrug.

I was stunned at what my mother had just revealed. It hurt. It hurt so badly, but it was also a RELIEF to hear what I must have suspected all along—what shrinks had tried so hard to help me see: that she didn't hate me just because I was me. She had had her own dreams—God, I'd never imagined that she could dream!—dreams that I had smashed. She was a victim, too, in a way. Not that I could help smashing them. If I'd been anyone else born to her at the same time, she would have hated them, too.

She wanted to just drink, now, and forget everything. We were on our third round. I had to say something. "Thank you for telling me all that. Um . . ." My voice was so tiny and fragile, but I couldn't make it stronger just then. "Do you think that now, um, since your dream has come true, and you're going to be rich and powerful managing Shell Oil in Singapore, do you, um, think that you could love me now, just a little?" God, how corny and pathetic that came out. I could NEVER have asked that of her if I weren't smashed. But that's what I felt. That's what I really wanted to know, so bless that Vodka Tonic, anyway!

And she must've been REALLY smashed, because she did something she's never done before or since: she hugged me. She didn't want me to see or know, but I know silent-crying too well: she was silent-crying on my shoulder. The tears weren't even very wet—she even cries tidy—but I still knew. I never hassled her to answer me, and she never did.

We stumble-walked to the free clinic (clever one that I am—Reubans' was just down the block) as if we were pals. Mother even giggled at the Jimi Hendrix posters: "good God, what is that?" She signed the necessary papers, and as we walked back, more sober now, she suggested—fully in control now—"perhaps you'd like me to drive you to and from the clinic tomorrow? You won't quite be out of the anaesthesia."

"Thank you. That would be great."

The Vodka Tonic glow with her didn't last, but from that day, I was definitely on speaking terms with my natural mother. I can't say that all the anger went poof! and vanished instantly, because it didn't. No. The anger is still with me—some, not all of it. But the hate is gone. I understand her so much better, and I just don't hate her. She, too, was a victim. She screwed up with me, but on her next kid, my brother, she tried to make up for it. If he'd been born first, maybe I would've gotten the nice mom. Whatever. I started to grow up, in many ways, that day.

* * *

Dear Little Sisters:

I want to talk to you about abortion.

I want you to know that I wish abortion had been legal when my mother was carrying me. And you might say, "oh! But then you wouldn't have had your wonderful daughters, etc., etc." Wrong. Someone else would've had them. Maybe I would've reincarnated, as a different fetus. Many cultures believe this happens, and who's to say it doesn't? I might've come to another mother who would've loved me, and to a father who wasn't a sicko. Or maybe I would've just slept forever in the mud, never reincarnating, but just blobbing in the mud. That would have been so much better than the early life I had!

I'll tell you something, from the bottom of my heart. If God came up to me and said, "Vanessa, you have a choice: live just one day of your childhood and get a million dollars—or die," I would take death in a minute. In one minute, little sisters, without even blinking. I've seen an awful lot of dead people sleeping in their coffins, and I'll tell you, it doesn't look nearly so bad as what I went through.

Please think about it. If you get pregnant, and you don't think you can love that child with your whole heart, think about ALL your options. Abortion is one of them. There are a lot of people going around with nothing better to do than hassle free clinics. They say that abortion is murder. They place the life of a fetus above the life of the woman carrying the fetus. They place the life of a fetus above the life of the child that fetus could become. And they are wrong. The pain of getting vaccuumed out of my mother's womb would've been NOTHING compared with the fifteen years of torture I went through once I was Out. And I'll tell you something else: I was able to forgive my mother most of the hell she put me through ONLY AFTER she told me that she at least TRIED to abort me: that she faced herself honestly, knew she'd give me a lousy life, and tried to do the kindest thing: spare me that cruelty. My mother is not a horrible person; she was simply a horrible mother. It wasn't her fault that the law did not allow her to do that kindness. I am glad the law did allow me to do that kindness, years later.

* * *

When I was two months away from turning eighteen, Carol flipped out and ran away – again. She couldn't handle the Johnsons' trip of harping on how great Karen and Lia and especially I was, compared with how inferior she, Carol, was. So Carol had gone into my closet and slashed all my clothes with one of my art razor knives, and then split.

I felt sorry for her, and angry with the Johnsons. (Sure, OK, also a little pissed that all my clothes were wrecked.) Why did they have to be so insensitive to the fact that kids with our backgrounds didn't need to HEAR how much better everyone else in the world was? We already KNEW we were shit, thank you very much!

I promised poor, frantic Mrs. Johnson – whom I'll always love a little – I'd find Carol for her. It wasn't hard; I found her at her boyfriends' parents' house. Carol was flying high (low?) on reds. Her eyes were all pupil, and she talked like a record playing on the slowest rpm.

"Hey, Carol, look. I'm not mad at you for wrecking all my clothes, and I'm going to tell you something else: I'm moving out, this minute, so it'll be better for you. Honest, now you'll get to be the Queen Bee. OK?"

Since her boyfriend's parents really didn't want her

around – she was a "bad influence" on her dope dealing boyfriend, they said – Carol returned. And I kept my promise and moved out, the hour she moved in. A couple months early, perhaps. I missed out on the little farewell party, but somehow, I couldn't see Carol and Vicki – I called them the Dopettes – convincing me I'd be missed. (They called Nerds Square, back then. I was very Square to Carol and Vicki.) Since all my clothes were slashed, moving was a breeze. Richard and I found an apartment a block from the beach, and I started living in sin.

* * *

Richard let me drive his Porsche only once, so I drove straight to the valley to see Elizabeth. I was almost eighteen, and I must admit: I felt that for the very first time in my life, I was not locked up. Freedom! What a special thing it is. I was set loose, with all my pent-up passion and rage and talents.

"Elizabeth! I'm FREE! I'm FREE! And freedom tastes of reality!" I sang to her from The Who's TOMMY album. The two of us jumped up and down on her couch and sang the whole song. ("If I told you what it takes to reach the highest heights, you'd laugh and say nothing's that simple ...") Elizabeth's boyfriend, Mark, walked in the room wearing boxer shorts and brushing his teeth: I deduced immediately that he lived there. He was a handsome jock-type.

Elizabeth was wildly happy to see me. I'm not sure WHY she likes me so much – except that having a link with a person you don't have to bullshit with about your institutional past IS pretty wonderful. We danced around the rented house in the valley, and she convinced me to come see her at THE SANDY BISTRO that weekend, where she was playing. I couldn't believe it; the Sandy Bistro was down at the beach, near my house. God, the whole sky exploded with joy that day, in the craziest sunset. My rib cage had to stretch hard, to hold all the happiness.

I introduced Elizabeth to Richard as the girl who'd lived in the "orphanage" with me. The four of us snuggled into a booth at the Bistro, which was one of those steak houses where it's too dark for anyone to see what they're eating. I think it had the world's first salad bar. We could only have a free dinner if we ate it at four in the afternoon, because Elizabeth started singing at five for happy hour.

Elizabeth climbed onto the tiny stage in the bar. She looked long, small-boned and beautiful as she curled around the fat body of her guitar. Her thin, straight hair made her look innocent, and those white-blue Malamut eyes shone — at me. This was such a longtime fantasy come true for the two of us! She sang Judy Collins and Joni Mitchell songs with not just a rich, mellow voice, but also with power and guts. The cocktail waitress wasn't bothering about ID's, so when Richard ordered red wine, I did, too. Why not? My first experience with alcohol had certainly been momentous. This occasion was also momentous.

I liked the wine; it warmed my insides and helped the music melt into my skin effortlessly. Elizabeth and I were going to be happy and have all our dreams come true: I could hear it in her warm, vibrating voice. The music hummed and melted, and flowed from her to me, and I gave it back to her again. From my seat, from my heart, I sang the chorus with her. I joined her for "Clouds", a Joni Mitchell song then made popular by Judy Collins. "I've looked at life from both sides now, from up and down . . . from win and lose . . ." And we sang loud and rich, in perfect harmony, as if our hearts had practiced this moment for years.

The bar was crowded for happy hour, and though I was absorbed with singing the song and our joy, I could feel a big hush all around us. When the song ended, ("I really don't know life at all"), everyone clapped and shouted, and Rick, the young, hip owner of The Sandy Bistro, noted this with his nervous head, even while he darted around looking tense.

Elizabeth's smile was GLAMOUR MAGAZINE splashy. "Thank you. Thank you." People still clapped and shouted.

"Many thanks to my wonderful friend, Vanessa, for helping me out. Vanessa, come on up here. It's a little lonely on this stage, and I could use the harmony."

We sang until closing time. I'm sure it was the happiest night of my life. I quit my full time job at the Art Shop and began singing with Elizabeth.

This was no small sacrifice on anyone's part, as Richard's parents had disowned him when they discovered he was living in sin. I think they were devout Catholics. Or maybe devout Jews, or Baptists. I forget. But they were very religious, and somehow this massive crime of unmarried cohabitation (forget the fact that Abraham got it on with the cleaning woman!) was so against their religion that they wanted God to know that they weren't about to gamble their souls for the sake of their sinful, misguided son. As Richard was a full time Business Administration student at UCLA, and I was offered only ten dollars a night to sing with Elizabeth—who was paid twenty dollars a night— we sank (I, gleefully) into student poverty life. Richard was shocked that I would give up both my classes at UCLA AND my job at the Art Shop, but I tried to explain to him the drive: the drive to sing, to make music, that was bigger than school or money or us—or anything. Elizabeth and Mark moved in with us to cut down on rent costs, which meant that Richard had to give up his study. Looking back, I am horribly sorry he had to give up so much.

It is by no means easy living with musicians. We'd come in at three in the morning, high on applause and music. We'd talk and laugh and sing until four. We drove Richard and Mark crazy, and the thing is, we didn't care. I was guilty of the most insensitive behavior of my life, at that time.

For me, the wild-in-love-feeling I didn't have for Richard, I had for Elizabeth and me—for our music. Elizabeth and the music came first, and when Richard, depressed, sailed to Europe wearing a backpack and the remainder of his savings, I hardly noticed. I wish he were around now, so I could apologize to him for making him feel so ignored and unimportant in my life. He will always be important – for his goodness and his kindness. At that time in my life, I honestly thought there must be something really wrong with Richard to be so much in love with me. My subconscious figured, "if he loves me, he must be an idiot, therefore unimportant." I did my old trick of showing someone my worst traits to see how long before they threw me out. He never did; he simply left, with a broken heart.

When Mark-the-jock ran off with a cheerleader the next week, (he was a macho jerk, I must say), Elizabeth and I were shaken by reality-tremor number fifty seven: severe financial stress. We needed to move into a place that was as close to free as possible. What luck that in 1969, hippie communes were as easy to find as condominiums are today! And in decaying old Venice Beach, California, there were scads of abandoned, grand old buildings that had once been beach clubs for the upper crust. These filled up with colorful people who wore names like "Merry Sunshine" and "Golden Moondust".

We found the Billy Goat's Rainbow, a newly renamed, big, abandoned beach club. It was right on the beach – pure, soaring heaven for us! We moved into a corner closet; closets were fair sized in the grand old beach club days. Not that we had much choice: the rent – thirty dollars a month – was about our tops. Our two mattresses barely fit on the floor. When "Siddhartha Dayglow", the unofficial leader of the commune, discovered that we never took acid – and probably never would – he took two dollars a month off our rent. He and the others had a great time teasing us two straight-looking chicks with "foreign" names like Elizabeth and Vanessa who never dipped into the "magic acid bowl". But they all smiled big and wide when they heard us sing and play guitar, practicing new songs. Hippie living, I must say, was pretty friendly.

* * *

Our first chore was smashing out a chunk of wall in our closet-room, so that the sea air could blow into our room. It was summer, so we didn't have to worry too much about the ragged gaping hole in the wall freezing us out. We hoped to have the money together to put some glass in by the time the weather got cold. For now, all we wanted to do was sing and play. Now we could afford it, AND live by the sea. Once the hippie freaks warmed up to our music, and quit treating us as if we were narcotics agents, Billy Goat's Rainbow became a comfortable, happy home. We had a great time jamming with Sensimillia Jack and the Licorice Papers, out in the Rainbow's once-grand ballroom. The audience was a lot more spaced than at the Sandy Bistro, and they never got over our weird clean-cut looks, but they dug our music.

I loved living with Elizabeth. She was my sister, my friend, my partner. We spent hundreds of nights at least, sitting up and laughing. Being the two aliens at the Billy Goat's Rainbow bonded us, and gave us many, many jokes. Elizabeth and I were still insomniacs, but she never seemed to need sleep. Her long, wiry body replenished itself when she sang. Sometimes she sang a whole set with her eyes closed, releasing pain from her safe, faraway world.

One night, after work, Elizabeth and I were laughing in our tiny closet-room, staring out the huge "port hole" at the ocean. Wave sounds rushed in at us, and a full moon poured gold light all over the water and us. The room was so bright with moonlight, we didn't need to turn on our one red lamp. Elizabeth's face looked ten-year-old fresh in the moonlight as she laughed with me.

There was a quiet knock on the door. It was Sensimillia Jack. Even in the moonlight, we could see he'd been smoking lots of pot; his eyes were a thick red. His grin was enormous. He wore his guitar strap down his chest, but his broad, thin body covered the guitar behind him. For the first time, I noticed the grey in his long, thin hair. Jack was older than he looked.

"Hey! It's the Insomnia Twins! Ole' Sandman here can

help!" He laughed a ludicrous lecher's laugh and stumbled onto my mattress. I roared. Jack was a lovely, warm clod of a freak.

He swung his guitar around to the front, and when his fingers played the metal strings, he was no longer wasted Jack. He was an artist, tender and full, with great gifts to give. "You know 'Just Like A Woman', by Bobby Dylan?"

Elizabeth smiled, and in a moment had her guitar tuned. Our three voices climbed and soared; we sang a long time while watching the moon's pattern change across the water. We sang Leonard Cohen, Joni Mitchell, Joan Baez, with Jack pulling out a new joint during three different "intermissions", as he called them. "Whop. Whop. Whop. Intermission, ladies and gentlemen. God, you're beautiful!" The latter he said to Elizabeth, myself, and the joint he was about to light. He was a very generous man. By the time he'd passed out, his head thunking onto his guitar on my lap, the three of us were very, very stoned. Elizabeth, for the first time since I'd lived with her, slept a full eight hours. She couldn't thank Jack enough.

*　*　*

"Elizabeth," I asked her one early morning over our "Bedtime Cocktail Joint" after playing at the Bistro, "you don't have to answer, but I'd like to hear your story. I mean, why were you sent to the Child Center in the first place? After all, you know everything about me, but. . ."

"I've wanted to tell you, Vanessa. I don't know, though, you'll get depressed, maybe. My mother—she just hated my guts. Everything I did, she hated. She beat me and starved me and, and—well, she did weird things with burning cigarettes."

I gasped. "You mean, burned you—your skin?"

She quickly turned on the light and lifted up her shirt. I gasped. We stared at all the faint, little round scars all over her flat stomach. I'd noticed them before, but assumed they were chicken pox marks. They weren't. She inched the shirt up higher, and I winced, the same little circle-scars ran across her breasts. "In pretty private places, you know?" She snapped at the waistband of her jeans.

"But God, Elizabeth, that's so HORRIBLE!"

She smiled. "It really is, isn't it?" Her eyes were already glassy-stoned, the anaesthetic effect. "Screaming at me, always. Calling me a slut—at ten, Vanessa! Finally one night, she tried to strangle me to death with a pillow. That's when I became a bird—flipped out, I guess. I scratched up her face pretty bad, and got away from her somehow that night. I ran as far as I could run. Found a good, high climbing tree and made a nest at the top. I curled up in that tree for a whole day, cawing, I guess, before they found me and took me to the Child Center."

She was trying to sound casual about it, with a cocked shoulder and a smile. But she looked like a wounded bird, and I held her, and cried.

"Elizabeth, I'm so sorry. I never knew. You always seemed so smart and together, I always assumed it was either a mistake that you were put there, or that you were an orphan."

Elizabeth started crying bitterly, a hundred years' worth of tears. "God, Vanessa, I got so full of crazy hope when your natural mother apologized to you. Do you know what I did?" She pulled away from my shoulder and looked at me, wild-eyed. "I CALLED her. My natural mother. I looked her up in Washington, and I called her, Vanessa. It was so DUMB of me, because she screamed at me how much she hated my guts. 'Why, WHY?' I kept asking her. 'WHY DO YOU HATE ME? WHAT DID I EVER DO?' She said I was wicked. Wicked! 'You're wicked! Sinful!' She screamed it, and slammed the phone down. Jesus."

"But Elizabeth, she sounds absolutely crazy. I mean, seriously. She should be put away. God, hon, I love you!" I hugged her again.

"Yes, she is, Vanessa, but she's my mother, and I wanted

her to love me anyway—be proud of me! You know,
APPROVAL—the approval . . ."

"That never comes," she and I finished together. We
laughed a little. All of our shrinks had told us, again and
again: life must go on, without the approval. It probably
will never come from them, our natural parents who have
serious problems of their own. It must come from within
ourselves.

"Beautiful, beautiful Elizabeth the Queen," I cooed at her.
I'd always thought of her that way, only now I was stoned
enough to SAY the corny words. She lay with her head in
my lap, purring at every touch, every gentle word. "*I*
approve—so much! I'm so proud of you! You're brilliant,
and talented and beautiful, and I love you! Anyone who
doesn't agree can shove it. We don't need 'em." She laughed,
which made me feel fantastic to have given HER something, for a change. "Thank you so much for sharing," I
added.

"Vanessa, you're so strong. I feel so scrawny compared
with you."

"Funny. I always thought you were the stronger one—
making it in just one foster home, going out and ending up
a super-successful musician. You're still my ultimate hero."

"God. Why is everyone so insecure, anyway?"

"We just are. Everyone is. They put it—insecurity—in the
water."

We laughed, and got silly, and smoked another joint. One
of the men in the audience at the Bistro had put this joint in
our tips jar, so it seemed auspicious. The more stoned we
got, the more we celebrated ourselves. We had a great time
discussing some of the men who swarmed around us every
night at the Bistro.

"How 'bout the big muscly guy who was so drunk, he
ended up in the broom closet, peeing in the mop bucket?"
Elizabeth roared. "I almost choked, trying to stay cool and
sing. God! We were doing 'Blackbird', right? Such a quiet
song, and you could just HEAR his piss filling the metal

mop bucket!" We were out of our minds, laughing our guts raw.

"Gawd," I reminded her, "how 'bout that guy tonight — 'Mister Studly' — he thought we should just throw our panties at him here and now, because he's just TOO COOL! Course, he WAS absurdly beautiful, but STILL. I can't STAND people with that much self esteem!"

* * *

There was an endless parade of admiring men. The two of us were a striking pair, and though we let the guys buy us drinks and take us out, we made it very clear that we were married to our music. Elizabeth had called herself "a loser" when Mark left.

"But, Elizabeth," I'd tried to console her, "you and he just did not connect, you know? I never understood what you saw in him — besides his great looks, that is. He was BRAINLESS."

"But, Vanessa, he was such a HUNK, it made me feel like I could get a HUNK, you know? That made me feel womanly."

As for myself, I felt awful — still do — about hurting Richard. So we played it casual; we were "artistes", living in a commune in the midst of the Sexual Revolution — and The Pill Celebration. Even though I wasn't fooling around much, I took the pill; I'd NEVER get caught again! Guys, both the surfer-jock types at the Bistro and the hippie freaks at Billy Goat's Rainbow, loved our music and our bods: we were heavily in demand. Though it worked wonders for our self esteem problems, nothing serious, romance-wise, happened for either of us. On the other hand, nothing bad happened, men-wise; it was a carefree, happy, crazy time.

It was also a time of Social and Political Revolution. Elizabeth and I performed for a bunch of benefit concerts to help "the Revolution". We played right beside Joan Baez

once, to help raise money to get a lawyer for some con-
scientous objectors. Another time, all of us played to help
Caesar Chavez raise money to help the Mexican farm labor-
ers. It was at the Billy Goat's Rainbow that I heard the
Black Panthers speak, and Ron Hubbard (the founder of
Scientology) did a lot of motor-mouthing at the BGR in
those days. All of us surged with the electricity that comes
from struggling to fight the ugly wrongs in the world. And,
hey! It must be quite a surge, because I'm still doin' it!
Fighters never quit.

Our job at the Sandy Bistro continued to be unprofitable
but happy—until the Bistro met up with big competition
from the topless bars down the road. By then, nervous
Rick-the-hip-owner decided it was time to make a drastic
change in format if he was to survive.

* * *

Dear Little Sisters and Brothers,

Let me change the subject for a few minutes. I'd like to
tell you everything I've learned about sexual abusers and
their families.

Who are these guys, anyway?

The most important thing to know about them is that
they usually look very normal. They can act friendly and
charming. People like them. The first thing that neighbors
always say when they discover that their neighbor is in jail
for child molesting is, "I never would have guessed it! He
was so quiet and nice."

Sometimes, sexual abusers are pedophiles. Pedophile
means "lover of children." Remember your mom telling you
"don't talk to strangers?" or, "Never get into a car with a
stranger?" One thing she was afraid of was that a pedophile
would try to use your body for sex. Sometimes they want
to take pictures of you with no clothes on. If anyone ever
wants to show you pictures of naked children, run like hell!

The guy is a pedophile, and he doesn't want to give you candy just because he's a nice guy. Honest.

Sometimes, they have jobs working with kids; we have all heard of the horrible things done to children at day care centers. These stories surfaced from all over the country, and three year old kids can't read. Some of these kids got diseases from their abusers: from AIDS, which will kill them, to Clamydia, which can make them blind or infertile.

Pedophiles rarely use force. I watched one interview of a pedophile in jail in the film, THE SILENT SHAME, and he said that kids *want* sex. Pedophiles really believe that, except this guy admitted that he had to trick kids into having sex with him, or he had to bribe them with candy.

Studies show that almost all pedophiles were also sexually abused as children. They are, in a way, "getting even" with whoever abused them.

There is a book written by a Russian man, Nabokov. The book is LOLITA, and it shows perfectly the attitude of a pedophile. In the book, the little girl has a little girl's crush on her mother's boyfriend. She wants to sit on his lap and be loved and kissed by him, and this pedophile thinks that that means she wants grown-up sex with him. She is just a KID, roller skating and running around, but HE thinks she's a total sexpot. He rapes her, over and over. It hurts like hell, and she cries every day. He is always telling her how much he loves her.

What makes me furious is that our society has used this book in a horrible way against children. Many people talk of a sexy "Lolita type" to mean this really sexpot child. I am angry about it because Lolita in the book never, ever *wanted* to be raped over and over. No child does. She wanted the love and affection that all kids want. But that's a pedophile: he sees a child's wish for affection as if it were an adult's wish for sex. And, really, let's face it: he doesn't much *care* about the kid, or how much he will hurt the young boy or girl. He wants what he thinks *he* needs.

I read one case history of a young man in high school who was sexually abused. It is important that I mention a guy because *12-15% of all rape victims are male.* Anyway, we'll call him Joe. Joe was attacked by an older man—a stranger—who had a knife. The man forced Joe to have oral sex with him, behind a building. He was then going to sodomize Joe—rape him—when a car drove by slowly. The abuser ran off. Joe was in total shock, his pants were still down, and the driver of the car took him to the Emergency Hospital.

Joe was lucky that that driver took him to the hospital, because most boy victims don't report sexual abuse at all. Ever. They just let all the hate and fear rot inside of them. Joe and his parents went into therapy, but it took a long time before Joe was really well. He blamed himself for being a coward: "why didn't I fight back? Am I gay?" His parents blamed him: "What were you doing in that part of town?" His girlfriend, thank heavens, was really great. Between her and the therapist, he and his folks got over it. He's made it; he's now a happy, well-adjusted adult man who loves life.

Back to the guy in the car who wants to give you candy. Don't get in the car. You might know this guy, but he's acting weird. Say NO, even if he offers you a VCR or a Sony Walkman. What he might be is a child pornographer. Child pornographers take pictures of kids having sex with adults. They do not care how much pain the children suffer. They are the worst form of animals, because all they care about is money. If ANYONE somehow talks you into getting your picture taken with no clothes on, tell your teacher. Tell the police. Yes, your mother will be angry with you for disobeying her, because you got in the car with a stranger, or you went somewhere with a stranger. Mostly, your mother is worried. She might yell a bit, but really, she will be glad you're safe. Many kids get kidnapped, sexually abused, and killed, and she knows it. The main thing is, all the hassle will be worth it if you can get those suckers locked up in jail. TELL ON THEM. NOW.

Speaking of child pornography, there is this guy in Denmark, named Strauss. He brags about how rich he is off kiddie porn (that's what they call child pornography). He is such a pig that he made a movie of a six year old child being raped by a grown man. The child is crying throughout the whole movie, but does he care? He was interviewed by a reporter for the NBC documentary film THE SILENT SHAME.

The reporter asked him, "do you ever think about the children? Don't you think this harms them?"

"Yes," he said. He and his wife were proudly showing off their fur coats. His wife was smiling and laughing.

"How do you justify hurting these children in this way?"

"Well," he said, "if I didn't do it, someone else would."

I hate violence, little brothers and sisters, but I feel very violent toward this man. I can't help it.

So now you know a little bit more about the pedophile. You know a little bit more about what to watch out for in strangers. For most of you, however, the abuser is someone you know and trust. The abuser is a member of your family.

What is sexual abuse? Any physical contact that has to be kept a secret. If you feel you can only touch a kid in a certain way in private, or if you get something sexual from that touch, you as a parent have some problems you should deal with.

How Can It Happen?

The following is an explanation of "how" that I think is a good one. I found it in a book called FATHER-DAUGHTER INCEST, by Judith Lewis Herman, and I shortened it, and rewrote it in my own words.

Most girls and women reading this cannot imagine for one moment doing this to their kids. But remember, 99% of abusers are men. From the time they are small boys, men in our society are taught to be dominant in every area, and that includes sex.

For all babies, the first person they fall madly in love with is their mother. But in houses where the father is a bully, and the mother obeys him no matter what, right away, the boy learns that the person he loves most—his mother—is totally inferior. She is also not like him. She has no say in matters, so he doesn't want to ever be like her. He learns how NOT to cry (his mother cries) when he's sad. He acts disgusted by all things feminine, including empathy. Being loving, warm, and caring toward people is too feminine. Too bad, because if you care for a child—if you have empathy—you can never rape a child. At the same time, he's learning to reject the feminine in himself; he is learning that he can grow up to be just like Dad—tough, in control: the Boss. This is a position of great power, including sexual power over women who are weaker and younger.

For little girls, of course, it's different. Girls also fall in love, at first, with their mothers. They very quickly see, though, that their mothers are inferior to their fathers. Their mothers are also girls, like themselves, so they don't like the feminine in themselves. Maybe as early as age two, or three, or four, they start to take a serious interest in their father. Maybe the little girl hopes her father will "pretend" she's a boy, so she can be privileged. She shows her dad she can act like a boy, run like a boy. At this point, with the little girl craving her dad's acceptance, if he wants to get sexy with his daughter, she will not question it. She will not try to stop him. She will give in.

Throughout her life, a girl is encouraged to fantasize that someday she will "give in" to a man like her father: older, stronger, and more powerful than she. This is how the cycle continues. How do we break it? If women like themselves, and don't allow themselves to be bullied by men, their daughters will learn to respect their mothers. It will be easier, then, for them to respect themselves as girls and women. Little boys, likewise, will respect their mothers. They will allow themselves to cry and care and nurture. They will respect their wives and daughters.

The following will give you an idea of some similarities found in incestuous families. Please note: when I use the term "fathers," this can also apply to stepfathers, even to moms' boyfriends. I hope it makes you feel stronger and less weird: you are not alone.

In one Harvard University study of incest victims – all were now in their twenties and early thirties – some striking similarities among the victims' families appear. All but 5% of the families were religious; the largest group was Catholic (42.5%), then Protestant (35%), then Jewish (12.5%). They were mostly working class and middle class, but that's a little deceiving, because rich people often don't go to public treatment centers. They usually go to fancy private (quiet!) shrinks.

Most of these families were large, with four or more kids. Many had ten or more kids. The incest victim was usually the oldest daughter (42.5%). Sometimes, she was the only daughter (37.5%). One third of these women were "pretty sure" their father was abusing younger sisters.

All the women described their fathers as the absolute bosses in their homes. All the kids and their mothers were afraid of these big, macho bosses. These fathers were the only breadwinners; their mothers stayed at home.

Here is a quote taken from FATHER-DAUGHTER INCEST, by Judith Lewis Herman. "Marion" is describing their family, which is very similar to many incest victims' families.

> "Yes, we were what you call an intact family. My mother lived at Church and Church functions. My father sang in the choir, and he molested me while my mother was at Sun- day School class parties. There was no drinking or smoking or anything the world could see. Only God knows."

These fathers were respected in the community. They worked long hours, and it was *very important* to them how they looked in the eyes of society.

The mothers were weak and submissive. They obeyed their husbands, who utterly controlled them. Half of the fathers were violent; their daughters saw their dads beat their mothers, and most of them felt angry with their mothers for being so weak. One third of the fathers had drinking problems. The drinking, of course, was not the cause of the incest; the drinking only allowed them to forget their conscience and do the abuse.

The interesting thing is that, very often, girls and young women blame their mothers, not their fathers. Some of the victims have pity on their fathers, and feel protective toward them. They will allow their fathers to abuse them, the little martyrs, rather than allow these men to be hurt.

There are two most common types of mothers among the families of sex abuse victims: the weak, sometimes sickly, mother-martyr, and the cold, unaffectionate mother. The first two quotes are from FATHER-DAUGHTER INCEST, and the third is from BETRAYAL OF INNOCENCE.

ANNE-MARIE: "She always said, give with one hand and you'll get with the other, but she gave with two hands and always went down. She was nothing but a floor mat. She sold out herself and her self-respect. She was a love slave to my father."

MARION: "In my case I put most of the blame on my mother. She is a cold person—cannot show love to anyone except babies. She started a large family and ignored my father from the day she got pregnant. I have seen her many times shove Daddy away from her. I feel she drove my Dad to this thing. He was starved for affection . . ."

"We were all starved in my family—not for food, we always had plenty of money—but for feelings. Nobody ever seemed to feel anything. At least when I had sex with my father I could feel *something*."

Mothers are often referred to as "the Silent Partner", because, in 80-90% of incest cases, the mother helps the incest happen, on an unconscious level. (Of course, that means that in 10-20% of the cases, the mothers were not silent partners. They were innocent.) A silent partner mother cannot give affection to her husband or her daughter, so she pushes them together. When their behaviors start getting suspicious, she grows more distant. She chooses not to see. For example, in the case where one father raped five daughters continuously over a period of many years, his method was to creep into his daughters' beds at night. (Very common method.) Now, if your husband gets up, night after night, and you don't hear the toilet flush, but maybe there are some funny, muffled noises, and he smells different when he returns, wouldn't you, shouldn't you, maybe check it out?

One girl, interviewed in the film THE UNTOLD SECRET, hated her mother for always leaving the house at night. Her dad was gentle in bed, she said, but she hated it — what he did — because "it didn't seem right." She wished her mom would stay home. She was only eight years old, "so how could I have stopped it? I just stopped talking. I never talked to anyone." She, and many other sexual abuse victims, *long* to have their mothers rescue them.

Sometimes, the silent partners are not so silent. These women, many of them, came from abusive homes themselves. They figure, "that's just the way things are." Whenever one, very wealthy father raped his young daughter, the girl's mother would go out afterwards and buy her an expensive present.

Usually, incest continues in a family where the mother and daughter are not at all close. In the Harvard study, 61% of the abuse victims were on hostile terms with their mother before the abuse. One teenage daughter who was interviewed on Phil Donahue said that she was afraid to tell her mother about what her father was doing because she thought her mother would hit her. For some of these victims, their mothers have made it very clear that they never want to hear one single word about anything sexual. So how DOES a kid go about telling her mother this VERY SEXUAL secret? This quote is also from FATHER-DAUGHTER INCEST.(A truly great book.)

> JANET: "My mother is a terrible prude. I don't remember any of her sayings, but I remember the feeling behind them. It was so ugly, it made sex sound like the dirtiest thing around."

This is a common feeling that daughters/incest victims have. The sad truth is that, sometimes, when daughters do tell their moms, their mothers get furious with their daughters. They protect their husbands, lie to police officers, and tell the police their daughters lied. If they do believe their daughters, these mothers consider the entire episode the daughter's fault. Having been there, with one of these mothers, I can tell you: it hurts.

But, hey, think of the poor mothers' point of view. They are terrified! They'll lose their home, their breadwinner, and their other kids won't eat. They don't protect their husbands because they hate their daughters; they protect their husbands to save their asses. To save their homes, and the rest of their family. It is ALL THEY HAVE. Whatever these mothers say to you about it being your fault, believe me, they feel guilty.

These mothers, then, need a LOT of help. Do you know that many of these women were also sexually abused as children? You and your mother might have more in common than you think. The difference is that *you* can choose, right now, to break that cycle forever. It is NOT "just the way things are." You can change things. You can grow strong and love yourself enough to let good people love you. When you're older, you can find a good partner who won't abuse your children.

The good news is that, after the sexual abuse treatment programs, the silent-partner-mother becomes stronger than she's ever been in her life. She and her daughter are taught how to become close friends, maybe for the first time ever.

The father who enrolls in the sexual abuse treatment program definitely loses some of his macho power, but he gets to learn what it's like to feel people hug him without sex. He gets to learn what it's like to show real affection. He gets to cry. He gets to be a real part of a real family, instead of just bossing and frightening people. Everyone wins, after the painful "family surgery" in therapy.

* * *

One Friday evening, I raced into work at the Sandy Bistro, late again. Elizabeth was breathless when she met me, and I panicked.

"Does he know I'm late?" I assumed I was fired.

"Vanessa, he wants to pay us fifty bucks a NIGHT!"

"You're kidding! Who died?" It didn't make sense, because all he'd done lately was bitch about the shrinking patronage after every set: as if it was OUR fault.

"But he wants us to dance."

"To our own music? Hell, for fifty bucks, I'd do a square dance to Mozart—I mean, I love dancing, but our music isn't . . ."

I stopped, because my neck was crawling with the itchies that meant some guy was getting turned on, leering at me. I was not wholly used to this awareness—that is, I hadn't learned to ignore it—and I whirled around to find Rick, the hip-nervous owner of the Sandy Bistro. Weird. He'd never acted this way before.

"So, Vanessa. Are you with us?" He asked, leering.

"Sure, Rick! What do you want me to wear?"

Elizabeth nearly choked to death, she needed to laugh so badly. Something was definitely up. "Come on, Vanessa, I'll take you to the dressing room." And she led me away by the hand. Once inside the dressing room, she emptied herself of all the laughter she'd just choked down.

I am incredibly slow at times, but I was beginning to figure it out.

"Vanessa, we're supposed to dance TOPLESS."

I squealed, and then she squealed. (We've never grown out of our grammar school-girl squeals, and I don't care who knows it. We were forced to repress them for many years—hell, even if that's not the reason, there's nothing like a good squeal with a close girlfriend.) "Are you SERIOUSLY considering DOING this, Elizabeth?"

Suddenly, she looked ashamed. I was sorry to have done that to her. "Kind of, yeah." But then she recovered her original naughty-wicked look. I was glad. The Malamut eyes went defiant. "The human body is nothing to be ashamed of. I mean, in a couple weeks, Vanessa, we could quit, we'd be so rich. We could work with Big Ocean full time. And, hell, it's only dancing. You're a great dancer, and you've even got tits."

(Here I should note that fifty dollars was an enormous sum of money, back then.)

I sucked in my breath, hoping something funny would come out. "If only Brutus could see us now. I guess it is just dancing, after all."

"We will be amazing," Elizabeth laughed, and danced out to "decorate the stage".

It seemed that the world drastically changed during the hour I sat staring numbly at myself in the dressing room mirror. When I walked out, still tingly-numb, the walls of our little stage were coated with stick-on mirrors. A huge, loud stereo blasted the Iron Butterfly: "Ina-godadavi-da, honey . . . " WOW. Super-straight, innocent little Elizabeth and Vanessa were going to do WHAT? The idea was that you danced around on the little stage in a bikini, and then at some crucial moment you unpopped your brazziere and danced around some more. Easily said.

Rick walked up, his usual businessy self again. "OK, you first, Vanessa."

God. What an awful moment.

Walking around in a bikini when everyone else is fully dressed is an odd, uncomfortable thing. Men looked at me as if I had suddenly become their property. It felt ugly;

there was definitely some hostility in those looks—as if they were angry with me for taking away some of their power. They were angry with me because I turned them on; if they got too turned on, they would lose control. That's what seemed to be going on. Anyway, the clientele had suddenly changed: from the carefree college folkie crowd to the leering macho guys crowd.

When it was my turn to dance, Rick put on an outstanding dance song: "Live With Me" by the Rolling Stones. I went into my old survival routine: I forgot everything but the music—the joy and freedom of allowing my body to soar as it may to the purring, thumping rhythms of a song. I also conveniently forgot to take my top off, I was so lost in the beauty of the beat. At the part of the song that says, "don'cha wanna live with me?", three sleazy guys in the front row yelled, "Yeah! Take it off! Whoo-hoo! Yes, Ma'am!"

Oh, yeah. I smiled at myself in the mirror when I turned my back to them. "You're supposed to take off your brazziere, Vanessa," I mental-telepathied to my face in the mirror. Right. So, while the sleazy guys were watching my backside shimmy, I reached around and unhooked my top. It fell, and I looked at myself in the full length mirror. I mouthed to myself, "this is SO WEIRD," and turned around so all the guys could see my naked bazzooms. It was funny; they got quiet-shy for a second. Only a second, and then they let loose: howls and hoots shook the place. It was time for me to leave my body, which never lost a beat. (It's true, what they say about the body's memory being far superior to the brain's. Leave the body alone, and it performs better on its own.) In my imagination, both brain and body were at the ski lodge in 1966 with Mimi and Scott and Albert—the first time I'd ever danced. I could feel my Apres Ski sweater steaming while I threw myself into the music all over the floor.

When the music stopped, I picked up my top and ran into the dressing room. Sweat, tears, and mascara had streaked

down my face, onto my chest; I looked like some exotic
jungle woman painted for war.

*   *   *

"Jesse, do you think I'm cheap for dancing topless at
the Sandy Bistro?" I asked him, next visiting day. He was
the same, except he was getting thinner. I'd splurged and
brought him three boxes of Van de Kamp's cookies.

"Vanessa, you've known me long enough to know I don't
think it's wrong. *Killing* is wrong. Jesus, I'm a little sick of
your little game of, 'gee, if I tell him this really bad thing
I'm doing, THEN will he hate me . . . ' " He sucked in his
breath and continued, really exaggerating, "even if I'm a
topless dancer? Grow up, Vanessa!"

It was maybe the only time I'd ever seen him in a bad
mood. I wanted so much to cry and feel sorry for myself—
that one had hurt!—but he needed me. "Jesse, are you OK?
You want to talk about it?"

He sat for a long time, doing the three-deep-breaths routine he'd taught me to do when I needed to collect myself
fast. "I'm sorry, Vanessa. I didn't mean to snap at you.
Quick recovery, though, woman! I'm proud of you . . . I'm
on a bummer, all right. Elaina dropped by. She's leaving—
no, she's left me. I don't blame her a bit. It's not as if I can
satisfy her in here, when there's a SEXUAL REVOLU-
TION going on out there. But it makes me so damned
angry, Vanessa. It's all Nixon's fault, and that fucking war.
Damn!"

He smashed his fist on the picnic table. I jumped—as I
always do, still, at the slightest threat I'll get hit. When he
lifted his head, I saw he was crying. I was frightened, and I
felt awkward, but I held his head. He slumped onto me and
cried into my shoulder.

"Vanessa, I wish I'd listened to you and gone to Canada.
It's horrible in here . . . I had these great visions of Elaina
and me, another Joan Baez and Richard Harris, sticking

together for a beautiful cause. The little baby, even, visited his daddy in jail . . . damn! It's just me, getting the shit kicked out of me—and I haven't made it onto one single album cover," and at that, he laughed a little through his tears.

"Jesse; you're so good, so strong. You'll make it. And you ARE teaching us—all of us, something. Jesse, I'd be dead if it weren't for you." God, I loved him: my shrink, my friend, my brother. If he'd asked me to smuggle in a file to get him out, I would have.

Jesse wiped himself off. "Nope. You're the strong one, Lady Vanessa. I sure wouldn't have the guts to dance topless."

We both laughed. "Shut up, Jesse!" I boxed him playfully. "Do you think it's bad for me to do it?"

"Not even a little bit, dummy. But I think you think it's bad, and maybe you don't respect yourself as much. But I don't know.. Maybe I'm wrong. Did you proudly announce to Mrs. Johnson, when you visited last week, in a loud voice with your head held high, 'I am the best topless dancer in town!'?"

I laughed; the idea was ludicrous. I couldn't tell anybody. Whenever Mrs. Johnson or anyone asked me what I was doing, all I'd tell them about was the band, "Big Ocean", that Elizabeth and I had formed: two guitarists and an upright bass player. We were pretty hot, and practiced all day at the Billy Goat's Rainbow. Jesse, of course, knew that, and he answered my embarrassed look.

"You see?"

"Jess, is there anything at all I can do to . . . get you out?"

He laughed. "Yeah. Put a real good file in the cookie box, next time."

"I will. I swear it!"

"Hold it, hold it. Just joking . . . God! You could call my lawyer. That might help. And don't ever stop smiling that beautiful smile. It's helping a lot."

Jess had no idea how much he gave me. And that night, a

miracle—one that usually only happens in the movies, but that I swear to God, really happened to me, happened that night. Jess swore up and down he had nothing to do with it, but I somehow think even he might tell a lie if he thought it could help someone.

* * *

"Hi, tits," Rick said to me when I showed up for work. God, I hated that! Suddenly, I was his property, too. He'd never once said, "hi, voice," when I was his *singing* employee. I wanted to smash him, but instead, I chewed up the inside of my cheek while he motioned me over to him. "Listen," he said, "there's a very well-to-do looking gentleman who's been waiting to see you. You might want to have some clothes on when you talk to him."

I walked up to a handsome, grey-haired man who was wearing a classic Brooks Brothers suit. The way he said to me, "Miss Morelli?" made it clear that he was not in his usual environment.

"Yes, sir?"

"I'm a very big fan of yours."

Oh, great, I thought, completely disappointed. Another one of these. I'd run into a few of them, some of them even claiming they could "make a big movie star out of me". Right! All I had to do was one little dance for them in their hotel room. No way, suckers. Yuck. But this guy looked so different. Maybe he really was a big fan, of all of me.

"Oh?" Was all I (very tartly) said.

"You have an absolutely beautiful voice. I've come here many times to hear you sing, and I was wondering if you might be willing to teach young children to sing. A mutual friend said you might."

I greatly enjoyed quitting before my show that night, and ushering Mr. Graham out before Elizabeth went on. He wasn't a rock fan, anyway, and was only too happy to leave. Thus ended my twelve day stint as a topless dancer. Outside, I shrank beneath the massive, blinking TOPLESS sign we passed in the parking lot – surely Mr. Graham had noticed it! – but he was utterly unconcerned with it. Maybe the whole world didn't think I was a dirty person. We headed for Reuban's – my official "Momentous Occasion" restaurant, and he elaborated.

He ran a school for toddlers and nursery school kids that had gained some great press as an innovative school. I remembered the newspaper article entitled, "A Truly Caring Place". He was doing great things for kids, some of whom came from homes without hope. Mr. Graham had received all kinds of government grants so that economically stressed kids could get into his school, which was a rather pricey establishment. Now, he hoped to start a children's choir.

"I got the idea simply from listening to the children. Their voices are absolutely superb!"

He loved kids, and he was rich; you could hear both in his voice. "I'm at the age where I should be a grandfather – would've been, in fact, if my daughter Jeanine hadn't died as a young girl."

"I'm sorry, Mr. Graham."

"Thank you. It's something you never quite get over, I guess. But caring for these kids has given my wife and me so much. They are wonderful, these children! We're constantly learning from them – they're astonishing!"

I thought he was going a bit overboard; I mean, kids are great, but, come on! I hadn't been around any kids, lately, though – except for the two kids at the Billy Goat's Rainbow. Their names were "Mellow" and "Sunshine", and they didn't wear diapers because Peyote Flower, their mother, said that diapers were unnatural. I tried never to spend too much time around old Mellow and Sunshine, therefore; they always seemed to "get natural" all over me when I did.

So, anyway, my expectations were not high, but I was on a new road – one that suited me better, perhaps. I'd start the next day (Wednesday), meeting the kids and listening to them.

"Play with them," Mr. Graham urged. He sounded like a football coach's coach. "Get their confidence up. Then I want you to plan a teaching program tailor-made to each child. I understand you're just shy a few units from getting your degree in Education, is that correct? You probably should have a credential as soon as possible."

"No problem, Mr. Graham." Thanks, Jesse, I thought to myself. "Just a few" was stretching it, but I could easily go back to school and pick up the rest.

I couldn't wait to tell Elizabeth when she got home. Unfortunately, she was furious.

"Thanks, Vanessa! You could've at least told me before you walked out! . . . Shut up! Don't talk to me. I'm PISSED! I had to dance two extra times because of you, and it's not like I got paid extra to do 'em!"

"Elizabeth, I'm so sorry. I freaked out when Rick called me 'tits' like that's all I am now is two walking boobs, . . ."

"That IS all you are!"

"Elizabeth, please don't be so angry. I just got the most wonderful job, you wouldn't believe it. Teaching children to sing!"

"Great. And what do I have, Lady Vanessa? I get to wiggle around in front of a bunch of asthmatic sleezebags for the rest of my life, and MY BAND HAS JUST FALLEN APART BECAUSE MY SINGER'S GOING TO GO PLAY WITH CHILDREN!"

The band. Big Ocean. Elizabeth and me. If I went on the road with these kids, I couldn't be in Big Ocean, which was Elizabeth's lifetime dream coming true. All of a sudden, I felt selfish and awful. Shit! I would never ever have opened my mouth to sing if it hadn't been for Elizabeth, over ten years ago. And she was the one who'd gotten me the Sandy Bistro job. But I was just chucking her, without a thought. I was really a rotten person.

"Elizabeth, I'm such a shit. Can you please forgive me? I'm not going back to Rick, ever, but I will tell Mr. Graham I have previous committments, and I can't do it."

"Oh, Vanessa, don't be dumb. I'm proud of you, I'm happy

for you, I'm just jealous, OK? Not an admirable emotion, but an honest one. A real one. Big Ocean is my dream. It's never been yours. So, OK, you've found something you want to go after. Our lives start to change from here—we'll never be this close again—and I'll miss you. That's all." She cried until she was exhausted, and collapsed onto her mattress on the floor. She didn't even wake up when I took her shoes off and straightened out the bunched-up blanket at her feet so that I could cover her. It was unusual for her to sleep so soundly; she looked ten years old, clutching the sheet tightly next to her bunched-up fist. I kissed her forehead. What if she was right? How could I live without being this close to her?

"Thanks, Elizabeth, for everything. I love you," I whispered, and crawled onto my mattress. Tomorrow I would have a different life.

* * *

It was the children who taught me everything. With the children, I finally grew up. They taught me how to respect myself, and how to demand respect from others.

With the kids, I was relaxed. It felt natural and lovely, spending time with these talented, wise beings. I didn't get paid much, if certainly more than the ten dollars a night I'd pulled in singing at the Bistro, but I almost felt guilty taking anything. Teaching children to sing never felt like work. When the mothers came to pick up their kids, I was always amazed that the day was over. Best of all, I was doing some good, for kids whose parents were some of the poorest I'd ever seen. This school was a glowing sun in lives that knew nothing but struggle. Yes, there were middle and upper class kids in the school; their parents gladly paid the high tuition. But Mr. Graham's biggest excitement, I think, came from giving the really poor families some joy and promise.

Mr. Graham wasn't crazy; these kids were wondrous.

When he introduced me to them the first day, he asked
them to sing "When the red red robin comes bob-bob-
bobbin' along . . .". Their ages spanned three to five; I
walked among them with my face fully grinning. There was
some real quality in these tiny voices! Best of all, they were
having a ball, singing at me; you'd have to be strange not to
lose your heart to those shiny black, brown, and white
faces.

We organized a repertoire of kid-songs, and I taught
them some harmony. It brought back memories of Choir at
the Child Center with Elizabeth — and other, less pleasant
memories that strayed in with the good. When I wasn't
teaching them choir, I was supervising their crayon coloring and swingset sliding. And I was learning from them
constantly.

It was important for me to treat them with respect, but
even if it hadn't been so important to me, they would have
demanded it. They were wise; they wanted to be reasoned
with.

"Why, Miss Morelli, why is it wrong for me to hit Jimmy?
He took my swing, and I hate him."

"Because, Kevin, we use words, here. Those are the rules.
You need to tell Jimmy that he doesn't get to take your
swing. Kevin, you need to really listen. Now go out there
and try again."

"OK, Miss Morelli, but I don't think it'll work!"

They would not accept a "no you can't have it because I
said so" answer. I wanted to give these kids everything I'd
never had, in the way of respect and appreciation. Caring
Kindness: it became my crusade. I never spoke baby talk to
the kids, because I didn't know how; no one had ever spo-
ken baby talk to me. Fortunately, the kids seemed to be
happy enough without it. Kids are so honest, that if they
hadn't liked me, or the way I dealt with them, they definitely would've told me.

Of course, not all the kids were so easy; I had to get
creative. One kid, Casey Daniels, would walk in the school
yard every single morning and punch the first kid he saw.

That was only the beginning of a reign of terror that could last all day.

"Casey," I told him, "you just can't seem to control those hands of yours, so you know what? You get to put your hands in my coat pocket here and walk around with me all day today."

"Oh, boy!"

Needless to say, he was bored by my activities pretty quickly. "Pu-LEASE, Miss Morelli, can I go play, now? I cross my heart I'll control my hands."

* * *

Dear Little Sisters and Brothers:

If you can, get a job working with little kids for awhile. They'll teach you interesting things about yourself, and about getting your lives happy again. You also get to play with them! Play in the sandbox with them, and swing on the swings: be a real kid. GROW DOWN! Childhood is something you were robbed of when abuse forced you to grow up fast. See how much fun you can have, smearing peanut butter and jelly all over your clothes. (That one was Major Rebellion City for me!)

They'll help you learn how to respect yourself, and how to treat other people with respect. Kids are funny: when they're not in their own home, they demand that everyone treats them with respect. Some of them are little tyrants! In their own home, of course, they might be a lot more intimidated; I could guess a little about some of the kids' home lives, and I did everything in my power to help them. That is an excellant thing for once-battered kids such as you or myself to learn. The children will help you get stronger. They might even help you see that you CAN someday beat the statistics, and NOT beat your own kids. They teach you patience, and patience is something every-one on earth can use. The children teach you not to be in such an all-fired hurry: if you go SLOWLY, you are more likely to get there, and you'll notice all the scenery along the way. And I can tell you, all this is a hundred times easier to learn from SOMEONE ELSE'S KIDS than from your own!

And besides that, right here I'm going to put in my own personal little plug for WAITING to be a mom or dad. The older you are, the more you will have learned to know yourself and love yourself. If you've worked at learning and loving, it is less likely that you will make the same mistakes with your kids that your mom and dad made. You'll make other mistakes, but the chances are good you'll get better at loving with each passing year.

* * *

Elizabeth's new band, still named Big Ocean, had made it. A slightly too hip (for my taste) producer-type had booked a zillion engagements all over the country. I was a little frightened for her: Jimmy Hendrix, Janis Joplin, and Jim Morrison were famous rock 'n rollers who had all died of drug overdoses. But maybe I was just jealous, I told myself. I was also incredibly proud and happy for her as she went out on the road. She'd been right, though, when she said that our lives would never mesh together as in the early Sandy Bistro days. I'd become (horrors) a day person, and I can't say I blame her for not sharing my enthusiasm over what the toddlers had said and sung each day. You had to be there, folks, to appreciate it. We'll love each other until death, but our dreams and paths changed. Music will always be Elizabeth's husband and her life. I, on the other hand, was bound for heaven knew where.

"This is really sad, Elizabeth, but it's really happy, too. A dream come true for you – God, going on the road with your band, and getting paid, even, big bucks."

"But I wanted it to be US going on the road, together, Vanessa."

"I know it sounds dumb and corny to you, Elizabeth, but I'm really happy here, with the kids. I feel as if I'm doing something IMPORTANT."

"I'll miss you and this crazy place so much."

"Take me with you in your heart, and, please? Take care."

"OK."

Shortly after Elizabeth went on the road, the Billy Goat's Rainbow was condemned. Sensimillia Jack and Siddhartha Dayglow were "going down with the building," they swore. Not I. Clapping the guys on their shoulders, and taking a few joints out of the last communal Magic Acid bowl, I walked away from the mattress, the airy closet, and an interesting chapter of my life. I'd saved enough money to get a real apartment, and I carried quite a lot with me: a few clothes, some great memories, a big empty loneliness, and more dignity than I'd ever carried before.

* * *

We made some money with the choir, which was a good thing: Mr. Graham was bigger in the heart than in financial matters. He wanted to save every kid in Los Angeles from ghetto life; the school wanted to give more than it could afford. I became a businesswoman, for a very good cause. I was lonely, anyway, so I had the hours. I got into promotional work, showing slides and tapes of the kids, (nobody had VCR's, back then), and getting them booked into paying shows around town. I made a fool of myself more than once, and I guess that's an important thing: I don't think it's possible to be successful in business unless you're willing to look foolish at times.

"Cute. Very cute, honey, but I'm afraid we only do sex shows. It's not quite in our line. You have anything sexier than this?"

(Yes. That really happened, one time; that was one of those foolish-times. A friendly middle aged woman I'd met on the bus had struck up a conversation with me. I hadn't

been working so much with the children's choir as I had the
promotional end of it, so I told her I was a promoter. She
was kind enough to give me the name of this guy in Holly-
wood who "booked some real talent. He might be interested." Live and learn.)

When we'd gotten enough bookings so that I could concentrate on the choir, I had some glorious, wonderful days.
Listening to the kids' voices singing fat and joyous gave me
goose bumps. They were an easy joy to deal with, too,
because they never minded the work. When we'd been practicing for a long time, and I could feel their restlessness, I'd
say, "OK, kids, time to run." "Yes, Miss Morelli!" They'd
shout, and burst out the door. They ran until they were
tired, then returned to work with flushed faces and
giggles.

We played at auditoriums and charity league lunches all
over Los Angeles, San Diego, and Santa Barbara. The kids'
mothers covered me with bright pink kisses after the Los
Angeles TIMES featured an article about us. We made a
couple local magazines, too. The kids were hot. I'd start
crying every time I heard them sing "Michael Rode the
Boat Ashore"—especially the part about "the river is deep
and the river is wide,// milk and honey on the other side,
Alleluhia!" I'd come so far since I'd sung that song in the
choir at the Child Center! I was lonely, but I was free. And
blissed out, listening to the purity and joy of children's
souls lifted in song.

* * *

Mr. and Mrs. Graham were like an amazing set of
grandparents to me; I gladly ate dinner at their place often.
Mrs. Graham taught me everything I know about country
French gourmet cooking; she was from France, originally—
"Alsace Lorraine," she stressed, "where is the best food in
France." Their dead daughter, Jeanine, was always there, in
the house with us: a pensive little spirit-sprite that seemed

cheered by my presence almost as much as her parents were.

"You are such a joy to us," Mrs. Graham would say to me in her thick accent, taking my face in her two hands. It was a gesture that brought back Ginny Barnes to me: down through the years, a shaft of light that had somehow kept me struggling through the darkness, to here. Through the years, gentle souls here and there had loved me, and saved me. Now, I had learned to love in return. I gave it back — the love — and I'd been able to help Elizabeth, Jesse and the Grahams through some rough times. Love IS a miracle!

The Grahams and I were there to hug Jesse when he was finally released from prison. He'd done the same two years in prison that he would have done in the army: "a perfectly fair exchange," as he put it. Mrs. Graham and I cooked all day to give him a fancy French feast. (That magical man was the one who had given the Grahams to me — and me to them. It never surprised me at all that Mr. Graham was Jesse's uncle.) All of us ended up with glowing French wine-eyes that night, even the ghost Jeanine. The Grahams' elegant, country-French dining room was warm and full with love all around. The funny thing was, though I could have stayed in that room, in that night, forever without getting bored, I could sense that there was another change about to go down in my life.

* * *

The Children's Choir was perfect, the dates were booked, and the truth was that I was no longer essential. My salary, tiny though it was, was also a drain on the Grahams — something they never would have mentioned. The other thing was, I frankly wanted a little more financial security than the ten dollars, on a good day, in my checking account afforded me. So when I met this incredibly nice guy, Ben, in the back of a limousine, and all my hormones red-alerted all over my face (SO embarrassing!

But Ben swears to this day he never noticed), I didn't slam on any brakes.

Ben was Tammy's father. Tammy was a heartbreakingly beautiful child in the children's choir. Tammy was five, and crazy about me. I was drawn to her as I was to any child when I sensed that all was not right in her home. She clung to me, and often whimpered, "Mommy, Mommy" to me.

One day I was walking her out of the playroom toward the street. She would not release my fingers. Suddenly, she jerked them and screamed, then buried her face in my skirt. I patted her head while I eavesdropped on the huge fight in front of the school. It was ugly, a man and a woman were screaming at each other. The two of them stood beside a limousine; one door of the limo gaped open.

"God DAMN you, Helen," the man shouted, "Tammy is never going to be hurt by you again! KEEP AWAY FROM HER, OR I SWEAR, I'LL KILL YOU!"

Tammy was sobbing into my skirt, so I folded myself protectively around her. I never knew what hit me. THUNK! A hard, heavy blow to my back knocked me onto Tammy; my chin crashed onto her head.

"YOU BITCH! GET YOUR HANDS OFF HER!" Helen screamed at me. She was pulling at Tammy and whacking me at the same time.

I punched her hard in the stomach and ran, BUT FAST, for the open limo. Tammy was holding me fiercely. We scrambled in, looking like a crazy mother monkey and her clinging baby. The guy who'd done all the yelling at Helen—Ben, who was Tammy's father—wanted to finish his chat with Helen, but I grabbed him hard, and pulled him into the limo. All this happened in about thirty seconds.

"Save it, would you? That woman is CRAZY!"

Ben jumped in, yelling, "let's get the hell out of here, Bill!" Helen threw her body at the door. Thank God, it locked automatically when Ben slammed it. The car jolted forward, and Helen crashed onto her enormous fanny, still screaming. We burnt a LOT of rubber, removing ourselves from wild Helen.

For a while, nobody talked. I was in a real live limousine when it was nobody's funeral; I'd just been attacked by a strange woman I'd never seen before, and a child was clinging to my neck so hard, I couldn't breathe.

"Is this a weird movie, or what?" I finally asked, in a funny, choking-to-death voice.

Ben (I didn't know yet that his name was Ben) laughed, releasing a lot of his frantic pain. But not all of it. "I'm really sorry." He bent toward Tammy. "Hey, Muffin? Daddy loves you."

Tammy leaped from my neck onto her father's; I couldn't believe how good it felt to breathe again. Ben kissed Tammy all over her head. It was the first time I ever saw a kind, gentle daddy. In my whole life, I'd never known that a little girl could be hugged like this. It is hard to describe what that did to me. I wanted imlnediately to know this person, Ben, better. I had no idea where "Bill", the limousine driver, was taking us, but that didn't matter. I wanted to be there.

Ben smiled. "I think we've earned a cocktail. What can I get you?" He opened the beautiful wooden cabinet in front of him and pulled out two crystal glasses. He reached over and pulled the top off another richly varnished wood cabinet and plucked some ice. I wanted to bounce up and down yelling, "oh, boy! Oh, boy! Cocktails in a limousine!" I wanted to sniff like an excited puppy at the rich leather seats, and shriek. But I stayed cool, and acted as if this was the most normal, average day. "Scotch and soda OK?" Ben asked finally, when the only answer I'd given him was a dumb grin.

"Sure!" (I HATE Scotch and soda.)

"Daddy, can I stay with you?"

"Absolutely! Forever and ever."

Tammy's eyes went bright again. "Oh, goody! And Miss Morelli, too? Can she be my new mommy?"

Ben blushed as brightly as I did. Our heads wheeled in

opposite directions, toward opposite windows. When his normal color returned, Ben said, "my ex-wife and I, we're, um, having differences of opinion over custody."

There was more: more he wanted to say, also more that he never wanted to say. This was my territory; something was very wrong. I would join this father's fight for a kid who I knew had been through something awful. I felt strong, filled with all this resolve, but I spoke softly. "I'm really sorry. I'd be happy to testify or anything like that. That lady should be locked up."

"You have no idea."

Ben's suit and shoes were beautiful, and his face was kind. He didn't look smug-rich; he looked more the fairytale nice-prince. He was the first gorgeous man I'd ever met whose smile relaxed me.

"You've done an amazing job with the Children's Choir," he said. "I just got back from a business trip in New York, and they'd heard of it back there! The kids sound like angels. You must've worked very hard." He gave Tammy a squeeze, and looked down at her face, which was shining into his. "I am so proud of you!" He told her. God, what a million kids would do to hear their mom or dad say that!

One of the biggest rewards of working with the Children's Choir was seeing that, over and over: parents loving their children, parents proud of their children, and children proud of themselves. This happy feeling, mingled with a raging hormonal high, came close to knocking me out with a full-on swoon, one like the old fashioned ladies in the corset-days used to do. In those days, however, everyone carried a little vial of smelling salts wherever they went. It would be just TOO corny of me to pass out, so I grabbed a handle as we went around a corner, hard enough that my knuckles turned white.

"I don't want you to get the wrong idea, Miss Morelli."

"Vanessa. Please . . . my first name, I mean." Total blushout. God, I was being such a jerk. This guy had class, and I could barely manage to sound adult – that's not an easy thing, anyway, when you spend your days talking to preschoolers.

"Vanessa. What a beautiful name. Listen, it's not as if I'm rich or anything. I work for a company that sells used limousines . . ." He was staring at my white knuckles clutching the handle on the door. "I mean, if you know anyone who wants to buy a limo, let me know."

"But Daddy gets to use them, sometimes – one time we went to Disneyland, for my birthday, with my five best friends, and we got to take a double stretch limo," Tammy bragged. "You can come, Miss Morelli, on my next birthday – right, Daddy?"

Now, thank God, Ben was embarrassed, the blush monster passed from me to him. "Well, sure, sweetheart, if you'd like. You can invite anyone you want for your birthday."

Ben had Bill drive to Bob's Big Boy – Tammy's favorite restaurant, "because you can make your own ice cream sundae there, anything you want!" Tammy explained. The three of us made outrageously artistic sundaes, and talked and talked. By the time I'd finished half my sundae, I was stuffed – and madly, wildly in love for the first time in my life.

* * *

I started working at Cagney's Class Autos with Ben shortly after that, and I was a natural, I must admit. Ben says I did so well selling the cars because I love cars so much: the way the new paint shines as if it's still wet; the way the insides smell, and the way the dash lights come on at night. I say I did well because I was in love, and people were happy being around me: "sure, lady, I'll buy the car – but can you slip me some of whatever drug you're on?" I'd smile, but in my head, I sang, "Love is the drug that I'm thinking of" by Roxy Music, as my theme retort.

That was the summer I discovered what an amazing thing sex is when you love and trust someone with your whole heart. What I am saying is that, all of a sudden, ANY WOMAN CAN! included ME, TOO! We're talking orgasms, multiple ones, even, complete with exploding skies and clanging bells: the works!

"Elizabeth!" I babbled over the phone, long distance. "It's UNREAL! I mean, you know, THE BIG O! I—wow—there's just nothing like it!"

Elizabeth laughed a little on the other end. "Congratulations, Lady V. . . . I miss you, crazy one."

Tammy lived with Ben all summer while Ben and Helen's court custody battle raged. (Much as we wanted to be together every moment, I couldn't move in, because it might hurt Ben's case.) It was a bittersweet time for me. I suffered during court days, because of the ugly memories it brought back. Court was a thousand times better for Tammy than when I'd been there. She didn't have to sit and listen to her parents testify; she and I had a nice waiting room outside the courtroom where we sat and colored in coloring books. She also had someone—her father—on her side. Tammy was much braver than I'd been, also remarkably straightforward.

"Vanessa, why do you think it is that my mommy, who loves me so much, is so mean to me, sometimes?—I know she loves me, more than anything. It's obvious. But why does she get so nasty?" She asked me once.

Tammy's mother abused her. She beat her, Tammy said, "when she doesn't like me. Just because of that. But then, the next day, she cries and says she's sorry. She says she loves me more than anything. And I love her, too, THEN, when she's nice." Tammy also told us that Helen's boyfriend had sexually abused her. "He put his finger down here. I HATE him." Knowing that she'd been hurt this same way I'd been hurt, long ago, made Tammy more precious to me. It also brought the nightmares back: the big fat monster worm in the ugly dead garden sometimes chased me in the night. It was terribly hard to answer her question, just then.

"Tammy, it's not that she doesn't like you. It's just that

she hates herself, sometimes," was all I could say to her. I held her close. I knew that Helen and Ben had "had to get married"—how I hate that phrase!—because Helen was pregnant. It's such a lousy excuse, I wasn't going to load it onto Tammy.

That night I woke up screaming and thrashing angrily in bed with Ben.

"Hey, hey, hey, it's OK, sweetheart. Sh, sh, sh. It's only a dream."

But I cried and cried, clutching him. I could not let go. "Listen, Ben, I have to tell you everything. About me. I'm so afraid, though, that I'll lose you if I do."

"What, you think I'm crazy? Not a chance. Vanessa, I've never been loved so much—ever. Not by anyone. You've made me feel whole, and rich."

"Really?" I asked, feeling teeny.

"Really. Trillions' worth. So let 'er rip. Tell me."

"But it's so gro-ooss," I sobbed.

"I'm a pretty gross guy, myself. Trust me. I can take it." I couldn't talk.

"Is it grosser than this?" and he—SO grossly—gulped air and belch-talked, "THIS is gross!" Belch, belch, belch.

"EEEEW!" I thumped him with a pillow, but then I started crying again. Finally, it came out. Everything. My father with the ice cream cone routine, the courts, the institutions, the foster homes.

"I'm gonna' KILL that son of a bitch! How DARE he?" He was furiously pacing the bedroom floor. "Him and Helen's boyfriend, man. They are HISTORY. God! I am so SICK of all the perverts in the world!" He smashed the TV with his fists. Broke the whole thing apart. That—the violent response to violence—infuriated me.

"That's real helpful, Ben. God! I'm just SO glad I told you. You're a big comfort. Thanks a LOT!" I threw my clothes on, and slammed the door to his apartment. I'm real tough, aren't I? But I collapsed on the other side of the door. He was my life, the first lover I'd trusted with the ugliest parts of myself. And he'd blown it. In my mind, anyway—not that I knew just then what I'd expected, or would have liked him to do, exactly.

He opened the door. And read my head. "So what did you think would happen when you told me? I'm no Mother Theresa, you know, and I've got a really bad neck, so it's a little hard for me to swiftly turn the other cheek. Is that what you wanted?"

"I want you to make it so it never happened! I want you to take it all away!" I held him tightly, crying. "I need your kindness, the same kindness you give Tammy!"

"OK, OK . . . I'll do my best. But I'll blow it sometimes with you, just like I do with her. I get mad at the bastards, and I want to kill them. I don't think that's so unnatural. OK?"

"Just try."

"I can try."

They became my family. My very own, real family. Ben was incredibly generous, and wonderful-corny-romantic. "Sweets for the sweet, my dear?" He would actually say, (SO corny), before giving me a big box of incredibly expensive Godiva candy.

I think that because it was such a difficult time for Ben and Tammy, the three of us became close faster than I'd ever known closeness could happen. They were amazed that I could purr like a cat; Tammy'd put her hand on my throat, trying to figure out how I did it. I told them about Krayta—not everything, not with Tammy in the room.

"You see, Tammy, when I was little, my house was a sad house. A really sad house. So I made up this magic kingdom in my mind, called Moravia. A beautiful queen, Shalimar, ruled the kingdom, and she gave me this huge black leopard, called Krayta, who would love me and protect me."

"God! That is so neato!"

"Krayta was the one who taught me to purr."

"Did your mother hit you?"

"Yes. And it made me very sad."

"Did she have a boyfriend who, um, abused you, too?"

Oh, Tammy, do you know, do you have any idea, how hard it was to answer? "My father did. A lot."

Her enormous, grown-up, brown eyes searched mine. She held me tightly. "Then you and I are like sisters."

"That's right." I was crying onto her beautiful curly brown hair.

I slept alone, that night, in my apartment; Ben was paranoid that Helen had some private-eye type watching us. The fat worm monster in the dead ugly garden came that night, and tried to choke me to death. I woke up alone, screaming. Crying hysterically, I called Ben.

"Oh, God, Ben, it's so awful!"

"Baby, I'm coming over right now. But listen to me. I want you to breathe really deeply, and remember what Miss Grant taught you. I want you to go back to sleep and KILL the monster. I'll be there with a billy club, right behind you. I swear it. Can you do that?"

"Yes." But I must admit, I kept one eye open until he got there, and THEN I went to sleep. It was as horrible as ever, looking for the monster in the garden, but I could feel Ben's love making me stronger. I borrowed Ben's billy club, and I bludgeoned the shit out of it. The next morning, I felt great.

"We killed it!" I yelled at Ben, as soon as I woke.

When I met him at his place after work for dinner, there was a big picnic basket on the table, tied up with a big red bow. A small tag hung from the bow that read, "For Vanessa". I opened it. Inside, a black Persian kitten stared up at me with wise, golden eyes.

"His name is Krayta," Tammy announced proudly behind me, "and he already knows how to purr, real good."

Ben stood behind her, grinning his, "aren't I bitchin'?" grin. "He's little, but look at his head, Vanessa. Look at the size of those paws. The breeder says he'll be huge. He'll be a real monster-killer, for sure."

"Boy am I lucky!" I said quietly, hugging Krayta, Ben, and Tammy.

* * *

I was holding Tammy and Krayta on my lap, purring in two-part harmony with Krayta, when the phone call came.

"Is this Vanessa Morelli?" A really tense man's voice asked.

"Y-yes." I was terrified. Someone wanted to lock me up; the tone of this man's voice made me positive I'd be put in jail.

"Vanessa, listen, this is Jimmy."

Jimmy?

"Big Ocean Jimmy. Shit, Vanessa! You better get here, quick! Elizabeth, she . . . she . . ." he choked. He was crying.

Oh, God. No! "Jimmy! Jesus. Is she . . . what happened?"

"She's OK. We got to her in time. She hasn't been sleeping so well, this tour. She-she took like a whole fucking bottle of pills, and . . . I don't know, she's been really down. But she's OK. They pumped her clean. I think she needs to see you. Bad."

"Where, where are you?"

"San Antonio. Um, there's an afternoon flight out of L.A. on Delta."

"I'll be there."

Ben loaned me the money—not that he had any to spare. Legal fees were breaking him, and neither of us were exactly into selling cars just then, so there was nothing coming in. I would've done just about anything to make that afternoon flight to San Antonio. Tears streamed down my face silently the entire flight. Two Bloody Mary's just made it worse. It was all my fault, all my fault: Elizabeth had sounded sad and lonely, and I had not rescued her. I was so into myself and my heavy duty romance, I'd just blithely babbled on, ignoring her pain. God, I was a good-for-nothing, selfish shit.

Elizabeth must've lost twenty pounds since I'd seen her last; she looked wrecked, even with her little girl's smile when she saw me. "Lady Vanessa! Please don't look so cross, Babe. It was an accident."

"Accident, bullSHIT! You can't DO this to me, Elizabeth! I'd DIE without you."

"Really? You've seemed pretty tied up with Mr. Right, every time I've tried to talk to you."

"So, OK, now I'm punished. We even? TALK to me, Queen Elizabeth."

"You're SO corny. Some queen, huh?"

"What's going ON, Elizabeth? PINBALL LOVE was a gold album. You're rich as hell, you're insanely gorgeous — WHAT IS YOUR PROBLEM?"

She looked guilty, and, as always, ten years old. "I don't know." Tears slid onto her pillow. "I've just been. . . .feeling abandoned. Really lonely. And dumb."

I climbed onto her hospital bed and cradled her. Elizabeth the wise, older queen lay in my arms like a frightened child. She needed me to be the strong mother, so I did my best. We cried and cried. People walking by in the hall looked at us really strangely, but I didn't care. Well, until one farty old doctor stuck his fat face in, all blown up with disgust.

"Excuse me, sir, but would you mind leaving us rock and roll perverts alone?" I asked him. He left in a hurry, and Elizabeth laughed.

"Oh, God, Lady Vanessa. I've become a cliche: the messed up success. Too many drugs, too many dumb men in dumb beds. And . . . and . . ." she started crying.

"What? What, Elizabeth? You can tell me ANYTHING. I'll love you to the death, remember?"

"Vanessa, I think I'm a fag!"

(The word "gay" wasn't yet happening.)

I was a little shocked, I have to admit; she sure could've fooled me! "But, well," (I was blowing it), "really? Why do you think so?"

"I just like it better with women." She pushed me away. "Will you hate me now, now that I'm a fag out of the closet? Will you be afraid of me — avoid me?"

I laughed. "Don't be DUMB. So you're a fag, Elizabeth. Who CARES? I just want you to be happy. I mean, loving anyone is good. Remember Lia, the girl I lived with at the Johnsons' house? She came out of the closet YEARS ago, and she's happy and rich. She's in love with a really pretty, sweet woman. Love, roses, holding hands – the whole bit. So quit torturing yourself. God, Elizabeth! Don't be so bourgeois."

"But what about my foster parents? I mean, if I fall in love, and this woman and I want to get married, it's not like they'll come to our wedding or anything."

"But I'll come, and Big Ocean will come, so you'll be fine. And EVERY one will get used to it. We just want you to be happy, Elizabeth!" Funny, funny thing: I was feeling jealous. "So, um, is there – I mean, someone you're serious about?"

She touched her finger playfully on my nose. "You'll be the very first to know. Always. Thanks for coming. You're my rock, you know – don't leave me alone for so long."

"Never. God, Elizabeth, I'm so sorry – I always assume everyone's strong except me. Listen, take a rest when this tour's over, OK? At my apartment, in L.A., OK? Promise?"

"OK."

Life was just complicated, we decided during the two days I stayed with her in her penthouse suite in San Antonio. She was quickly her old, graceful self again. "And we have tremendous NEEDS," we also admitted. That's just the way it is: it takes a lot of love for each of us to get through the heavy load of crap that life dumps onto our brittle shoulders.

It was a good thing that I had that time with Elizabeth, because all the love it had taken to pull her through had made me a stronger person. And what I faced when I returned to Ben would take all the strength and love I'd ever be able to muster.

* * *

I walked in feeling pleased with myself, and pleased with life, just as if it was I who'd been given a second chance. I'd missed Ben, and I was wildly eager to see him. I turned the key to his apartment.

There's a smell in a house when everything is wrong. There is no mistaking it. It is grim, musty, and cold. I shook, wondering what could have happened. What should I do?

"B-Ben?"

I walked toward the dining room table. It was piled with papers, two empty scotch bottles, and coffee mugs. I saw him, and caught my breath. Ben sat there, half-dressed in dirty clothes, emptily staring ahead. His eyes were raw, red and swollen. Jesus.

He thudded emptily onto my chest, and I held him. He was making dry, rasping sounds with his throat. "She's gone. Gone. Helen's taken her. Stolen her. Stolen my baby! Vanessa, Tammy is gone!"

We searched, and called, for years: lawyers, cops, private detectives, the FBI, and Missing Children Support Groups. Tammy and Helen had simply vanished. Helen was afraid she might lose the child she loved, so she took her baby and ran, God knows where. For years, we couldn't look at Tammy's huge brown eyes and curly brown hair in photographs without crying. Both of us still hover, depressed, by the telephone whenever her birthday rolls around. It's been almost eleven years.

This was the hardest I ever had to love someone; Ben was a fragile, broken shell for months. Losing a child is the worst. The absolute worst. Ben losing Tammy proved to me once and for all that there is no FAIR in this life. You can bust your buns livine a good life – or, being SUCH a GOOD FATHER – but that is NO guarantee you won't get crunched. Life dumps on people, absolutely without discrimination: just about everyone gets dumped on. So if you've gotten dumped on recently, take heart: you have massive company. You are not a bad person. BAD STUFF HAPPENS TO REALLY NICE PEOPLE, REALLY

GOOD PEOPLE. There are crowds of people out there as sad as you are, who need you as badly as you need them.

We spent exhaustive, long days and weeks, months. We spent the days in a protective Numb Bubble we'd made for ourselves: we couldn't talk about it. We simply functioned. We took turns calling the detective, the lawyer, and filling out forms. When we weren't calling someone, we sat numbly by the phone. We ate many a TV dinner staring at the telephone. At night, we sobbed in each other's arms for hours, then washed tears of sadness away with the golden tears of beautiful, passionate lovemaking. There was nothing else. Our lives had been reduced to two things: this constant raw pain, and each other—our love. For me, this was it. This was the love and the lovemaking I'd always assumed that my past had taken from me. Kids like me never get the ultimate passionate love, I figured. Wrong.

Six months of searching and crying passed before Ben was ready to collect himself. He'd made himself ill with worry and anguish; his body was a mess. I felt honored to help him get through those days. I'd been learning and learning all my life how to love and be loved. This was the test. I'd needed every lesson, but finally, I had it wired!

Not that all his anguish didn't get to him sometimes, and make him moody and nasty. I'd take a little pissiness, but not a lot. And that was a sign that NEW Vanessa had really emerged. OLD Vanessa never would have made a squeak that she thought might endanger a love like this one with Ben.

One time, he just blew up at me as we were carrying groceries up the hallway of the apartment building. (I hate fights in public.) He was having a fit—really putting me down, because I'd bought a whole new set of sheets. Yes, they were pricey; yes, we were broke. But the old sheets had rips in them that Ben's goddamned too-long toenails were enlarging nightly, so when I made my first reasonable-sized commission, I "invested" in some fancy sheets.

"Good, God, Vanessa, you spent your whole goddmaned

commission on some SHEETS? What got into you? How could you DO that?"

God. As if I'd poisoned his favorite goldfish or something. "Aren't you getting a little carried away, Ben?"

"I don't think so. I think this demonstrates that you have a serious lack of good judgement, . . ."

That was enough for me. He was getting wound up for a long spiel. No thank you. New Vanessa ran a little quickly, opened the door to our apartment, and then slammed it behind her. I clinked the chain lock closed.

"Vanessa, open this goddamned door!" Very loudly, he shouted. Old Vanessa would have a) cowered before such display of authority, or b) opened the door out of sheer embarrassment.

New Vanessa, however, started dancing behind the door, screaming like Aretha Franklin at the top of my lungs: "I'm about to give you/ all my money/ and all I'm askin'/ for the time, honey/ is gimme a little respect when you come home. Just a little bit, just a little bit. R-E-S-P-E-C-T. Find out what it means to me. R-E-S-P-E-C-T, baby, baby! Sock it to me, sock it to me, sock it to me." Well, I thought I was being the most adorable woman on earth. I opened the chain lock a little bit, and I must admit, SHRANK when I saw that five doors to five apartments were open. People were staring, and Ben's face was flame-red. He was pissed.

"That was very good, honey." He turned, smiling, to the "crowds". "Isn't she something?" He turned back to me, with a REALLY-PISSED-nice-guy-fake-smile. "I guess I deserved that, so, now, if you'll just let me in . . ."

I did. Two days later, he started speaking to me again. I hated the silent routine, but at least I got to throw out the old, torn sheets without any further argument. .And those early-relationship-fights are great in a way, because they're not over really BIG things, and you learn about each other's unusually sensitive areas. Ben doesn't like to make a scene, and I need some respect. So we got to figure out those two very important things over torn sheets. And we survived.

"How'd I get so lucky?" He'd ask on the good days, when I'd come bounding in with a big check. I was selling limos well at Cagney's again, which was very necessary. We were Broke City.

"God, honey, I don't know," I would laugh, "I AM pretty hot stuff!" Remember Natalie Wood, in WESTSIDE STORY, singing, "I feel pretty, oh so pretty, I feel pretty and witty and gay? I'm so pretty, that I hardly can believe I'm real." That was Vanessa, for the first time in her life.

Eventually, Ben decided to get on with life, and get well. "Couldn't have made it without you, Babe," he said one evening, when I could see that the color was returning to his cheeks. He'd gone out and bought a couple new suits, and was giving me a fashion show. The worst was behind us. We had to console ourselves that Helen DID truly love Tammy, and that Tammy knew it. Helen had also left the pervert-boyfriend when Tammy told on him. That's certainly better than I ever got. Tammy was strong and smart, and we could hope with all our hearts that her own big heart would get her through. We hired an answering service so that, should we ever be away from the phone when she called, Tammy could get to us. Then we started to piece together our own life as a couple.

* * *

Now, I declared to myself, I might after all be worthy of such a man: a man good and smart and lovely and gentle. A man who has built his world around me. I'd moved in with him the day Tammy was taken, and from the beginning, I felt easy with Ben. I opened my entire soul to him, both the ugly and the beautiful. I introduced him to Jesse, the Grahams, and Elizabeth, who was again on top of the world as the Queen of Rock 'n Roll. This time, though, it was without the booze, drugs, and men. Ben folded perfectly into all of their hearts: all the ones who love me, I rejoiced at learning, love him for loving me so well.

I then developed a deep, rich craving to somehow find Mimi and Scott and all the Ramseys: I wanted them to see what a happy-ending kid I'd become. Ben said yes, of course; he said tender things about how I'd opened him and made him blossom. (Really personal stuff.) He spoke to me with amazing tenderness, and he never flinched when I showed him my worst characteristics.

"I've never felt this well loved in my whole life, Vanessa. Anything—anything in the world I can give or do is not enough."

This love—his, mine, and ours—had surely made me strong enough to look up the people who'd actively gotten it all going in my life. If they'd forgotten me, or if they'd never forgiven me for the T-Bird incident, or if they refused to see me, or to love me again, I could take it. I had Ben's love, no matter what. And I had my own self respect. That doesn't mean my whole body wasn't shaking like hell, the day we drove one of the limos up to Mimi and Scott's new house on the fancy west side of Los Angeles.

* * *

The house was absolutely Mimi: it was a perfect good-fairy witch's house, set high off the street, above a hill of green lawn. Every possible space was splattered with a garish riot of flowers. The house was pointy on one side (it looked as if there were a magic attic, up there beneath that spiky witch-hat roof!), and turreted on the other side, with a cheery bay window. Ben fell in love with Scott and Mimi before ever meeting them: their personalities were splashed all over the outside of the house.

"They must be great people. This place is fantastic!"

"Oh, Ben, they are! I can't wait for you to meet them, but I'm so scared!"

Ben laughed a little, but he wasn't making fun of me. It was a soft laugh that relaxed me. "Honey, NO ONE could stay mad over the T-Bird thing. They probably don't even

remember it." I never did convince Ben what an awful thing
it was that I did, but he was still shocked by it. "Was that
really YOU that did that? I can't picture it!"

It seemed to take hours to climb all the steps up to their
house, and we were a little out of breath when we got to the
bright red door. I was glad I could cover up my nervous
hyperventilating with Out-of-breath excersize-puffs. Scott
opened the door, and smiled. As if it were the most casual
thing in the world.

"I'll be damned. Son of a gun! Well, come on in, girl, don't
stand there hyperventilating!" He hugged me hard. Just as
in the old days, his hug was more like a football tackle. "Let
me get Mimi—she's in the shower." And he went off shouting, "Hey, Meem! MIMI, get the hell out here!" We could
hear him shouting, "they don't care what you're wearing,
for Christ's sake, just get out here! . . . Come on, come on,
Meem, this is not a goddamned fashion show . . . Never
mind WHO, it's a surprise."

"Scotty, I am dripping all over the goddamned carpet.
Would you at least let me dry off?"

By now I was laughing. Nothing had changed; they were
still the same crazy Mimi and Scott. Poor Mimi walked into
the entry wearing nothing but a skimpy towel, all drippy
from the shower. Sopping wet, with her hair full of white
shampoo lather, she was still the most glamorous, beautiful
lady in the world.

"Vanny!"

Oh, it was good to hear her call me that! She hugged me
hard, getting shampoo all over my face. I couldn't think of
anything brilliant to say—or anything at all. It was one of
those thick-air moments.

"Hello," Mimi said, super-embarrassed, to Ben. "Vanny,
would you mind if I finished my shower, now?" She cocked
her head back funny, and looked down her nose at Ben: "I'd
like to meet you when the shampoo's not running down my
nose." And she trotted off, painfully embarrassed. "Honey,"
she said to Scott, who was thoroughly enjoying all this,
"would you get our guests a drink while I get the shampoo

out of my eye? Huh, would you do that? You're real proud of yourself, aren't you?" We could hear Mimi giggling as she headed for the shower. She also thought he was cute. (I would have KILLED Ben, if he'd pulled that.)

Scott was still laughing. "So! What can I get you two?" And, after he'd handed us a couple beers, he came right to the point. "Vanessa, you sure grew up gorgeous! Damn, I had no idea. Ben, did you know she used to be plump? You been ripping off any more T-Birds, Vanessa, since you left this neck of the woods? My old man got quite a kick out of that one! You should've seen him trying to keep a serious look on his face when he told me. I told him it was his own fault for driving such a hot rod car at his age—and then ducked. He didn't appreciate that too much."

It was as if I'd left last week—which is how you know which friends are your best friends: the ones you feel you never left. We were slipping back into our old routine, where nothing was sacred. There was absolutely nothing you couldn't laugh at. Ben fit right in, and the four of us became friends for life. One funny thing was that I still felt like a "bad girl", living with a man I wasn't married to. I don't know what it was: maybe all the Catholic stuff from when I'd lived with Scott's parents, or maybe it's just that I wanted them to think I'd turned out PERFECT. Very dumb, but real.

"So," Mimi said, "you live alone, Vanny, or . . . ?"

"Um, I live with, um, Ben. We're . . . engaged."

Ben's eyes grew soft and wide. We'd all had a couple glasses of wine. "We ARE?" He exclaimed. "Vanessa, when did we . . ."

Scott laughed, and teased me. "You blew it, Vanessa!"

I felt like the ULTIMATE nerd. Except that Ben (swear to God!) took my hand and said, "so, let's get engaged again, hon. This time, you'll have witnesses."

A couple embarrassment-tears ran down my face; one thing nice about feeling loved and free is that you can cry whenever you want. "Absolutely." And then I stuck my tongue out, at Scott.

* * *

Mimi and I spent as many days together as we could possibly squeeze into our busy, businesswomen schedules. Mimi was getting famous as an interior decorator, and I was pulling some good moves in the limousine business. And planning a wedding. What an amazing thing, to be getting married! Mimi wanted to make my wedding dress — as if she didn't have enough to do, with two sons in Little League and a flourishing business! But that's Mimi: the giving sources within her never seem to dry up.

I was able to call my mother in Singapore; I felt that I should. No. I wanted my natural mother (all my mothers!) to be present at my wedding. I loved and forgave the whole world. If she couldn't come, well, the many miles between California and Singapore would make a damned decent excuse for her.

She was efficient and polite. "Congratulations. Let me look at my calendar. Well, I am a contract negotiator, so I should be able to make arrangements accordingly."

I guess that meant she was coming — that she wouldn't miss it for the world (just kidding). Still, I was excited for her. She'd realized her dream late in life, but she'd done it. She'd persevered. Unlike many people who've screwed up along the way, my mother realized it — and even apologized for it. I don't think one in ten abusive parents do that. I knew I was damned lucky. Ben caught me hugging myself a lot, before the wedding: I was vibrantly alive with goodwill for the universe.

Ben and I excitedly accepted Scott and Mimi's offer to hold the ceremony in their backyard: it would be lovely, with the swimming pool, the gazebo, and Mimi's gorgeous flowers everywhere. The dress Mimi made me was simple and elegant — and perfectly me. Everyone fussed over me, telling me what a gorgeous bride I was. (But, really. Has anyone ever seen an UGLY bride?)

But what I was absolutely unprepared for was my

father's presence in the audience. Instant rage. I yanked my mother aside before the ceremony was supposed to begin.

"How could you DO this to me, TODAY? I don't believe this!"

She seemed startled, uncomprehending.

"HIM, Mother. How could you bring HIM?"

"He's my husband, Vanessa. I married him again last year. I thought you knew . . ." She stared at me, feeling rotten, maybe? "He's so different, Vanessa—and all that's past. A new life is about to begin for you—let's forgive, and dwell on the good things, shall we?"

God. It was the first time my mother ever came off like a preacher, but I wanted to be happy. So I shrugged my shoulders and concentrated on Ben—his love for me. And I let the bastard stay, but without ever once looking at him.

"Vanny, Vanny, Ben's running up the stairs! Quick! Get in the bedroom—he's not supposed to see you 'till the music starts," Mimi yelled.

I sat in the bedroom feeling strange: the bride-queazies had finally attacked. Could I make Ben a good wife? He'll want kids someday—such a wonderful father should have them, but what would I do? What if marriage changed everything between us? I'd known more than one couple who lived happily together, but divorced within six months after getting married.

Scott knocked on the bedroom door, and shouted in his pretend-gruff, big-brother voice. "Vanessa? You decent?"

I laughed. "Never!" Silence. "Oh, Scotty, you know very well I'm dressed. Come on in."

He was dressed in white tails, and he carried a two liter bottle of Cutty Sark. "Fortification. You don't want to go out there unprepared, do you?"

I laughed. "Scotty, you're great. I need this." And I lifted this enormous bottle to my mouth, trying to somehow drink without wrecking my lipstick.

"Jesus Christ, you look like an old wino. Shit, don't laugh, you're going to get it all over the dress my wife made. She'll kill me. Here, let me put some in a bota." And he pulled a bota out from under the bed.

"Here." he watched me drink. "You look great. Are you happy?"

"Yeah. Nervous, though—and pissed that that asshole is here."

"Ignore him. Don't let it spoil anything. Ben's a really great guy . . ."

"Were you nervous on your wedding day?"

"Naw. My old man fortified me—only with Old Crow. Then, when I saw Mimi, so incredibly beautiful . . . it's a good time. You'll like it."

"I hope we'll be as happy together as you and Mimi."

"We are pretty great, aren't we?"

I slapped his knee. "You're so vain!"

He got up to go. "Don't worry about it. You will be. So, come on, kid—put the bottle down, and let's get this show on the road."

And he held his arm like a professional usher.

The sun glared, in hot white strips that bounced up from the pool. The brilliance of the sun, the pool, and the riotously clashing colors of the flowers threw me into a swoon. (Jeffrey Scott had teased Mimi, "Mom, why do you have to have so many different colors out here? It looks weird. Why can't we just have ONE color of flowers?")

Scotty caught me, though, so we never missed a beat. "Whoa, girl, steady. You're all right, now—this is the home stretch," he was murmuring.

Elizabeth was playing accoustical guitar, and was singing, "Like A Bridge Over Troubled Water", by Simon and Garfunkle. God, it was beautiful! She grinned widely at me, tears streaming down her face, as she sang,

". . . sail on silvergirl, sail on by. Your time has come
to shine. All your dreams are on their way. See how
they shine."

("Bridge Over Troubled Water" by Paul Simon
©1969)

She looked like a Renaissance flowerselling-gypsy, with a wreath of flowers in her hair, and long ribbon streamers on her dress. Jesse, the Johnsons, the Grahams, my little brother—ALL the people that mattered—were there for me, and filled with love and hope for us.

When Elizabeth finished singing, she started playing "If I Were A Carpenter" on the guitar. What a beautiful surprise! Ben began to sing the song to me.

> "See my love through loneliness, see my love through sorrow. I've given you my only-ness, come give me your tomorrow."
> ("If I Were a Carpenter" by Tim Hardin ©1966 by
> the Faithful Virtue Music Co.)

By the time I got to him, under the white, flower-laden gazebo, we were all bawling! The three of us, Elizabeth, Jesse, and I, put our arms around each other for one small private moment before I took Ben's arm, and the ceremony began.

When we were officially husband and wife, the party started; the champagne flowed. It was an elegant affair, and everyone bubbled with love and happiness for Ben and me. It was while I danced with Jesse (amazing luck: Big Ocean played rock 'n roll dance music for free) that I finally looked my father's way.

"Hey, Jess, you know what?"

"You're happy, and I'm happy for you. What else?"

"See that tall older man in the fancy suit who seems so very charming? That is my natural father—the one that fucked up my life."

Jesse was astounded. "I'm really sorry, Vanessa. Who invited him?"

"He remarried my mom. He's her date, for God's sake. But I'm so happy I don't even care."

"Way to go, Vanessa!"

"I'll tell you something, though—if he makes one single crack, he's going in the pool."

"Seems fair to me."

And he, my co-conspirator, smiled his old, crooked smile at me. I felt incredibly strong that day, and high on love: high on the love of all the people who'd stuck their necks out, over the years, to help me survive. And love for me, too: I was proud of me, for making it through hell to get to the other side. (Ben says I have a Dante complex.)

I was staring down when my father approached me; his gleaming leather dress boots must have set my mother back three hundred bucks. He was slightly drunk, and feeling jovial, charming, and handsome. "Well, well, Vanessa, let's give the photographer a picture of the father and the bride." He went to put his arm around me, but I swung away from him.

My arms throbbed hard; they surged with an electrochemical wisdom of their own. I shoved with all the strength behind my weight, and in he went: Frank Morelli, his French designer suit, AND the Italian leather boots were all one wet poodle, floundering around in Scott and Mimi's swimming pool.

Did it make up for all the hell he'd once put me through? No. But did it feel absolutely and thoroughly bitchin'? You bet it did.

Nevertheless, he still had massive powers of intimidation over me. I was shaking as I clapped my hands together, as if ridding myself of unwanted dust on my fingertips. "Takes care of that!" I said calmly, but my voice was shaking. I walked past the startled guests—most of whom didn't know what to make of it—over to the bar. I broke the startled silence by cooly ordering, "champagne, please!"

Ben, who hates scenes, walked up to me. I was tense. (Through my side vision, I watched as Scott and my mother helped my father out. I wouldn't see him again for five years. It would take about three years before I'd lose my terror that he would retaliate someday, by sneaking up behind me and slitting my throat.) I stared into the bubbles in my glass.

"Feel better?" That was all Ben said. I looked up. He wasn't pleased about the scene, but at least he was smiling. "You betcha! Let's dance, honey—it's party time!" At many, many levels, it was a perfect day.

* * *

As Vanessa Morelli Ferris, I can tell you that the glow between Ben and me has never faded; in fact, it's warmer and richer, now. But, my God, we have known some soul-trying times! Working together, we have played on the real-life Monopoly board. We did a little dabbling in highrolling capitalists' favorite roulette game: Real Estate.

We bought Cagney's, and let it roll. We started new branches all over L.A. Ben and I took our earnings and invested in Real Estate. The seventies in Southern California were bulging with R.E. Big Deals. We collected all kinds of red and green houses and condos during the fat times. We got RICH, and it was FUN! I started indulging in manicures, pedicures, and all kinds of rich-people things. We cruised the Mediterranean, and walked along the ancient sands of Greece and Egypt. We dined at the Ritz in Paris; we drank Ouzo and danced in the Plaka.

Did/do the horror memories from the past return, ever? Like, in bed, with sex, etcetera? Yes, I'm sorry to say. Sometimes they do. But less and less. The love that my husband and my friends wrap around me gets me through the bad spells of moody fear. A good shrink—Miss Grant or Jesse, in my case—teaches you how to expel it from your mind. Using visualization, I take the hideous memories and put them in a giant missle. I then launch them to Pluto, where they stay for a long time.

One of the reasons I fell in love with Ben was that he was a great, loving father to Tammy. Frightened as I was of myself and my past, when the pregnancy test read positive, I locked myself in the bathroom. And deep-breathed, and prayed. "Please, God, please let me be a good parent." Ben,

Mimi, Jesse and Elizabeth all cheered me on through my
bouts of serious depression and self doubt. But none of
them knew what it was like to live inside me, during that
time. Ben, Scott and Mimi, and Jesse—now a proud father
of two—were all proven parents. Elizabeth was living with
a woman she adored, and was radiantly happy, but what
the hell did she know about being a mother, and not beating
it, as the stats all say you will?

So my first pregnancy was especially tense. I was terrified, and the doctor was an asshole. I pleaded with him,
every time I saw him, "please help me get through this,
doctor. I was beaten and sexually abused as a child, and
this whole thing scares the hell out of me." In classic
Asshole-Doctor fashion, he completely ignored me and
talked about dilation. NO ONE understood my fears, not
even Ben.

"Come on, honey, anyone can have a baby. It's no sweat."
Right! Let's see YOU get through it, boys!

When birthing time came, I told the doctors, "just give
me the drugs, please." Unfortunately, the Birthing Move-
ment, with its emphasis on drugless, natural births, etc.,
had erupted. Doctors had completely reversed the attitude
of the decades before, when they had LOVED giving mothers drugs—it made things so much easier for the doctors.
So it was just my bad luck to be in labor in 1979 instead of
1959; it was also my bad luck that my childhood made the
whole thing so terrifying, and that no one even TRIED to
understand. They treated me like I was a bona fide baby
killer-drug addict.

Twenty-five hours of hard labor later, it wasn't happening. The baby was turned around inside me, and I was
COMPLETELY out of gas. Pooped. Ready to die. Some
jerk yelled, "PUSH!" at me, again, and I wanted to kill.

A fresh nurse who'd just replaced another nurse walked
up to me, as if this were my first hour of labor. "Hello, Mrs.
Ferris," she sang. "Let's try and push this baby around,
OK?"

"Hey, look, lady! I don't give a fuck WHAT you've got in

your needles around here, but I want it, and I want it NOW."

"Doctor," the nurse sang cheerfully, "Mrs. Ferris is very upset. I think you'd better come."

And they put me out-scout. Charisse, my first daughter, has taught me everything that is important to know. Wise, sensitive child that she's been from day one, she eased me gently into motherhood. Loving her without ugly force is as effortless as breathing, nine-tenths of the time. I attribute my best mothering strengths to her: gentle, lovely one, she has made me strong, the mother I've always hoped I could be. The mother I wish I'd had.

So I wasn't quite so tense with the second pregnancy; in fact, Ben and I were testing mattresses, lying and bouncing on them in a Bedroom shop when I went into labor. My water broke on a Sealy Posturepedic! I was so much stronger with the doctors: "no episiotomy this time, fellas." We have the right, women—all of us: except for in the most rare, dire emergencies, this cruel operation is unnecessary, and we have the right to refuse. And don't let ANYONE tell you that your sex life will be ruined if you don't get sliced up: Mumtaz Mahal had thirteen kids with NO episiotomies, and her husband still was crazy enough about her in bed that he ignored his forty other wives AND built her a Taj Mahal! So there. Couldn't resist. But seriously; for all women, but especially for women who were sexually abused as children, an unnecessary episiotomy is genital mutilation. And that's not all. The nurse started to take off my fingernail polish, and I just about flipped OUT inbetween contractions.

"I spent thirty bucks on this manicure, and no one's touching it!"

I raised quite a fuss over this—something I never would have done in my meeker days! But no one could give me any reason for taking off the polish, until one kindly doctor explained to me that in the old days, they needed to see if the skin beneath your fingernails turned blue. That meant you were losing it on the table: dying.

"Excuse me, doctor, but isn't there a more advanced method, nowadays?"

There is, he told me, so I got to keep the polish. It seems foolish, now, but it did take my mind off contractions for awhile. And doctors, just like car mechanics, should be required to tell us the what's and why's. We're paying them; we have the right to ask questions.

Danielle, my second daughter, also came out healthy and perfect. Everything that Charisse hasn't taught me, Danny has. And watching Ben splash in the pool with the girls, or hike in the woods, or color with them, gives me tremendous joy. My life is good. The financial hassles, and the various health problems with Ben and the girls, still make life hard. We work damned hard, and we have hard problems, but our love life, and our life as a family, is great. After all those years of asking God, "why me?", I am blessed – a very fortunate woman. Consequently, the next, most painful part of my story to tell, I tell to you with great sadness, but not in self-pity.

* * *

OK, here goes. The hardest thing in my life to confess, to reveal. I've blocked this from my mind long enough. I give you this most painful chapter, little sisters, only because it may help you. Read it and take note. It is a warning. The next episode I describe was harder to bear than much of the sexual abuse I endured as a child.

* * *

It began with a phone call, on a strange, "Earthquake Weather" day. Still, heavy air and limp clouds.

"Is this Vanessa Morelli?" A shrieking woman's voice asked. "I think I'm your half-sister!"

Needless to say, the news did not overly thrill me. The

woman, Terry, WAS excited; she babbled on and on about how my father and her father were the same. She'd spent the last three years tracking her real father down. She'd lived all her life with her mom in Minnesota. Her mother had told her Mr. Morelli was dead, but she'd found "clues", she said, snooping around her mom's room. She JUST KNEW he was alive, and she determined she would find him. Terry had a definite case of "Roots Fever".

"My roots! You and my real father are the ROOTS I've been searching for!"

She sounded about my age (30-ish). I felt enough compassion for her NOT to say into the phone, "hate to break it to you, honey, but your true father is a child molester," and hang up. She sounded nice, and innocently joyous about all this. And, hey, let's face it, the idea of a new sister—I'd never had a sister—DID sound intriguing. We agreed to meet each other for a Mexican lunch.

I liked her; she was bubbly, pretty, and ecstatic at meeting me. Her mother was Kathy, my father's second "interim wife" before he remarried my mother. Terry and Kathy got along "OK", Terry said, until Terry hit her rowdy teens.

"And then, you know, the usual 'generation gap', as they used to call it," Terry laughed across the table. She had thick, brown hair that she tossed around with tremendous energy. "Anyway, I'd started suspecting that Daddy— listen to me—'Daddy', I haven't even met him yet!— anyway, that Daddy was really alive. I just know I'll like him. I've seen his picture. He's GORGEOUS! So tall!"

"Terry," I started. Her gushiness was getting to me. "He's not perfect. I mean, he may not be someone you want to spend a lot of time with."

"I know, Vanessa, but, hell, I want to KNOW—ALL of you. You know? Hey! I've got a GREAT IDEA! Let's have a big reunion. A giant bash, with all the Morelli's on your side. Vanessa, you're so great to introduce me to all this California stuff—guacamole, and tostadas, and these Margaritas are great! Please, let me put on a party for your family."

I didn't say no. She seemed to breathe from exotic, colored helium balloons that day, and was floating out of reach. The next thing I knew, she was staying in the guest bedroom of our home, planning a huge family reunion. My daughters loved their new aunt; she and her two young sons were like red rubber suns bouncing off all the walls. I would be lying if I said I didn't want to believe the fairytale of a joyous, loving, family reunion. A new beginning.

I dialed my mother's phone number, and Terry spoke to her new-found, "real" father with tears streaming down her face. "Daddy?" She shrieked. "It's YOU! I knew you were alive! Daddy, it's ME! Terry!"

I rolled my eyes. I couldn't help laughing to myself. If "Daddy" was sober right now, he sure wouldn't be for long!

So. We set up a party for that Saturday. Charisse and Danny were delighted with the idea of meeting their grandfather. They'd met Grandma Barbara, and had found her a bit cold. —To put it mildly. When they'd presented her with their gifts—beautifully colored drawings—she peered at them the way I might peer into an open bucket filled with oozing, green, toxic waste. So, anyway, my stomach was a mess all week, but I swear that I wanted it all to go well. I called my mother.

"Mother, are you SURE your bozo husband no longer drinks?"

"Not a drop. Quit your worrying. He'll be FINE. Vanessa, you know, you really should forget the past. It can eat at you like cancer."

Jesse had also said, "hate can eat your insides, Vanessa. If you can forget about it most of the time, if you can keep from hating, most of the time . . . Do you realize how much freer you would be if you could ever forgive? I know, easier said than done, but . . ."

Oh, Jesse, Jesse, I WANT to forgive, I don't WANT to hate. I swear it.

* * *

My brother Johnny arrived first, with his beautiful wife and kids. That made it easier. Terry bubbled and gushed all over them, and now there were seven kids tearing all over the house. Ben and I were kept busy cooking and watching children. Ben squeezed me once, saying, "hey, Killer, you can handle this. It'll be OK, and then it'll be over."

"Mommy, Mommy, Grandma Barbara's walking up to the door, so maybe it's my real grandfather with her," Charisse ran in with a flushed face to tell me. She was flushed with the excitement, and she'd gotten caught up with all this "real father" talk.

Terry and her real father's meeting WAS moving, I guess, but corny enough for me to get a serious case of the rolling eyeballs. The good news is that my father did not drink a drop, was charming to all of the grandchildren — WITHOUT, thank God, laying so much as a pinkie on any of them. (The fact that I carried a cast iron skillet with me the entire evening could have had something to do with that.) He told the children funny, CLEAN stories; he let my daughters bring him drawings, and he oohed and aahed over them perfectly. They loved him.

I never let him or the children out of my sight the entire evening, and I, too, stayed rigidly sober. But despite MY tension, everyone else had a fabulous time. Even tense, I enjoyed the seven children, the flushed faces, and, frankly, the large family feeling. It WAS there, in that room, that day. When John and my parents had gone, Terry collapsed in a dreamy swoon on our couch.

"GOD, that was wonderful! Thanks, you two, for letting me do this tonight. It meant everything to me."

So, great. I'd been a good guy and survived without getting hurt. Yet.

* * *

Three days later, I was on a plane to Texas. Ben and I

were doing a big real estate deal, and he felt I was the one to deal with the woman tycoon who owned the property we wanted to buy at a discount. I kissed the kids – including Terry's Jeremy and Tyler – and thanked God that Terry was there to help Ben watch Charisse and Danielle.

"I'm so proud of you girls for being so good with Jeremy and Tyler," I told them as we said goodbye. They were so adaptable, so generous with their toys. "You are my little treasures. You make me rich."

"We LOVE our new family, Mom," Danny told me.

* * *

When I returned home two days later, Charisse was in bed, scrunched up in a ball with her arms folded over her chest. Her face was grey. I thought she was dying.

"Honey, are you sick?" I asked her, rubbing her forehead.

She jumped in my arms and clung. And sobbed. I had no idea in the world what was going on. I never heard Danny, the boys, and Terry enter; Charisse and I clung to each other in pain, crying.

"Danny, take the boys out to the playroom and turn on Sesame Street. Could you do that, please?" Terry's voice.

I barely heard them go. Terry shut the door, and sat down timidly at the foot of Charisse's bed.

"Vanessa, . . ."

"What in the HELL is going on?"

"There's been an 'accident'. There's been . . . hell, Vanessa, it's so UGLY. I don't know . . ."

"Quit your dribbling and tell me RIGHT NOW. Did someone hurt my baby?"

"Yes. And no. Well. Daddy took us all to dinner last night, . . ."

That word. Daddy. An animal sound came up my throat with the bile. The ugly animal sound escaped, and Terry inched away from me on the bed. She started motor-mouthing, fast.

"So we went to dinner and had the best time, all the kids, Ben, and me. He and I got to talking and talking, when we got home. All those years to catch up on, you know. Ben put the kids and himself to bed early, and Daddy and me just kept talking – and drinking just a couple of those Margaritas."

"He drank."

"Not much, I swear, but enough so I, well, I didn't think he should drive, so I got a blanket for him, and he slept on the couch."

My clinging daughter's body froze, and stuck to my frozen skin. My stomach froze. "Did he hurt you, Charisse?" I wish my voice had not been filled with rage.

"It wasn't my fault!" She sobbed. Oh, to say those words I'd desperately needed once – if only I could unfreeze my mouth.

"Honey, no, no, it wasn't your fault. It wasn't your fault." I buried my forehead in her neck and breathed the words, "God . . . It wasn't your fault. . . .." I wept silently, then collected myself. "Can you tell Mommy exactly what happened?"

She sobbed, and choked, and tried to talk. "I was lying in my bed, and it was morning. Well, it was almost morning, but it was still dark. Super early – no one was awake. Grandpa walked in Danny's and my room. It was a little weird, because he was naked, but I was so happy to see that my Grandpa had spent the night, that at first I didn't care, but then I saw. His thing, it was sticking out. I thought maybe he didn't know, you know, like maybe he forgot to put his clothes on after his shower, so I said, 'Grandpa, I think you, um, forgot something.' And I, like, pointed. It's not like I STARED or anything. But then he said, 'Oh, no, sugar, it's for you – a present. You get to lick it!' And that was just SO weird, so I said, 'Grandpa, I don't think that's very polite.' And then he said, 'It's real polite, honey, and you'll love it – it's just like an ice cream cone.' But, Mom, I just didn't want to. He was being so WEIRD, and NAKED, so I said, 'NO, Grandpa – I don't want to, and he got kind of mean, and said, 'I think you better do what your Grandpa says', and I-I-I ran. He grabbed my hair, just like this, but I didn't care, I ran right into Terry's room, and . . ."

She was hyperventilating, sobbing, and I did my best to give her what I knew she needed. "Honey, you did the right thing, and Mommy's very proud of you. I love you so much, baby . . ." and that was all I could give her just then. My tears would not stop.

Terry was suffering. "She came in hysterical, and told me. I swear, Vanessa, I jumped up and ran in to get Danny, and to get him the hell out. I wanted to beat the shit out of him, but he was gone, Vanessa. He left the front door open and just walked out of tile house. All the commotion had wakened Ben, so I had to tell him . . ."

Ben. Had he given Charisse what she needed, or had he blown up, done the macho-violent thing?

"Daddy was really nice to me, Mommy. He cried and kissed me, but then he said he was going to kill Grandpa. He called him the name with the f-word. He said, 'I'm gonna' kill that . . . f-word' Mommy, I was so scared that Daddy would hurt Grandpa. OK, so he was a little mean, but he's my Grandpa, and I love him a lot. I mean, I don't know, maybe I was wrong . . . "

"No. You did the absolutely right thing." Shit.

Terry spoke. "Ben, was furious with ME, Vanessa, for letting him stay over. I mean, what did I do? How did I know he'd turn out to be a pervert?"

I slowly rose from the bed, quietly went into the bathroom, and puked. I then cried a million silent tears, sitting on the bathroom rug, and feeling all the feelings I'd felt as a child. As if I were there, again, in my mother's house. The hot, crazy, fury of life's injustice whirled around my head, suffocating me.

I don't know how long I sat there. When I emerged, Terry was gone. Charisse gave me a quiet hug. "I'm all right, Mommy. Please don't worry about me. Terry says you're worried I was hurt, but he only pulled out the tiniest bit of hair off my head, Mom, and I promise, it will grow back."

Over the weeks, I'd catch myself clinging to Charisse, telling her over and over, "I love you, little Dear," and she'd glow. She'd comfort me with her wisdom: she knew what I needed.

"I love you, Mommy. You're the BEST Mommy in the whole world." And then, "honest, Mom, he didn't hurt me. I'm OK. They talk about this kind of stuff at school—we read books about it, you know, child abuse, and everyone says it's not my fault, that it's like a sickness Grandpa has. So, like, it's OK, and even though he's a little bit sick, I still love him, so when can we see him again? I won't point at his thing ever again if he forgets to put his clothes on."

My mother and father left the country immediately; she, as always, was protecting him. There would be no prosecuting. I had to break the news to the girls that their grandpa and grandma left the country on business, and we would probably never see them again.

"And we are never going to talk about them anymore, do you understand?" Ben added. We started to get on with things, but I would never be quite the same.

* * *

Jesse was right: you can take the statistics about battered children who grow up and beat their children, and shove them. IF you stay conscious. We never spank the kids, because we don't need to. We reason with them, and tell them the consequences of their behavior. Still, the girls are old enough now to get absolutely wild, sometimes. At the moment I'm running two businesses out of our home, and their exuberance—I will be honest—can get to me as nothing else can. Senseless rage sometimes bubbles up inside me. Senseless, because if I were logical, I'd say, "heck, it's only little girls having a good time. Relax." I'll yell—"girls, Mommy's trying to work!" Sometimes it works, but when it doesn't, I lock myself in the bathroom and tell Charisse, "you have driven me to a bad place. Stay away from me for awhile." This method works: I have never beaten my children, and, generally, when I get out of the bathroom, much calmer, the girls apologize to me.

"We're sorry we drove you there, Mommy."

And that's a big part of the happy ending of my story: I have broken an evil chain. You, little sisters, can also break your evil chain. And if a lot of evil chains are broken? We can replace them with warm, gentle hands held together with love. Beating and spanking your kids does not "discipline" them. Studies have shown that children who get spanked score much lower on IQ tests than kids whose parents divert the kids' aetention when they're small, and reason with them when they're old enough. Respect your children, and reason with them. And let them know that you love them — ALWAYS — even when you are angry with them.

* * *

Funny thing about big Real Estate booms: sometimes they blow up in your face. Whether it was due to the oil embargo or the soaring interest rates, or foreign countries flaking out on their debts, who cares? The real estate boom shriveled, and Ben and I ate it. Just like on the Monopoly Board, ALL of the little red and green houses and condos we'd worked so hard for were collected by the banks, one by one. The truth? It hurt like hell. As superfluous as my home delivery dry cleaners and pedicurist may sound, I'd enjoyed every bit of it. I miss them, maybe more than I miss the fancy dinners in Beverly Hills. I LIKED the first class cruises to Europe and Egypt and the Carribean, dammit! There wasn't anything great about losing it all, except, of course, that our marriage survived it. But combing the carpet for quarters to put gas in the tank so you can drive the kids to school is no fun. Hiding your car around the corner at a neighbor's so the Repo man won't get it—and then he finds it and takes it anyway—is NO fun. Material girl that I am, I'd like the big bucks back, thank you, and I won't rest until I get them. Meanwhile, I keep looking in the Classifieds under "Oligarchs Wanted", but there just NEVER seems to be an opening.

The Christmas before last stunk. Some jerk came and took our car, and we were three payments behind on our house: it was REPO CITY around here. I had no idea where I'd come up with money for the girls' Christmas presents. "It's OK, Mommy. We understand," Charisse tried to console me, "you don't have to give us presents this year."

The tension was on. If there ever was a red-alert season for a bad ugly family scene, this was it. Ben and I spent a great deal of time in stinko moods. There was this one fight, though, that was amazing. I don't even remember what it was about, but all four of us— Ben, the two girls, and I, each behind a separate, slammed door, shouted simultaneously at the top of our lungs. It's a great way to yell! You can't hurt anyone from behind a slammed door, and the joke of feeling your hot breath on a door makes you laugh at yourself. The comedy of the scene got to us, and soon we were all laughing.

The money scene is bad; I won't lie. It has, since then, improved tremendously, only because of too many eighteen hour days, working, working. We've managed to stay quite current on the house payments; that's a biggie!

"Mommy, I don't want to grow up and have to work as hard as you and Daddy work," Charisse told me.

"It's not the work, honey," I told her. "Work is a wonderful thing. It's just that there's sometimes not enough TIME in the day for everything I want to do. The good times with you guys are worth it, though."

And they truly are.

* * *

I told you already, at the beginning of the book, about

my next door neighbor's daughter trying to swallow poison. Her stepfather had been raping her for two years, and she wanted to die. It hit me that I would never escape child abuse. I had to speak out and do whatever I could to end it.

As these thoughts were firming up in my mind, Scott invited us over to his house to watch the Rose Bowl football game with his family. My first feeling was panic: what if Scott's dad gave me that evil, bloodshot-eyeball look? But I had to go; I had to see Albert, Kelly, and Beth, and I had to see Mr. Ramsey and thank him for rescuing me when he did. It was important to me.

He was older, and, BOY, was he different! "Hi, Buckeroo!" He shouted at Danny when she entered. She laughed, and walked right up to him. He'd become a happy, if somewhat frail, jolly old man! God, I thought, let's hear it for the wonders of modern medical science.

"Mr. Ramsey, it's good to see you! Remember me?"

He whirled around and looked at me very closely. "What's the big idea, growing up like that? Cut that out, dammit, you'll make an old man out of me!"

He was adorable, and for the first time, I could see why his family was so crazy about him. It was really no giant effort to gather my courage during half time.

"Mr. Ramsey, could I talk to you for a minute?"

"Better be damned quick. I have a nap to take."

"I, um, just really needed to thank you for all you did for me, you know, when I was—during a really hard time. I mean, you took me in, got me out of that horrible place, even though you were ill . . ."

"I'm a helluva nice guy, aren't I? . . . You drive any better than you did back then? Kelly said you scared the hell out of him, and he don't scare easy."

Mrs. Ramsey laughed politely at that; funny, it was clear that she had no idea what we were talking about. She didn't even REMEMBER the T-Bird incident!

I laughed, and looked in his brown, no-longer-bloodshot eyes. "You saved my life, Mr. Ramsey."

"Don't mention it." Suddenly, he whirled around and gave

Charisse a really ferocious look. In that terrible, low growl, he asked her, "How'd you like to get your eyes poked out?" And he held two ominous fingers right in front of her eyes.

Did my Bear flinch? She laughed, and threatened, "I'm gonna' poke YOU!" And she did, right in his ribs.

Albert, Beth, and Kelly were pretty much the same. Albert wasn't so tan and sunbleached, Beth wasn't so scrawny, and Kelly was tall, but they still spent much of the evening arguing with each other. They didn't really concern themselves with my presence, at first. (What did I expect?)

Beth was jubilant when the game was over. "I HATE football!" And she and I had a great time "yakking" as Mr. Ramsey called it.

"Are you two going to sit there yakking all night with every goddamned light in the house on?" He called to us as he was leaving.

"Goodnight, Dad!" Beth called cheerfully to him. We yakked and yakked while Danny and Chelsea colored. Scotty'd bragged to me, down through the years, about Beth's fancy Stanford honors and stuff she'd published as a writer, so I knew. Talking to her that night, I realized that she was the one I wanted to write all this.

First, though, I had to tell her. Everything, after the kids went to bed. "Beth, would you be interested in writing a book about, um, child abuse?"

She laughed. She had the same freckly smile and big teeth. "Gee, Vanessa, I don't know. I mean, I hadn't planned on it. Why?"

"Well, I think we could help a lot of people if we told my story—you know, about the sexual abuse and everything."

"What! Vanessa, what are you talking about?"

"You mean, you didn't know? . . . Well, why did you think I was living at your parents' house?"

"Is that why? Vanessa, I had no idea!"

She got up and walked over to my side of the table and hugged me. She stayed there for a long time. "I'm really sorry I never helped you through it, back then. I mean, what a dummy I was – I thought Mom and Dad went to an orphanage to find a live-in babysitter for us, or something. Vanessa, I'm so sorry. How awful. God, how did you survive, all those years?"

And that was the beginning of many, many long evenings, talking. Her questions were hard, and sometimes it took days to answer them. She taped our talks, sometimes above the clatter of video games in dark restaurants. And then, my God, did she get into it! Piles and piles of research on the sexual abuse of children, the treatment for child victims AND for Adults Molested As Children – that's a group she strongly suggested I attend.

She got to know my kids pretty well – had a great time, skipping everywhere with them. Ben and I spent vacations with the kids, sometimes staying with Beth and her husband on their little farm. One day, Charisse, Beth and I were talking about our relationships with parents. Charisse had just turned nine, and loved nothing more than adult conversations.

"With me," Charisse said, "I tell my Mommy everything, because she and I are like really good friends. Like, like that time when I told you, . . ."

And she started crying. I held her, and she continued, "you know, about Grandpa, and then I never saw him again. It wasn't my fault!" She sobbed. It had been two years since "the incident", and she was still suffering. Beth and I looked hard at each other. We had to do something.

Beth left Charisse and me alone while I comforted her. When both kids were asleep, Beth gave me three addresses of Sexual Abuse Treatment Programs right in my area in southern California. "Honest, Vanessa, it's all so much better than when you went, years ago. She needs to get over this."

I made the appointment, and had a long talk with Charisse. "Honey, I'm going to tell you some things I never told you before. When Mommy was your age, your grandpa did those things to me they told you about in school. He did them a lot."

"NO! Really? Poor Mommy."

"He's very sick, like we've said before, but if you'd like, you and I can go to a place where we can talk to some really nice, professional people about all of it. It will make us feel better."

"You mean, like therapy?"

"That's right, honey, you and I can go get some therapy."

"I'd like that, Mommy."

So we went.

* * *

Dear Little Sisters and Brothers,

I want to tell you exactly what therapy was like, for me, and for Charisse. That doesn't mean your therapy will be the same. Yours could be very different; each person's therapy has to fit the person in order for it to work. However different it might be, I can tell you: it helps! My daughter and I are feeling better, about everything.

The building wasn't ominous. A small sign read "Family Center". I was glad that it did not read, "All loonies or people who have been molested and brutalized, Come here." Inside the clean, cheery office, a woman in brown velveteen was very busy answering phones. When the phones stopped ringing for a second, she smiled at me, took a deep breath, and handed me some forms to fill out. While I filled out the forms, a really beautiful woman and her twelve year old daughter were ushered from the waiting room. I couldn't help wondering, "gee, what are THEY here for?"

The forms were easy: circle this, circle that, yes, no. "Why are you here?" was one question. I wrote, "because my daughter and I want to feel better. We were both sexually abused." Just as I was writing this, a tall, slim, arty-looking woman with blonde hair who reminded me of Elizabeth walked by. She was wearing fun, folded-up pirate boots, and she carried a cup of coffee. "Good!" I thought to myself. "Another caffein freak. I hope she's my interviewer."

She was. "Ms. Ferris? Hi, I'm Christy. C'mon in." She read over my forms while I grew nervous.

"Um, do you think I could have a cup of coffee?"

She smiled. She was really sensitive-looking. She brought me a cup, and then started asking me yes and no questions, about everything. All my yucky past with my father was dredged up again, but at first it was easy, because the graphic details of "what he did" were simple yes-no questions. No details, until it got to questions like how many times; did you ever take money for it; what is your relationship with your husband like; any sex problems?

"What about your relationship with your mother?" She asked.

"Well, you know mothers." I know. Pretty feeble answer.

Christy changed, right then. She got bitter, and strange. "Yeah . . . I guess I really do."

So Christy had some bad things in her closet, too. We never talked about them, but I knew, right away, and felt closer to her.

"Why did you wait two years after the incident with Charisse to come here?" Christy asked.

"To tell you the truth, I don't have a lot of faith in the system, or in any kind of bureaucracy."

"I don't blame you."

"I heard that it's different, now—better than it used to be. And, I thought she was over it—it was only the one incident. But she's still suffering, and I won't have my bear suffer for one minute the way I did."

I cried. She cried a little, too. "I thought all my demons were put to rest," I told her, sniffling. "God. How do you kill a 7-headed dragon?"

"I know. It will never go away entirely, Vanessa, but we can help you feel better. And I swear to you we will be able to get Charisse over all her worst nightmares."

I told Christy my whole financial situation—pretty bleak, just then—and she told me about their motto: "you pay whatever you can afford." I would be doing some individual therapy and some group therapy. Charisse, we both agreed, was simply too sensitive to go into a group and hear the much-worse stories of other kids. She would only need a few individual therapy sessions, the first one being next week.

I'll tell you: that day was the hardest, because that's the day we pulled all the musty old garbage out of the heap. I cried all the way home, and called Beth.

"Bethy, I feel so terrible. I-I mean, I thought I was OVER this, but all the old hate, all the old fear . . ." I broke off.

"You're so brave," she told me. "This is the hard part. But you're doing it for you, and you're doing it for Charisse. I'm so proud of you."

I felt sick all night, and couldn't eat dinner. Ben was quiet, and put his arm around me. I didn't want to talk about it: I just wanted to limp out on his shoulder. That was OK, he said. It was a bitch, but each time I went, it got easier and easier. More about the process, later.

The first day I took Charisse went much better. I picked her up from school early, at ten in the morning. She loved that! She had an individual session, first alone, and then with me. The woman who interviewed Charisse and me agreed that a few individual sessions would be best for her. Because hers was only a one-time thing, AND because Charisse feels other people's pain so intensely, we agreed that group therapy would be too traumatic for her.

Outside, I asked her what it was like.

"Well, we went into a room that had toys everywhere."

"Did you play with puppets?"

"Oh, Mom, puppets are only for the real little kids who are too nervous to talk. They play with the puppets while they talk, and the interviewer asks them to show with the puppet everything that happened to them. You know, since I'm a big kid, I just talked. We read a book called, "It's Not Your Fault', about this other girl and her grandfather, and we talked about everything. I think it's really good for me. Very positive. Marla, she was my personal interviewer, you know? She is really beautiful, and so nice about everything. She'd say, just like this: 'now, take your time. You don't have to answer if you don't want to'. I like her a lot."

Charisse went on and on, clearly enjoying being out, "just you and me together, Mom. I mean, I am having such a big week!"

It was only the fourth of December, but all the lights and Christmas decorations were up at the malls. We decided to do our shopping for the Giving Tree. The Giving Tree is a plan where you get a wish list from someone in an institution, and you buy whatever you can afford on their wish list. This year, we offered to buy four wish lists, one for each person in our family. We had an eighty-eight year old woman, one teenage girl, and two teenage boys. Having endured a couple of institutional Christmases, this is a huge part of Christmas for me—no matter HOW broke we are.

We picked out a fluffy pink robe and slippers (on sale at KMART) for the elderly woman, who'd scrawled "anything at all" on her wish list. Then we had to find a camouflage backpack for one of the boys. Charisse lifted her eyebrows when she saw the price tag—she's just like her dad, that way!—and started to complain.

"Why do we have to get him just what he wants, even if it costs too much?"

"Because, honey, Mommy was once in one of those institutions, just because my parents—well, you know, your grandpa had his illness."

"God, Mom, I keep forgetting you were in one of those. I keep forgetting you don't have to be poor, like an orphan, to end up in an institution. Sometimes people go there for sad reasons, like they have problems with their family or something."

"That's right, Bear, and believe me, we need to do anything to help make their Christmas better."

"I know, Mom. This has really been a great day."

* * *

OK, so that was OUR first day. Yours might be different. At these treatment centers, they do have some basic kinds of therapy, for different age groups and different experiences. Some things are the same for everyone, however: for everyone, they ask "those questions", over and over, in great detail. It is boring, and hard, but qualified therapists know exactly what they are doing. They HAVE to ask those questions. Just get through it.

Many states also have "Victim/Witness" Programs, which is a state fund that pays for therapy *after* a police report has been made, and all the proper papers have been filled out. BE AWARE of this! I've seen some victims really get hurt over the big push to report to the police. If the agency you go to seems to care a hundred times more about getting that report to the police than it does about helping you feel better, GO SOMEWHERE ELSE. They're too worried about the money to be sensitive.

GROUP THERAPY is very important for pre-teenagers and for teenagers, especially those who endured the sexual abuse over a long period of time. As one teenager put it, "No matter what anyone told me, I really believed the whole thing was my fault. I really thought I was the scum of the earth, but when I listened to the other girls in the group talk about their experiences, I realized that they really hadn't done anything wrong! It wasn't their fault, and they weren't bad people. When I was done with the group, I started doing individual therapy, and it finally dawned on me: it wasn't my fault, either!" So, for her, and for many like her, a combination group-and-individual therapy was perfect. She'll make it.

THE SELF-HELP PROGRAMS:

> Parents United (PU)
> Daughters and Sons United (DSU)
> Adults Molested As Children (AMAC)

The three groups work on a principle similar to Alcoholics Anonymous. In each group, members know they are with people who understand them. They've been there! Women who are now grown, but who've never gotten over being molested as children, can speak aloud, maybe for the first time in their lives. They can confront the devils in their nightmares, surrounded by caring, fellow-sufferers.

In Parents United, a member admits, "I was to blame," yet fellow members forgive. Some of the members who forgive the fathers were themselves molested by their fathers. They come to see the abusers in the group as human beings who are desperately sorry for the past. They help each other heal and move forward: to a life of self awareness, self control, and self esteem.

In Daughters and Sons United, children from five to eighteen are grouped according to age: young children, pre-adolescents, and adolescents. They help each other through the toughest crisis stages. "It wasn't our fault!" They remind each other. They help keep each other from destructive behaviors, such as drug abuse and promiscuity. They help each other become more self assertive, so that sexual abuse can never happen again. They help each other learn to love themselves.

All three groups are led by strong but caring counselors. The counselor is trained to lead the members toward self awareness, self control, and self esteem.

AMAC – A FEW SESSIONS

Many times, women molested as children who join the AMAC program are self destructive. Maybe they are battered wives, or they take drugs, or drink too much, or screw around a lot. They think they're dirty, so they act dirty, and they don't take care of themselves. We work together, to change all that.

Gestalt therapy is used. That is a process by which you get to know yourself. You become aware of yourself, then take responsibility for your actions.

Members feel safe at the meetings: Safe to act out and finish the unfinished feelings in their past. It hurts to confront all that anger, but it's so much better than having the anger quietly rot out your gut. You get to act out old feelings at meetings. It is frightening, and hard sometimes, but you get rid of so much crud when it's over! You sleep great after you get these feelings out.

AMAC pushes for confrontation, with both parents, if possible. It has been exciting to watch Eileen, a thirty-five year old woman, "practice" on us. All those years, she and her mother didn't talk about the incest. Her mom had caught her father on top of her, screwing. Her parents agreed to "never bring this incident up again!" Period. No discussion allowed.

"Yeah, Eileen, my mom is a lot like that," I chime in.

Jody, our facilitator, has me play Eileen's mom, which is weird for me. I get chills, because I feel as if I'm also becoming my mother. Eileen starts screaming at me. Her face is all distorted.

"How could you just DROP THE SUBJECT of your husband raping me? Why didn't you care about what it did to ME? Do you know what that DID to me? I HATE you! I HATE you! Worse than I hate HIM!"

I'm not me anymore, because if I were me, I'd be crying. I'm her, Eileen's mother. My mother. My voice is cold. I respond.

"Do you think I'm proud of myself for the way I treated you? Do you think I like myself?"

"Mother, why didn't you help me?"

"Because . . ." I don't know what to say. My mother couldn't help me. She is so cold, she doesn't know how to thaw out. The words come. "I don't know how. I didn't want you to see me break down, so I kept a stiff upper lip. That's what my father always taught me: stiff upper lip."

Eileen screams at me. "Cry for me, you bitch! I need to see you cry for me! You ruined me!"

At first, I sit there, cold. Her-mother-my-mother. Slowly, my mother's hard, silent tears fall. Eileen throws herself in my lap, sobbing. I am stiff and cold, but I make myself touch her soft, blonde hair. We are all silent.

Eileen will be leaving soon, to fly to Missouri to really confront both her parents. "Wish me luck!" She says as she leaves. She hasn't had a cigarette or joint or drink in over three months. They were killing her. We are proud of her, we tell her. She's finally putting the past behind her. She's no longer punishing herself, and she has taken responsibility for her own life.

Many other AMAC members practice for confrontations with their abusers, but not me. I have no idea where my parents are, only that they are in some foreign country. Carolyn, too: her father is dead, so she certainly can't talk to him about things!

Jody tells us we must write letters to our fathers, telling them everything we feel. She wants us to put every vicious feeling we have into that letter. We can use all the cuss words we want. We also have to write another angry letter, to our mothers. Carolyn and I have similar mothers, so I know that it's no coincidence Jody has paired the two of us. Her mother was always busy working, or with friends. She was also a clean freak, and a perfectionist, just like my mother. Jody tells us that we will be reading our letters aloud at the next session. This is all part of the "Ventilation Exercises" series.

I write a letter to my father. It is filthy with hatred and rage. The letter I write to my mother blasts her, too. I am up until four in the morning, writing these letters. Ben can't believe it: "good God, Vanessa, what're you trying to do, rewrite WAR AND PEACE in one night?" I surprise myself; the letter to my mother is angrier than the letter to my father. It feels fantastic, writing these letters.

> "... so you just stay with your Bozo husband. You're much sicker than he is, and I'm goddamned glad you're finally out of my life!"

I wish I had her address. I would love sending it.

Jody has Carolyn and me sit in two chairs facing each

other. I go first, and scream at Carolyn (my father), telling him everything I feel. Some of this stuff I didn't even know I felt; it just gushes out of me.

"You blew it, asshole. You had a chance to make it up to me for fucking up my life. I COULD HAVE FORGIVEN YOU if you'd been a decent grandfather. They LOVED you, and you betrayed them!"·I was sobbing. "I'm going to slice you up with your precious Bowie knife. I'm gonna' skin your hairy hide and feed you to Krayta—the real Krayta in Moravia. Krayta will tear your eyeballs out and roll them in the mud on a rainy day," and I went on.

Carolyn-my-father was horrified. She-he just sat, and took all the punishment I heaped on him. He hung his head. He accepted all my rage. He'd waited for it. He wanted it.

It was different, being Carolyn's father. She loved her dead father. All her feelings were those of sadness and tremendous loss.

"We were both so lonely, Daddy. I needed you, but not that way--you made our love strange, and shameful. Why couldn't we have just stayed friends, like we were at first?"

I cried. I was Carolyn's father, feeling what he felt. I was my father. I was me. My father and I had been lonely—abandoned by her, Barbara, my mother. We could have helped each other . . . As Carolyn's father, I weep: I have let this child down. "My beloved Carolyn, I never meant to do you any harm. I was weak, so weak. Can you forgive me?"

We hug, as friends. "Daddy!" Carolyn is crying.

I get a fun exercise, next. I hold a tennis racket. My mother's favorite sport is tennis. There are two chairs in front of me, with fat pillows tied to them. They are my parents. I beat them, both of them. I slam the racket on their heads, and jam it into their guts so they feel the gut aches I've felt "all my fucking life!" I yell. I spit in my mother's face; she LOVES that! I wack my father's nuts off. I continue, until the racket is ruined.

"Here you go, Mom. Happy tennis. You can use his balls."

I am exhausted, and well-ventilated. I sleep ten hours, that night.

At the next meeting, Jody makes me try to remember one good time I had with my family as a child.

"Wow." I smile. "That's a tough one." I try. Other people are doing exercises, while I think and think.

It comes. "There is one!" I yell, interrupting a quiet-time exercise. Everyone laughs. I remember, for the first time in almost thirty years, a trip to Disneyland. Johnny and I were laughing, and my parents seemed to love us. They loved each other. My father was sober. The four of us went on the spinning teacups ride together, and laughed and laughed. It was pure joy, being together, that day.

Tears are rolling down my face. "God, I'd forgotten all about that day!"

"They would have been good parents, Vanessa, if only they'd known how," Jody tells me. "They would have loved having more happy times like that, being loving parents. All people want to be good, loving parents."

I leave that day feeling changed and happy. I am finally learning to forgive, and to put the past behind me. This is healthier; I am healthier. My future looks outrageously bright to me, that day. I'll make it. I will forgive and love them, someday. All my past pain has made me better and stronger. I'm Vanessa, because of it, and Vanessa is good: a kind, caring, loving survivor. I am strong, but I am gentle, too. I have faced my fears and my weaknesses. I have faced my beauty and my strength. I can love. I love me.

* * *

So that's my story.

I tried not to make it too long, but it's still pretty long. I tried to mention only the parts of my life that you, abused children, might find helpful in your own lives. The truth is that almost EVERY part of my journey made me stronger, or taught me something. It's been a long, winding journey—and it's not over, yet, for me or for Charisse. It's a journey I had to take to get strong, to love myself, and to love others. I wanted to take you through my journey so that your own journey might not be so hard. If you haven't begun your journey, DO IT! Start the long hard road to your own happy ending. If you're in the midst of your journey, and finding it damned hard—as, God knows, mine was!—may my story give you a little strength to keep going.

The main thing I hope I've helped you to do is open yourself. That sounds like the craziest hardest thing to do after what you've been through! Probably, all you really want to do is curl into a little ball, and close yourself off forever from the pain of life. Maybe, in your case, the people who you love most—the people who should love you—have betrayed you. But like a tough little flower, you must open again! You will only feel the beauty and warmth of the sun if you open yourself to it. Like the open flower, you will get rained on, even hailed on. But if you open yourself to love by finding friends who are GOOD to you, honest!—the warmest rays of the sun will heal you. If you don't love yourself, you'll try to hurt yourself, with drugs, or with drinking too much, or maybe by letting boys use your body. If you don't love yourself enough, you'll make friends who treat you rotten, and hurt you. If you have friends who are mean to you, DROP THEM! Tell yourself "I deserve better!" And try again, just like the toughest flower that straightens up after getting rained on. Make another friend, and another, until you feel the warmth of their total love for you, and your love for them. Love is what will save you, so never give up on it until it works—and that includes the love that you must develop for yourself.

So. Learn to love yourself, then go out and find people who love you, too. I know I've said this many times, and that's because it's the hardest thing for an abused child to do. A child loves her parents and trusts her parents, so when they are cruel to her, or don't protect her, she thinks it is because she is a bad person. But that's not true! They are cruel to you because they have their own problems. They have a sickness, a hate for themselves, that is just like cancer. It eats up their mind and their heart.

We still have hard, grown-up problems that make some days a bitch to get through. But it's so much different when you're working WITH a family—your OWN family, that loves you. When the most essential ingredient, love, is full in your life, everything else somehow works out. You struggle through some bad days, but you never feel that dreaded anguish you felt as a battered or sexually abused child.

NOTHING EVER FEELS THAT BAD AGAIN. What I'm saying is that when you get through that, life does not suddenly become easy; life never does that! But when you end the abuse, you have ended the very worst. Everything is better after that.

And my story isn't completely over: I'm not old, and I'm not dead. I'll never be famous, and though some days I think we might be rich again, other days, I'm sure we won't. Put it this way: we'll never be Sylvester Stalone, or Prince. What IS fairly cleaned up, though, for the most part, is the mess my parents made of me. Charisse and I are still attending our AMAC and DSU meetings, and we'll continue doing so until we feel we don't need to anymore. I have tried to make all the bad stuff in my past make me stronger. I think that maybe I am a better parent BECAUSE OF all the bad stuff. I am more sensitive to other people's pain, so maybe I can do the right things to help them. In short, I have become strong, and I urge you to do so, too.

Farewell, little sisters and brothers!

Do you know someone this book could help?

To order, please send $12.95 plus $1.00 postage and handling, for each copy, to:

FREEDOM LIGHTS PRESS BB
P.O. BOX 87
CHIMNEY ROCK, COLORADO 81127

ORDER FORM:

NAME: _____

ADDRESS: _____

_____

_____

Number of copies: _____

* * *

CHILD SEXUAL ABUSE TREATMENT PROGRAMS

There are child sexual abuse treatment centers in every state in America. Unfortunately, due to a shortage of funds, their addresses and phone numbers are always changing. Hence, I can't really give you all the current addresses and phone numbers here. It'd be pretty depressing if you were to call one, and instead you got a disconnected recording. For a current address or phone number of a treatment center in your area, you can call either 1-800-4-A-Child— toll free, 24 hours a day—and ask them for help, or you can call 408-280-5055, 9:00 am to 5:00 pm, Monday through Friday, Pacific Standard Time. The second number is in San Jose, California, and is the headquarters for: Parents United/ Daughters and Sons United/ Adults Molested as Children United/ the Child Abuse Treatment Program/ and the Institute for the Community as Extended Family. Tell them where in the U.S. you live, and they will connect you with the treatment center in your area.

Don't forget, also, the inside of the telephone book in your area, where it reads: "Emergency Numbers:" places you can go any time of day or night. To write for a current list of Child Abuse Treatment Centers, write to: ICEF; P.O. Box 952; San Jose, CA 95108.

MY SOURCES

I. BOOKS

Burgess, Ann Wolbert. SEXUAL ASSAULT OF CHILDREN AND ADOLESCENTS. Lexington, Mass: Lexington Books D.C. Heath Co., 1978.

Daugherty, Lynn B, PHD. WHY ME? Help for Victims of

Child Sexual Abuse (even if they are adults now). Racine, WI: Mother Courage Press, 1984.

Forward, Susan, MSW, and Buck, Craig. BETRAYAL OF INNOCENCE – Incest and its Devastation. Middlesex, England: Penguin Books, 1978.

Geiser, Robert. HIDDEN VICTIMS. Boston: Boston Press, 1979.

Guggenheim, Martin and Sussman, Alan. THE RIGHTS OF YOUNG PEOPLE. New York: Bantam Books, 1985.

Herman, Judith Lewis. FATHER-DAUGHTER INCEST. Cambridge, Mass: Harvard University Press, 1981.

Kempe, Ruth and Kempe, Henry. THE COMMON SECRET. Sexual Abuse of Children and Adolescents. New York: W.H. Freeman and Company, 1984.

McNaron, Toni, and Morgan, Yarrow. VOICES IN THE NIGHT. Women Speaking Out About Incest. San Francisco: Cleis Press, 1982.

Morris, Michelle. IF I SHOULD DIE BEFORE I WAKE. New York: Dell Publishing, Co, 1984.

Nabokob, Vladimir. LOLITA. New York: Berkeley Books, 1983.

II. FILMS

These films were loaned by the Henry Kempe National Center for the Prevention and Treatment of Child Abuse and Neglect in Denver, Colorado.

MIT Teleprograms, Inc. INCEST: THE VICTIMS NOBODY BELIEVES. Northbrook, Ill.

ODN Productions, Inc. NO MORE SECRETS.

University of Calgary, Canada. CHILD SEXUAL ABUSE – THE UNTOLD SECRET.

NBC News Presents. SILENT SHAME – THE SEXUAL ABUSE OF CHILDREN.

III. Television Programs – 1986.

Phil Donahue – 8/29/86, Channel 7, 4p.m., PST

Oprah Winfrey – 11/10/86, 3p.m., PST

IV. PAMPHLETS

American Association for Protecting Children, Inc. HIGH-LIGHTS OF OFFICIAL CHILD NEGLECT AND ABUSE REPORTING, 1984.

De Francis, Vincent, JD. American Humane Association. THE FUNDAMENTALS OF CHILD PROTECTION – A STATEMENT OF BASIC CONCEPTS AND PRINCI-PLES. Englewood, Colorado, 1978.

Gil, Eliana, PUD. THE CALIFORNIA CHILD ABUSE REPORTING LAW. ISSUES AND ANSWERS FOR MENTAL HEALTH PROFESSIONALS. 6/83.

ICEF, Adults Molested As Children United. ON BECOM-ING WHOLE. San Jose.

Van de Kamp, John, Attorney General. CHILD ABUSE PREVENTION HANDBOOK. Office of the Attorney General, 8/85.

V. PAMPHLETS OFFERED BY THE CHILD SEXUAL ABUSE TREATMENT PROGRAM IN SAN JOSE, CALIFORNIA.

"Legal Aspects of Incest."
"Members Guide to the Criminal Justice System"

"California penal code – chapter 1071, Child Abuse."
"Felonies/Misdemeanors"
"General Guide Through the Criminal Justice System"
"Supervised Own Recognizance Procedures Manual."
"Work Furlough Program – Samta Clara County"
"Parents' Guide to the Juvenile Justice System of Santa Clara County"
"Parents United Guidelines to Confidentiality"
"The psychotherapist-Patient Privilege Under the Welfare and Institutions Code"
"The Freudian Coverup" by Florence Rush.
"Interviewing Child Victims – Guidelines for Criminal Justice System Personnel" – prepared by the Law Enforcement Assistance Administration, US Department of Justice
"Special Techniques for Child Witnesses". Berliner, L. and Stevens, D.
"Military Memorandums," chronicling incest cases of military personnel and their successful treatment in Sexual Abuse Programs.
"A Comprehensive Child Sexual Abuse Treatment Program" by Henry Giarretto, PHD, founder and Director of the CSATP in San Jose.
"Treating Sexual Abuse – Working Together" by Henry Giarretto
"Humanistic Treatment of Father-Daughter Incest" by Henry Giarretto
"Ventilation Exercises" by Henry Giarretto
"Assimilation Exercises" by Henry Giarretto
"Counselling Methods and Techniques" by Ellie Breslin
"Sexual Child Abuse, the Psychotherapist, and the Team Concept" by Roland Summit, MD

VI. NEWSPAPER ARTICLES

Brooks, Jim. "EVENING OUTLOOK Author Wants to Expose Child Abuse – Focuses on Destructive Secrets". SANTA MONICA EVENING OUTLOOK, 8/26/86.

Dreyfuss, John, TIMES Staff Writer. "The 24-hour-a-day War on Domestic Violence. Counselor Helps Assault Victims to Rebuild Lives." 6/30/86.